THE POWER OF CRISIS

HOW THREE THREATS—
AND OUR RESPONSE—
WILL CHANGE THE WORLD

IAN BREMMER

SIMON & SCHUSTER

New York   London   Toronto   Sydney   New Delhi

Simon & Schuster
1230 Avenue of the Americas
New York, NY 10020

Copyright © 2022 by Ian Bremmer

First Simon & Schuster hardcover edition May 2022

SIMON & SCHUSTER and colophon are registered trademarks
of Simon & Schuster, Inc.

For information about special discounts for bulk purchases,
please contact Simon & Schuster Special Sales at 1-866-506-1949
or business@simonandschuster.com.

The Simon & Schuster Speakers Bureau can bring authors to your
live event. For more information or to book an event, contact the
Simon & Schuster Speakers Bureau at 1-866-248-3049
or visit our website at www.simonspeakers.com.

Interior design by Joy O'Meara @ Creative Joy Designs

Manufactured in the United States of America

10 9 8 7 6 5 4 3 2 1

Library of Congress Control Number: 2022932427

ISBN 978-1-9821-6750-9
ISBN 978-1-9821-6752-3 (ebook)

To a glass half full.
That first half was tasty.

CONTENTS

Introduction   1

CHAPTER 1
Two Collisions—
Us vs. Them, at Home and Abroad   15

CHAPTER 2
Pandemic Politics   63

CHAPTER 3
Climate Emergency   87

CHAPTER 4
Disruptive Technologies   127

Conclusion   175
Addendum   205
Acknowledgments   209
Notes   213
Index   241

THE
POWER OF
CRISIS

INTRODUCTION

Away from the cameras and warmed by the fire, Ronald Reagan opened his first private conversation with Mikhail Gorbachev with a startling question: "What would you do if the United States were suddenly attacked by someone from outer space? Would you help us?" Gorbachev didn't hesitate. "No doubt about it," he replied. "We would too," Reagan assured him. That moment took place in a cabin in Geneva on November 19, 1985, but it wasn't publicly known until Gorbachev told the story in front of a live audience at the Rainbow Room in New York City in March 2009. Only Reagan, Gorbachev, and their interpreters were present when that first exchange took place.

Gorbachev's revelation made news for all the wrong reasons. Discussion began anew about whether Reagan, who had died nearly five years before Gorbachev shared this story, had been soft in the head. Smirking pundits speculated over which of Reagan's favorite Hollywood sci-fi movies had inspired the question. (Historical consensus has settled on *The Day the Earth Stood Still*.) The anecdote embarrassed many of Reagan's admirers.

I open with this story for two reasons.

First, Gorbachev has said that their first private chat was an important moment for relations between the two men, leaders of the world's two superpowers. It certainly didn't guarantee peace or remake the Cold War. There was plenty for Reagan, Gorbachev, and their negotiators to fight over in the following years, and the Cold War ended not with a grand bargain but with Soviet implosion. But by sowing the seeds of trust and goodwill, Reagan's question and Gorbachev's answer laid the foundation for a working relationship that had never before existed between US and Soviet leaders, one that created the possibility of cooperation, even coordination, between hostile, nuclear-armed enemies on questions of vital importance for both countries and the world. At various times, leaders of the United States and the Soviet Union had persuaded themselves and each other that the two Cold War powers were on a collision course. Reagan and Gorbachev understood the need to take them off that path—and that shift allowed for the progress toward more widely shared security and prosperity that the world has enjoyed since the Cold War's end.

Second, world leaders really *do* face threats to the survival of those they govern. We can start with a global pandemic that inflicted damage and pain that will be felt for decades, especially in the developing world. COVID-19 started a war, and nobody won. Many governments made critical mistakes, almost every country lost too many lives, and every country suffered a sharp economic slowdown and saddled itself with new debt. Political finger-pointing within and across borders made things worse by shutting down the flow of vital information and resources that would have limited the damage for all of us.

In the coming decade, we will face much greater risks. To survive the challenges detailed in this book, we must all learn the lessons the pandemic can teach us, even if world leaders aren't ready to agree on them. US, Chinese, and other governments will continue to compete, both openly and secretly, over hundreds of political, security, and economic issues they don't, and will never, agree on. But on the big risks that menace us all at the same time, we can share responsibility, information, burdens, blame, and credit as we learn from past mistakes.

Unless leaders of the world's most important countries can build enough trust to work together on the threats we share, we will all suffer catastrophes that sci-fi fan Ronald Reagan never imagined.

CRISES TO COME

Two years after the worst global health crisis in a century, the world still struggles to regain its footing, but our future is now coming into focus. Let's first face two facts. One, domestic politics inside the United States, still the world's sole superpower, is broken. Two, the relationship between the United States and China, which will matter more than any other for the world's collective future, is headed in the wrong direction. Both of these realities make it difficult to respond to global crises as they occur.

We face three such crises today. The world is still struggling to shake off the economic, political, and social effects of

COVID-19, and more deadly viruses will inevitably plague us. Climate change will upend the lives of billions of people and threaten the sustainability of life on the planet. The greatest threat of all to our collective future will come from the unexpected impact of new technologies that change the way we live, think, and interact with other people and will determine our future as a species.

America's broken politics and the intensifying US-China rivalry imperil our ability to build the international trust needed to meet the great crises of our time.

AMERICA'S UNCIVIL WAR

Americans no longer look abroad for their most dangerous enemies. They find them across state lines, across the street, across the hall. They see members of the other political party, neighbors, and even relatives as hateful, ignorant enemies who must be checked. Voters on the left and right deliberately seek out information (and misinformation and disinformation) about the world from sources they know will confirm their biases and make them fighting mad. Government—federal, state, and local—increasingly reflects these distortions in frightening ways. Even on issues where Americans of left and right sometimes agree—on the need to stand up to a rising China, for example—they don't agree on what the problems are or what to do about them. It's difficult for citizens of other countries and their governments to see the United States as a source of solutions to global problems when tens of millions of Americans consider tens of millions of other Americans to be violent radicals or irredeemable fascists. I'll say more about that—and its dire consequences for the US and the world—in chapter 1.

A NEW COLD WAR?

On several fronts, the US and China will engage in a new conflict whose consequences could well be more dire than those of the first Cold War. Neither side is seriously engaging the other to meet the global goals the two countries share. This rivalry had been building for years when new animosities created by COVID hardened attitudes in both China and America. Washington and Beijing have legitimate disagreements and grievances. They will continue to fight over many issues. But America and China are far more interdependent than the US and the USSR ever were, and the leaders of both countries have set themselves on a new collision course—and at a time when there's no Berlin Wall to protect them from each other.

There is only so much either can do to separate their national fates, no way to hide from the rest of the world's problems, and no chance that one will thrive without the other. Given the links between their economies and the scale and imminence of today's threats, a new Cold War would cost both countries—and the rest of the world—far too much. A new Cold War would itself be a form of mutually assured destruction.

The United States of America and the People's Republic of China won't become allies anytime soon, but they can step off the current collision course to become pragmatic partners. As we'll see, their leaders can work on shared threats to both countries and the world. Beginning in the early 1970s, a time when only Nixon could go to China and only a man as powerful as Mao Zedong could have steered China onto a new course, the two countries worked together to end the Cold War. As a direct result, their economic interdependence of the past quarter century created an era of global prosperity without precedent in human history. That historic accomplishment is now at risk, as I'll detail in the second half of chapter 1.

PANDEMICS PAST, PRESENT, AND FUTURE

In chapter 2, we'll look at the many ways that US dysfunction and US-China confrontation have crippled the world's ability to respond more effectively to the global pandemic. The COVID emergency wasn't just predictable. It was *predicted*, including by world leaders with the power to prepare us all to avoid its worst effects. And we know that there will be a next novel coronavirus, possibly one both more transmissible and more deadly than COVID-19.

But the COVID-19 experience has also provided us with lessons: genuine success stories in global cooperation and more than a few deadly failures that are relevant to our approach to other global challenges. To respond more effectively to future emergencies, we need to understand both.

OUR CLIMATE

In chapter 3, we'll turn to the climate crisis. Like Ronald Reagan's alien invaders, and like COVID-19, climate change doesn't care about borders or distinguish among political tribes. It has already destroyed millions of lives and livelihoods and will upend many more. If the pandemic was the biggest global challenge of our lifetime, climate change threatens our collective future on a larger and longer scale—by creating turmoil within the home all humans share, by making unprecedented economic demands on governments, by stoking political turmoil, by increasing inequality within and among countries, and by pushing more desperate people across borders than any war ever did.

To meet the many challenges climate change will pose, governments that don't trust one another, and whose peoples share no political or cultural values, must cooperate and coordinate on climate policy even as they compete in a dozen other arenas. As in the past, governments, private companies, and individual citizens must work together as if they were at war with a common enemy. Because they are.

DISRUPTIVE TECH

In chapter 4, we'll turn to the greatest threat that faces our species: the unchecked introduction of profoundly disruptive technologies. We'll look closely at the many ways in which new digital-age tools can and will improve certain aspects of our lives. But having survived COVID, we're as aware as ever that new drugs with potentially dangerous side effects must be tested before they're injected into the global bloodstream. That's a commonsense safety precaution. We're inventing new tools, new toys, and new weapons that are changing our lives and societies faster than we can track, study, and understand their effect on us.

Throughout history, innovation has strengthened and enriched us, and we can't expect people—or their governments—to agree completely on how new technologies should be used. But lethal autonomous drones, cyberwarfare, biotechnology, and artificial intelligence (AI) are no longer the stuff of science fiction. Nor is the shock that comes with algorithms that teach machines to replace people in the workplace. These technologies are shifting the relationship between the citizen and the state—and between us and our fellow humans—in ways difficult to predict. In the process, they're changing what it means to be human.

G-ZERO

Anyone watching the news during the pandemic's early days can be forgiven for thinking that COVID-19 created all the chaos now roiling the international system. The United States, the world's most powerful nation, and China, the rising challenger, could have set aside their many differences to collaborate on containing the crisis, developing a vaccine, and helping to heal the wounds the pandemic inflicted worldwide. Instead, they traded accusations. We might have seen the US, China, and Europe join together to develop the technologies needed to safely reopen economies everywhere. It didn't happen. Finger-pointing became the norm. Even the world's central banks, which did a lot to cushion the economic and social fallout for wealthier countries, were working in the same direction but not together.

Yet COVID-19 didn't create the rivalries and suspicions that blocked cooperation. The international system has been broken for years. In 2012, I wrote a book called *Every Nation for Itself: Winners and Losers in a G-Zero World*. The story goes like this: Once upon a time (1975–2009), we lived in a world run mainly by the leaders of the so-called Group of Seven (G7) industrialized countries—the US, Britain, France, Germany, Italy, Japan, and Canada. Their shared political values and share of the global economy gave these seven countries the power to make rules that other democracies and many developing countries lived by. In those days, the Communist bloc posed a military threat but lacked the economic clout to match the West's global influence.

By the middle of the first decade of the twenty-first century, things began to change. Countries including India, South Korea, Brazil, Turkey, Indonesia, Mexico, and especially China had emerged from earlier crises and built economies that gave them more independence from the rulemaking power of the wealthy West and new international influence. Russia, rather than joining Western clubs, tried to play spoiler, assembling a new, if smaller, empire. The formal end to the G7's dominance arrived with the global financial crisis (2008–2010), an emergency that made clear that no global problem could be solved without China and others at the table. It was the expanded Group of 20 (G20) that coordinated the crisis response.

But the G20 is a large, diverse group of countries that don't share common views on democracy and free-market economics. They worked together effectively during the global financial shock, when each government accepted that it had the same loaded gun pointed at its head at exactly the same moment. But once that crisis had lifted, they couldn't agree on much else. I coined the term "G-Zero" to describe this new reality, a world that lacks leaders willing or able to break up fights and force compromise on expensive and dangerous problems in the name of global stability and shared benefit. The world entered a kind of geopolitical recession, a bust cycle for relations among governments that occurs whenever the global balance of power changes much more quickly than the multinational architecture that helps govern the international system. Alliances, institutions, and the values that bind them together have been unraveling for the past twenty years. Geopolitical recessions don't come along nearly as often as economic recessions, but they are tremendously destabilizing when they do.

Then came COVID. Just as an earthquake shows us which buildings stand on shaky foundations, the coronavirus revealed the accumulated damage of a decades-long political neglect of growing problems and the inability of world leaders to solve them together. Both the terrorist attacks of September 11, 2001, and the global financial crisis encouraged some multinational cooperation against a perceived common threat. Not so with the pandemic. Among world leaders, accusations flew, tensions grew, blame was cast, and borders were hardened. The pandemic created the first true global test of the G-Zero era, and by failing to cooperate effectively for the common good, governments around the world failed it.

The geopolitical recession has shaken the international system to its foundation. It's a historic moment when more than seventy million people have been forced from their homes and many more have been pushed back into poverty by COVID's economic impact. Most multinational institutions no longer represent today's balance of international power. Elected leaders who run on a "country-first" platform are much less likely to support spending on international organizations, including the United Nations (UN), that help displaced people around the world and coordinate action to fight climate change. Three decades after the Cold War's end, growing transatlantic divisions over both interests and values leave ever-larger numbers of people questioning the purpose and utility of the North Atlantic Treaty Organization (NATO). Former US president Donald Trump showed populists everywhere how easy it is to withdraw from major trade agreements, climate accords, and the World Health Organization (WHO) . . . even in the middle of a pandemic. The inevitable consequence is a world that's more unpredictable, less safe, and less prepared than ever to build new agreements and institutions to meet twenty-first-century challenges. G-Zero is still the defining feature of our time.

THE CRISIS WE NEED

So what can we do now? Faced with dysfunction at the heart of American politics, poisoned relations between America and China, and a broken global system, and with vitally important questions to answer, what is the way forward? What will it take to get our political leaders—people who spend much more time thinking about tactical approaches to this week's petty problems than they do about strategic plans to tackle long-term global challenges—to invest in cross-border cooperation on the questions that must be answered?

History says we need a crisis.

To check the growing power of the expansionist racist nationalism of the 1920s and 1930s, to force construction of a new international system that recognized global interdependence for the first time in history, and to build new forms of multinational cooperation, the world needed World War II. It took dread of Communism to persuade Americans to support the Marshall Plan to help rebuild Europe. It took the near-death experience of the Cuban missile crisis to persuade US and Soviet leaders to install the nuclear "hotline," the teletype and telegraph terminals they could use to communicate securely when the stakes were highest. It's human nature; we need fear to help us overcome inertia and address the risks we've allowed to become deadly. But the unprecedented interdependence of all nations and the destructive power of today's technologies ensure that the human race can't survive a new world war, and we can't afford a US-China Cold War that will make effective global cooperation impossible.

That's why we must use the crises already breaking around us—the lessons of COVID, the destructive potential of climate change, and the existential threat posed by rapid technological

*developments we don't understand—to create a new interna-
tional system that's built for today's, and tomorrow's, purpose.*

We need crises scary enough to make us forge a new international system that promotes effective cooperation on a few crucial questions. The nations of the world don't have to become
friends or even partners on every project; global competition
can still power human progress. But we need enough collaboration to survive the potential catastrophes to come. We need crises big enough to terrify us, not ones so grave that they destroy
our ability to change.

A NARROW WINDOW

Solving the largest and most complex problems takes vision,
stamina, and a leap of faith. As I'll detail in coming chapters,
today's dangers are greater than those facing Reagan and Gorbachev in 1985. They have a life and momentum of their own.
Surviving them isn't simply a matter of shaking hands and
dismantling some weapons stockpiles. Hard as it was to work
toward nuclear reductions, it will be much tougher and more
complicated to create a new global public health system, reinvent the way energy is produced and delivered, manage the
massive fallout from climate change, and ensure that new technologies don't destroy our common future.

In truth, there's no guarantee our world will survive the next
fifty years. We share the universe with an unimaginably large
number of other planets, and yet we've found no evidence of
intelligent life. Is that because our planet is the only one that
can sustain life? The odds of that are infinitely small. But maybe
we're alone *for now* because there's a limited amount of time
between the moment life begins to form and the moment "intel-

ligent" life destroys the environment that sustains it. Maybe the window of time that opens when a civilization is first able to send a detectable signal into space and closes when that civilization destroys itself is much narrower than we think. Surely life has existed, and will exist, throughout the universe, but perhaps only for the cosmological blink of an eye.

That's what world leaders should be thinking about—and not just the leaders of China and the United States. These are now the two most powerful countries on our planet, in military, economic, and technological terms. But cooperation must extend far beyond them. It must be *global*. Europe, as I'll discuss in coming pages, remains a central piece of this puzzle, and many other countries and non-state actors in every region of the world can offer much-needed leadership. COVID, unfortunately, has pushed us further apart, but we can still hope that lessons learned from the pandemic will guide our first steps toward a new international system of crisis response, one based on the need to identify dangers and agree on carefully planned and coordinated solutions before our problems become too big to contain.

———————

Now for a bold prediction—Europe and the United States, China, and other countries, institutions, and people WILL work together on these common challenges. But will they work hard enough, quickly enough, and effectively enough to build the new international system we need? The global pandemic made clear that the biggest twenty-first-century threats don't give a damn about borders. An "every nation for itself" approach won't help us meet the challenges described in this book. The race to create and distribute a coronavirus vaccine proved yet again that smart and committed people of goodwill can solve new problems at record speed. Human ingenuity is in ample supply. But we'll need much more compromise, cooperation, and coordination than COVID was able to create.

Globalism has failed over the past four decades, mainly because it has been global in name only. In wealthy countries, people without a college education lost the ability to build a secure middle-class life on top of a manufacturing job. In poorer countries, those who weren't benefiting from the rise of a new middle class got the closest view they'd ever had of those more fortunate. Inequality hit new heights. Too many people in every country have been excluded from globalization's historic rewards, and we've seen the result in public rage worldwide and the rise of next-generation populists eager to exploit it. In coming years, more people will question whether their leaders can help them achieve the security and prosperity they expect from their government. They'll ask whether life will be better for their children. Their leaders had better have good answers.

The next decade will see US-China confrontation, a future pandemic, unchecked climate change, and life-altering technologies, each of which might do more damage to our species than any other crisis in history. I will illustrate the threats they pose and how they will change the world's balance of power, and I'll point to potential solutions, many of which history has already shown to be far more workable than we may think. By working together and sharing responsibility for the dangers that loom over all of us, European, Chinese, American, African, Japanese, Indian, and other world leaders can construct a new international system, one that can effectively address *all* global crises.

Ronald Reagan asked the question, and Mikhail Gorbachev answered it. If we face threats that are bigger than all of us, can we work together? "No doubt about it," said the Soviet leader.

That's the right answer.

CHAPTER 1

TWO COLLISIONS— US VS. THEM, AT HOME AND ABROAD

To survive our impending crises, we must avoid disaster in two relationships: the one we have with one another and the one between the US and China.

Ronald Reagan and Mikhail Gorbachev understood that nothing inspires cooperation like fear of a common threat. But for now, Americans on both the left and the right too often treat one another as the greatest obstacle to the nation's progress, and the US and Chinese governments have spent the past several years arguing over differences that both sides treat as irreconcilable.

Before we turn to the crises that will define our common future, we need to understand the forces most likely to prevent us from addressing them.

COLLISION COURSE 1: DYSFUNCTIONAL AMERICA

The United States is a nation of contradictions. When COVID hit, the US led the world in hospitalizations and deaths, and then set records for speed of production and distribution of game-changing vaccines. In January 2021, the country's stock market surged to new heights even as a violent mob stormed the US Capitol in hopes of reversing the outcome of a national election. A month later, millions of Texans struggled for days without electricity, heat, or clean water even as the nation's space agency was landing a vehicle on Mars. The American capacity for invention and innovation is unparalleled; the nation's politics are broken. The United States remains the only nation that can project political, economic, cultural, and military power into every region of the world. And it's at war with itself.

That's why the first great challenge facing leaders and citizens of the most powerful nation on earth is how to build enough trust and cooperation to help the American people, and everyone else, meet the critical global tests ahead.

For now, Americans are anything but united. A report from the Pew Research Center published in October 2019 offered grim conclusions. Some 78 percent of Americans polled said divisions between Republicans and Democrats were increasing. Just 6 percent said they were decreasing. A majority (55 percent) said there's a "great deal" of difference in what the two major parties stand for, up from about one-third in the mid-2000s. A startling 73 percent said that Democratic and

Republican voters disagree not only on policy but on "basic facts" concerning what's happening in the country and the world. Just 17 percent of Republicans said Democrats had at least some "good ideas," and 13 percent of Democrats said the same of Republicans. That was before the election of 2020, Donald Trump's refusal to concede defeat, and a deadly insurrection at the US Capitol.

Today, a majority of Democratic voters call themselves "liberal," double the percentage from a generation ago. The number of Republicans who call themselves "conservative" has jumped from 58 percent to 73 percent over that same period. Self-identified independents now make up nearly 40 percent of the total US population, double the percentage from the 1950s, but these voters aren't necessarily centrist. In a Gallup poll published in January 2021, fewer than half called themselves "moderate." Most independents identify much more with one party than the other.

There's also a geographic component to American partisanship. In the 2020 presidential election, voters in the nation's most densely populated counties voted for Joe Biden by a margin of 29 points. Those in the most sparsely populated counties went for Donald Trump by 35 points. Those numbers were higher than for Democratic candidate Hillary Clinton and Donald Trump in the 2016 election. More disheartening still for those of us who believe in cooperation and compromise, a YouGov poll conducted in February 2021 found that 41 percent of Democrats view Republicans not as "political opponents" but as "enemies," and 57 percent of Republicans said the same about Democrats.

Partisan bitterness is even more extreme inside government. In the 1980s, more elected officials of both parties could be called centrists, and there was more ideological overlap among lawmakers. Today, there's almost no common ground between the most liberal Republicans and the most conservative Democrats, and the number of legislators who almost never vote with members of the other party has risen sharply. There's now more division within Congress than at any time in over a century. That means less room for compromise among federal lawmakers on every issue.

DRIVING THE DYSFUNCTION

There is another important source of division: widening wealth gaps. Income inequality in the United States has reached its highest point since the Gilded Age. Within the thirty-eight-member Organization for Economic Cooperation and Development (OECD), only Chile, Turkey, and Mexico have a larger gap between rich and poor than the United States. In the US, average incomes for the top 1 percent of earners rose by 226 percent from 1979 to 2016, while working- and middle-class income remained flat. The top 10 percent of Americans now own more than 70 percent of the country's wealth. The top 1 percent control more national income than the bottom 50 percent.

Much has already been written on why that is so. The outsourcing of manufacturing and service-sector jobs to lower-income countries has driven down wages. Only about 5 percent of Americans still enjoy the advantage of collective bargaining offered by labor unions, down from about 20 percent in the 1980s. The earning potential conferred by a college degree is rising even as the cost of higher education rises beyond reach for many Americans. Households headed by someone with a bachelor's degree can expect twice the income of those without one. And with smart machines replacing humans in the blue- and white-collar workplace at ever-increasing rates—more on that in chapter 4—future earning potential for the less fortunate is under heavy pressure.

THE AMERICAN WAY OF CAPITALISM

For two centuries, US businesses have created extraordinary innovation, wealth, and economic growth. Generations of the world's most successful entrepreneurs and business leaders have been American—many of them immigrants and the children of immigrants who came to the US seeking commercial opportunities they couldn't find anywhere else. That trend drove American industry in the nineteenth century, produced remarkable accumulation of American power in the postwar twentieth century, and enabled American companies to establish early dominance in the twenty-first-century information technology sector.

America's capitalist culture reveres the "animal spirits" unleashed by market forces and the entrepreneur as the epitome of self-reliant individualism. According to a 2021 study, 68 percent of those who voted for Biden in the 2020 election and 61 percent of Trump voters expressed trust in their employers. Just 45 percent of Biden voters and 28 percent for Trump said the same of "government leaders." Americans expect laws and voters to enforce checks and balances on politicians and political institutions, but many believe that the primary check on entrepreneurs and private-sector companies should come from the free market itself.

This veneration of the private sector allows neglect of American workers, whose interests don't always align with their employers'. Some elected officials, many of them Republicans, fight hard to lower tax rates for companies and the wealthiest citizens while warning of the dangers of raising the minimum wage. Companies are allowed to deny growing numbers of their employees the health and pension benefits they need for present and future financial security. The regulatory environment is driven more often by the needs of the private sector than by the health, safety, and well-being of citizens in general. And as technological change makes labor less important to the future of capitalism, chronic inequality of opportunity will become an even bigger source of political tension. The flexibility of the US economy in response to the pandemic supercharged these trends and exposed social safety net gaps beyond anything seen in other wealthy countries.

Exacerbating these problems is the growing importance of money in American politics. US political campaigns have become exponentially more expensive since the 1950s, making elected officials deeply dependent on the goodwill of people and organizations willing to bankroll their careers. And this trend has only accelerated in the last decade, since a 2010 Supreme Court decision allowed corporations and other outside groups to spend unlimited amounts of money on elections. The 2020 elections for president and control of the two houses of Congress cost about $14 billion, more than double the previous record set in 2016. Much of that money comes from deep-pocketed individuals and companies that expect a return on their investment—a return that boosts large companies and wealthy individuals, often at the expense of the nation as a whole.

DISCREDITED MEDIA

Small donors are still a crucial source of campaign cash, and to reach these donors, politicians must grab and hold public attention. To build a following on social media, influencers have learned to stand out from the crowd, often by shocking viewers in order to go viral with their content. In US politics today, candidates play the same game. To raise the ever-increasing amounts of money they need to compete for power and influence, they make outrageous statements and take extreme positions to seize the spotlight. Social media trends have taught them that anger drives attention, therefore money, and therefore success. America's so-called culture war began long before the advent of social media, but these new tools give it new energy and urgency.

In fact, in recent decades Americans have lost more trust in the media than in any other institution. Tens of millions of Americans now receive their national and international news from sources they expect will confirm their worldview and political biases—and there is virtually no interaction between these information sources and those sought out by partisans from the other end of the political spectrum. MSNBC hosts tell left-of-center consumers of political news about the latest Republican moral outrage and then bring on the same guests we saw last week to tell us just how outrageous these outrages really are. Fox preaches to a conservative older audience who want to believe that every Democrat is a dangerous leftist radical. The genuinely radical messaging that we now see via incendiary information outlets and platforms like OANN, QAnon, and 4chan began with the market- and culture-changing popularity of political talk radio and the growth of cable TV news in the 1980s. All these trends began in the United States. In Europe, regulators place higher value on personal privacy, more restrictions on free speech, and harder limits on the influence of social media companies. In Japan, mainstream media is generally less politicized, and adults spend far less time than Americans and Europeans on social media platforms.

Social media algorithms have created a business model, driven by advertising dollars, that productizes the personal data of citizen-consumers. As I'll detail in chapter 4, this has brought online bots into the media bloodstream to shape public opinion, sometimes via disinformation that distorts reality and drives attention—and ad revenue—while consumers become inured to online shock and outrage.

RACE–THE PAST IS PRESENT

There are no sources of outrage more deeply embedded in American life than structural racism and the determined efforts of some to pretend it doesn't exist. Those who dismiss the importance of race in American life argue that slavery, segregation, and other forms of discrimination bear no relation to current events. But, to paraphrase William Faulkner, institutional racism isn't dead. It isn't even past.

As part of President Franklin Roosevelt's New Deal in the 1930s, the newly created Federal Housing Authority instituted a process of redlining neighborhoods, creating boundaries that segregated residents by race, to rigidify the separation of white and black Americans, even in communities where segregation was illegal. The inability of black Americans to get mortgages in redlined neighborhoods prevented them from amassing equity and savings they could pass to future generations. The 1935 Social Security Act didn't provide coverage for farmers or domestic workers, the two job categories that included most black Americans, leaving them without unemployment or retirement insurance. Black Americans were also cut out of the GI Bill, which provided other veterans with education, low-interest loans, and other benefits. Black veterans unable to earn degrees had little hope of building careers and little wealth to leave for future generations. That's part of why, for all the talk of a growing black middle class in America, the median wealth for a white family was $171,000 in 2016 and just $17,600 for a black family. Racial discrimination wasn't just confined to black Americans. Asian American immigrant women couldn't vote until they gained citizenship, and that didn't happen until 1952.

Despite these institutionalized disadvantages, other forces, including the civil rights movement, affirmative action, and one of the world's most permissive systems of immigration, have created unprecedented opportunities for Americans of color. The United States is the only majority-white nation in history to elect (and then reelect) a black head of state. And the country has become much more racially diverse—the US is expected to become majority non-white in about 2045.

But the Republican Party, now financed and supported overwhelmingly by white Americans, has found ways to rewrite voting rules to hold back the tide of history. Local laws targeted at making it more difficult for black citizens to vote, an American trend with a very long history, continue to be passed in dozens of US states. More broadly, many black Americans are driven to prove their lives matter by double standards they encounter every day. When crack cocaine devastated urban black communities in the 1980s and early 1990s, many in government and the media treated the problem as a crime wave. When the focus of addiction turned to white Americans hooked on opioids and other prescriptions drugs, the trend was treated as a tragedy.

White Americans accordingly do not see the police killings of black people suspected of petty crimes by white police officers as black people do. And as anger over injustice grows on one side, resentment, fueled by partisan media and online disinformation, drives politics on the other.

Other factors also drive division and dysfunction in the US, but I believe these are the most influential and durable. And each of these trends—corporate capture of governance; the dominant influence of money on US politics; the inequality of wealth and opportunity these phenomena create; the power of increasingly immersive new media to commoditize suspicion, dread, and anger; and the long-term corrosive effects of institutionalized racism—continues apace.

SOLUTIONS

Democrats and Republicans can prove to the American people that they understand the forces reshaping economies everywhere and can ensure that every working American has a reasonable chance to succeed in a changing world. They can invest in lifetime universal education so that the United States can draw on the highest possible portion of its human talent to build the world's most innovative workforce. Accept that the nature of work is changing and create more flexible health and other quality-of-life benefits to profit from continued expansion of the gig economy. Make social media companies responsible for mis- and disinformation published on their platforms. The corporate and individual supporters of television's Public Broadcast

System and National Public Radio could finance nonpartisan public social media to provide another source of information that isn't structuring its content to compete for media market share. Agree on a common set of rules to prevent the most egregious forms of partisan gerrymandering by either side. Experiment with ranked-choice voting in local elections to minimize extreme polarization. Challenge politicians to speak to voters who don't traditionally support them. Experiment locally with various forms of universal basic income, and be honest in appraising both the positive and negative results.

I'm not naive enough to believe that most American lawmakers will support any of these ideas, but the fifty US states and local governments have always been laboratories of democracy. Some of their inventions have damaged democracy and national cohesion, but others have moved the nation forward. States like California, Florida, Illinois, and Massachusetts—with two Republican and two Democratic governors and a total of more than seventy million people—are already heading toward a $15 minimum wage over the next several years, no matter what Congress does on this issue. New York City is already there. And the nation's largest metropolis also held its first ranked-choice mayoral election in 2021—almost certainly a bellwether for other counties, cities, and states.

Let's remember too that Obamacare, the plan to expand health-care coverage to millions more Americans, became much more popular after Democrats found the votes to push it through Congress and consumers saw the benefits for themselves.

More broadly, the two parties recognize the power of appealing to "working families." Democrats make economic appeals to the sense of self-interest in this group, while Republicans make cultural appeals to tribal solidarity. But both parties share an interest in finding ways to strengthen America by strengthening blue-collar citizens. All these experiments can help meet their needs. And Democrats and Republicans must learn one of the crucial lessons that the inequality created by laissez-faire globalization has taught us: not only must US foreign policy serve the needs of working-class Americans, but these citizens need to see and understand its benefits.

Americans and the US economy have recovered better and faster from the pandemic than have other advanced industrial economies, thanks mainly to the country's entrepreneurial business culture, pro-business regulation, a surge in government spending, and a willingness to keep interest rates low. The immediate relief provided by massive stimulus will convince many in power, and many ordinary Americans, that the crisis is over, and that life can return to normal. Unfortunately, that sense of normalcy is the biggest obstacle to change that America now faces, because relief allows complacency without addressing any of the bigger problems described above.

In a country as politically decentralized as the United States, state and local governments, in partnership with like-minded corporate and philanthropic leaders, can do more to help those hurt worst by the pandemic and to match an innovative business culture with a more innovative political culture. Political dysfunction breeds anger on all sides, increasing the risk that incompetent populist politicians more interested in dismantling government than in fixing it will gain new followers.

Meeting the global challenges that I'll detail in coming chapters will require leadership. Some of it must come from the world's sole superpower. America's dysfunctional politics cripples the nation's ability to provide leadership in two ways. First, it makes long-term investment in solutions for complex problems impossible to sustain. President Barack Obama committed the United States to a nuclear deal with Iran and to the Paris climate accord. Once elected, Donald Trump kept his campaign promise to withdraw from both. He pulled US support for the World Health Organization in the middle of the worst pandemic in a hundred years. When Joe Biden was elected, he restored the Obama-era commitments and reversed Trump's order on the WHO. If Donald Trump or an ally is elected in 2024, those decisions will be reversed yet again. During the Cold War, most conservatives and most liberals agreed that the Soviet Union posed the primary threat to world peace and American values. Democratic and Republican presidents committed to a consistent strategy of containment. In American politics today, there is no consensus on anything.

The second problem is that the first problem is no secret. Every American ally and rival knows that today's solemn vow can be shredded tomorrow. Democracies like Japan, South Korea, India, and Australia know that China's commitment to its increasingly assertive foreign policy is much more predictable that any long-term US response to it. European and Middle Eastern allies understand this, too. How can anyone expect the United States to consistently combat global threats like infectious disease, climate change, and new life-altering technologies when another headlong dive into "America First" might be right around the corner?

Just as international leaders must find ways to cooperate on the issues that matter most even as they compete everywhere else, so America's conservatives and progressives must learn to cooperate just enough to renew the country's strength. Neither side will eliminate the other. Both reflect deep currents in American life. They don't need to agree on everything. But they will have to agree on a few big things.

One of the most important is building a pragmatic partnership with Beijing to avoid a Cold War–style confrontation that America, China, and the world can't afford.

COLLISION COURSE 2: AMERICA AND CHINA

A smiling Xi Jinping waved to acknowledge the warm applause as he strode to the podium to begin the most anticipated speech of the 2017 World Economic Forum. It was the first-ever appearance at Davos by a Chinese president, and the usually jaded crowd, made up mainly of the capitalist world's political and business elite, was eager to hear what Xi had to say. Over the next few minutes, he told us the time had come for China to change history. Two years earlier, Xi had unveiled his "Made in China 2025" plan, a blueprint for global supremacy in AI, quantum computing, robotics, and other tech sectors. In 1990, then-leader Deng Xiaoping famously warned that China would be wise to "hide its strength and bide its time." But on that January morning at Davos in 2017, Xi made clear that China was done with hiding and biding.

"It was the best of times. It was the worst of times," Xi said. The invocation of Charles Dickens was surely meant to engage his listeners. He explained why China was wise to follow an economic development strategy laid down by the state, one in which the country's corporations were Chinese first and multinational a distant second. But the headline of the event was his forceful and energetic defense of globalism, the view that interdependence among nations strengthens us all. He condemned populism and protectionism, points all the more striking for their subtext: the other major news event that week was the inauguration of the famously anti-globalist Donald Trump three days later.

Fast-forward nine months to another podium and another Xi speech, this time to China's 19th Party Congress. At that event, he went much further in detailing his vision for China's future. He heralded "a new era" for his country and its people, one in which China intended to move "closer to center stage" in global politics. He presented China as "a new option for other countries," an alternative to Western democracy—and he outlined what he called the "Chinese solution" for the world's problems.

Under Xi's leadership, China has gone from pushing for reform of the current international system, to helping guide that reform, to making plans for leading it. Its leaders intend for China to dominate East Asia, in part by tightening political control in Hong Kong, pressuring Taiwan to stop resisting Beijing's push for unification with the mainland, and methodically building its military strength in the South China Sea.

Everywhere else, Xi wants China to become an indispensable economic power, with all the political influence that accompanies this role. In 2016, China created the Asian Infrastructure Investment Bank (AIIB) to invest in other countries. The country has joined the Regional Comprehensive Economic Partnership (RCEP), an enormous free-trade zone that spans more than a dozen nations. China's Belt and Road Initiative (BRI) is building roads, railways, bridges, and ports across Asia, Africa, and Europe. BRI is creating new opportunities in dozens of countries for Chinese companies and workers, and it will strengthen China's influence with their governments. Beijing's expanding influence in trade, investment, credit, and supply chains is making China the developing world's standards-setter for new technologies.

COVID-19 created new opportunities for China. Its authoritarian political system, backed by surveillance and other techno-social controls, and direct state intervention in the economy made China the first to emerge from recession in 2020. As the pandemic forced waves of defaults and bankruptcies of governments and companies in poorer countries, Beijing found itself with a unique ability to buy up suddenly cheaper assets—farmland, fossil fuels, minerals, energy resources, and infrastructure like highways, bridges, and ports. And while Americans bickered over how to measure and respond to the coronavirus threat, and the right of government to impose lockdowns to contain it, it was Beijing, not Washington, that offered equipment, cash, and advice to hard-hit countries.

Many of the products China offered were poorly made, provoking a backlash, particularly in Europe. And experts agree that the virus began in China—and that officials there made matters much worse for other countries by hiding the scale of the threat during the period when infections might have been contained.

It may well seem that China's burgeoning power is the inevitable result of President Trump's determination to withdraw the US from global leadership. But this change began with China's decades-long rise from poverty to economic powerhouse. It continued with President Carter's decision to normalize political relations with Beijing in 1979 and ramped up with President Bill Clinton's push to normalize economic relations with China by bringing the country into the World Trade Organization in 2001. But Xi Jinping's remarkable consolidation of power inside China and his grand ambitions for its central role in the international system began in 2012 and will accelerate when the country becomes the world's largest economy. Xi Jinping, not any American president, has put US-China relations on a more confrontational track.

China is home to 1.4 billion people and a middle-income

economy, an unsurpassed accomplishment. Add the Chinese government's ability to direct massive funds toward building projects—at home and abroad—that align with the national priorities of the state. Just as important, only China has a long-term global strategy that it will continue to execute as US presidents and European leaders come and go. None of us has ever lived in a world where the largest economy is governed by authoritarians. But that's where we're headed. And it puts the world's two most powerful nations—the United States and China—on a collision course.

Beyond the politics of today, the economics of tomorrow, and a growing risk of new forms of war—as if these questions weren't weighty enough—the US-China relationship is crucial for global peace and prosperity in other ways, too. If the world's governments can come to any meaningful agreement on how to tackle the historic challenges outlined in the chapters that follow, it will be because political leaders of the United States and China, with support from their respective peoples, have built what former Google CEO Eric Schmidt has called a "rivalry partnership." They will have found enough common ground to cooperate and invest in a mutually secure and prosperous future.

The US and China won't be allies anytime soon. But if they can become partners in addressing global threats to human health, climate change, and profoundly disruptive new technologies, then we will finally have the governance that globalization has never given us. The two countries will have created the foundation for a new international system, one that brings in the best ideas from Europe, Japan, India, and elsewhere to build a future we can all live in.

For now, however, the US-China relationship is headed in the opposite direction. Many in Washington and across the country see China's rise much as their grandparents saw the

Soviet Union's launch of Sputnik, the world's first artificial satellite: as an ill omen of American decline and a threat to its future. Many in Beijing and across China see US resistance to China's progress as a clumsy attempt to protect Western privileges by stunting China's growth—and they're determined to overcome this resistance. The US-China relationship is getting worse, and while the United States is by far the most politically dysfunctional and divided of the world's advanced democracies, China is by far the most cohesive and functional of the world's major authoritarian regimes. That adds to both the difficulty of improving US-China relations on American terms and the urgency of avoiding a destructive and costly confrontation.

CHINA'S RISE

China's rise, among the most remarkable accomplishments in history, has become one of the world's most familiar stories, but the numbers that tell it have not lost their power to amaze. Between 1990 and 2018, while the US share of the global economy fell modestly from 26.4 percent to 23.9 percent, China's share grew from 1.6 percent to 15.8 percent as hundreds of millions of Chinese rose from poverty toward the middle class.

Communist China is now the world's leader in trade. A generation ago, over 80 percent of the world's countries traded more with the US than with China. By 2018, China was the larger trade partner for 128 of 190 nations. It also holds valuable resources within its borders, including the largest reserves of many strategically valuable materials, like rare earth elements, which include minerals used in weapons and vehicles. Yes, anything multiplied by 1.4 billion people will be a big number, but China's success isn't just a matter of scale; it has also become a much more innovative country. In 1999, the World Intellectual Property Organization received just 276 patent applications from China. By 2019, that number had grown to nearly 59,000. China has also become a leader in taking on some of the international responsibilities that come with power. Since 2012, it has contributed more UN peacekeeping troops than the United States, Britain, France, and Russia, the other four permanent members of the UN Security Council, combined.

Hundreds of other numbers reveal China's ascendance, a source of deep pride for its citizens. The country's leaders have earned credit with them, not just because the state feeds them propaganda and dominates the flow of information into and around the country but because the Communist Party has transformed the lives of hundreds of millions within the living memory of most Chinese people.

China's continued rise is no sure thing. Xi Jinping has consolidated more power within the system than any leader since Mao, in part by purging potential rivals. There's a downside to that. If his government fails to deliver steadily rising prosperity, if he can't protect the Chinese people from crises, it will become harder for him to shift blame onto others. Public anger could become a force he will have to reckon with. Economic growth will become harder to deliver as China becomes more reliant for innovation and progress on a private sector that Xi expects to align with Communist Party development goals.

Jobs will be harder to come by as rising wages make China less attractive as an outsourcing destination and as more production is automated. Many of China's largest companies carry debt, and Beijing has never proven that it's willing to allow defaults that are destabilizing in the short term—by throwing people out of work and alienating investors—but crucial for long-term financial health. Increasingly combative trade relations with the United States and, in some areas, Europe will also slow China's expansion. The nation will need an ever-stronger social safety net as the population ages: the share of the population over sixty-five is expected to jump from 13.5 percent to nearly double that by 2030. And the risk of a financial crisis in China is rising as the need to prop up failing banks and a struggling real estate sector, and provide cash infusions for poorly managed state-run companies, triggers a wave of bankruptcies that throw people out of work and further burden the safety net. All of that could happen over the next decade.

But China's leaders have been managing these threats for decades. For now, its international influence will probably continue to grow, in part because more people around the world no longer consider America's global dominance a better alternative. Few Americans these days are demanding that their elected leaders fight for democracy and individual freedom far from US shores. Most Americans want President Biden and Congress to focus squarely on domestic problems like economic recovery, access to health care, job creation, gun policy, education, border security, protection against terrorism, and race relations.

And it's much harder for Washington to support democratic reforms in other countries when US elections are themselves the subject of intense dispute. How can Washington condemn human rights abuses in other countries when black Americans are so often brutalized by unaccountable police, and immigrants are treated as criminals? How can Americans promote free trade when politicians in both parties warn that free trade kills jobs? How can Washington lead coalitions of capable and like-minded allies when the former president publicly accused them of freeloading off the American taxpayer?

The idea of the "West" still has plenty of strength. Trade deals with rules to protect free markets continue to be signed.

NATO could be expanded to include Asia-Pacific members that give the organization its first truly global mandate. But China is offering alternative development models that are attracting much interest around the world, and public divisions among its leaders are rare. So when China approaches the government of what President Trump called a "shithole" country with an offer to boost economic growth and visibly improve living standards by replacing ramshackle infrastructure with twenty-first-century roads, bridges, hospitals, and ports—without asking for the painful economic reforms often demanded by Western lenders—many countries say yes. More will follow.

Some countries, however, are increasingly worried by China's rise, especially traditional US allies like Japan, South Korea, the Philippines, and Australia, among others. These countries want the US to continue to offer a true China alternative. They want US military protection to ensure their lucrative economic relations with China and Chinese companies, many of them owned by the state, don't create a dangerous dependence on Beijing. For many of these countries, the Trans-Pacific Partnership (TPP), originally a US-led twelve-nation bloc that was designed to form one of the largest free-trade zones in history, was especially appealing. President Obama committed the US to finishing that deal but couldn't get it done, and when Hillary Clinton, who once referred to the TPP as the "gold standard in trade agreements," backed away from the agreement while running for president in 2016, many of China's neighbors wondered whether Americans of both parties had given up on trade—and on their region. Then, three days after Donald Trump became president, he withdrew from the TPP negotiations. With leadership from Japan, a smaller version of the deal went forward, but doubts about the long-term US commitment to remain a power broker in Asia rose to new heights. Americans, if they'd been listening, could hear the cheers all the way from Beijing. China is here to stay, its leaders promised. Washington could not be reached for comment.

The United States still has plenty going for it—favorable geography, a historic surge in energy production, the privileges that come with the US dollar's continuing dominance as the world's reserve currency. But some traditional US advantages, particularly those relating to military power, mean less than they used to. The US has defense treaties with dozens of countries, while China's only military ally is North Korea, and thanks in part to its eleven nuclear-powered aircraft carriers and the eighty fighter planes that each can carry, the US is still the only country that can project conventional military power anywhere in the world. China has just two carriers, and both are much smaller than their US counterparts. The US has military bases in forty countries, while China is present in just three. The reach of the People's Liberation Army is limited almost entirely to East and Southeast Asia, and the country hasn't developed a nuclear arsenal large enough to compete with those of the United States and Russia.

But that military imbalance doesn't offer as much stability to build a "rivalry partnership" as it used to, because any future war between great powers won't be won by aircraft carriers or tanks or even boots on the ground. It's more likely to be decided by the superiority of one side's cyberweapons and its ability to wield power through trade and investment opportunities and restrictions. Cyberweapons are the great levelers. The outcome of this kind of war will be harder to predict than were those of wars of the past. A nation's cyber-arsenal can't be photographed from space like missile silos, military bases, warships, or other combat hardware. It's impossible to quantify the true balance of power in cyberspace, at least in the way that the potency of an arsenal in the physical world can be determined—because offensive and defensive cyber-capabilities are less well understood and changing so rapidly. History shows us that when the balance of power is unclear, conflicts become more likely.

THE EMERGING TRAP

Twenty-four centuries ago, the Athenian historian Thucydides made an observation that often crops up in discussions of today's US-China relationship: how emerging power Athens provoked fear in established power Sparta and made war between them inevitable. This idea that champion and challenger are doomed to clash is known as the Thucydides Trap, and though comparisons of different power dynamics at different moments in history can be deceptive, Thucydides's logic rings true for the twenty-first century.

There is dread on both sides. US policymakers fear that China will rewrite the rules that created and protected US dominance in the post–Cold War world—and that China's rules will undermine the global appeal of democracy and individual freedom. Many Chinese fear that the US is determined to curb their country's natural growth in order to protect its great power advantages, and that China can never realize its legitimate potential in a US-dominated world. There *has* been a sharp shift in the balance of power between champion and challenger over the past fifteen years. After all, the Peloponnesian War between Athens and Sparta ended with a Spartan victory—but at ruinous cost to both sides.

But over the past decades, there has also been a deepening interdependence that binds China and the United States together. China's rise has created historic profit opportunities for American companies, first as a source of inexpensive labor and then as an enormous consumer market for US-made products. At the end of 2019, there were some seventy thousand US companies doing hundreds of billions of dollars' worth of business in China. The Chinese, in turn, have benefited from the stability created by the US-led international system to grow their economy and expand their influence abroad. They've been a vitally important lender for the US government via the purchase of US treasuries. There is no more important symbol of US-Chinese interdependence than the supply chains that link the two economies.

Yet American apprehension, then fear, inspired by the sheer scale of China's success, has led US policymakers to challenge the methods China has used to ensure its lasting success. There are three broad US commercial complaints: China's government won't open more of its markets to foreign companies, it heavily subsidizes Chinese companies to give them an unfair advantage over foreign competitors, and it takes intellectual property from foreign firms by forcing them to share in exchange for access to Chinese consumers—or by simply stealing it. Given that new technologies are now fast transforming the global economy and, with it, the balance of power, the US and others have warned China that they will no longer tolerate large-scale theft of intellectual property perpetrated by Chinese companies and facilitated by the government. In the United States, this warning has the support of both Democrats and Republicans, not to mention growing numbers of US corporate and other interests. Many of the latter no longer believe that the benefits of doing business with and investing in China outweigh the drawbacks.

Donald Trump was the first president since Lyndon Johnson to reject an "engagement-first" approach to China. What began in March 2018 with US action against steel and aluminum imported from China became hundreds of billions of dollars in tariffs on a broad range of Chinese products. China responded in kind. Each government already had powerful political incentives to "get tough" with the other side, on all kinds of disputes. The trade war increased those incentives—and showed both governments that decades of deepening economic integration had created vulnerabilities the other side could exploit during a confrontation. That realization created new incentives for separation. The US and China are now "decoupling" by looking for every means of reducing each side's economic, financial, and technological dependence on the other. Their relationship is deteriorating on just about every front, making it harder for them to find common ground when they need to most—for their own sake and the world's.

China still needs access to US investment, technology, and consumers. The United States still has a large enough edge in military muscle to prevent China from dominating East and Southeast Asia and forcing US allies there to follow China's lead. But by 2030, when China will likely surpass the US as the world's largest economy, US advantages will have narrowed significantly, and future American presidents will have to be much more flexible and creative in negotiating with Xi Jinping or his successor.

Once the trade war began, Xi and Trump both had good reason to show their people that they weren't afraid of confrontation. Then COVID-19 provided fresh incentives for a get-tough approach. As COVID began killing large numbers of Americans, Trump tried to deflect criticism of his incoherent response by shifting blame to China for lying about the origins of the virus. And Trump was right: in the early days of the virus's spread, the Chinese government launched a large coverup to protect its reputation. It hid news of the virus, reprimanded the first doctor to speak publicly about the dangers it posed, kicked foreign journalists out of the country for reporting on it, withheld critical information from both the World Health Organization and visiting doctors and scientists, and allowed millions of Chinese, many of them infected with the virus, to travel across China and abroad. That failure and deception transformed COVID from a Chinese problem into a global pandemic.

But this widely accepted reality didn't force a Chinese retreat, because China was the world's second-largest economy and well on its way to being number one. It was a critical part of global supply chains—in desperately needed medical supplies and other areas. China was the first to restart its economy, and it began an international charm offensive. While Trump tossed personal insults at reporters and offered quack cures for the virus, Xi Jinping was touring Wuhan to tout the success of his lockdown, and he ordered local officials to offer a "solemn apology" for their treatment of the doctor who had become a hero in Chinese social media after dying while fighting COVID. China then sent medical advisers and humanitarian aid (much of it medical equipment) to hard-hit Italy, the third-largest economy in the EU and the first EU country to sign up for Belt and Road. More Chinese doctors and equipment went to help in Spain. Here was the "new option for other countries" that Xi Jinping had announced in 2017.

In fact, China had become much more than just an "option," because the Trump administration had little to offer the world in response. Gone were the days when, as in 2004, after a tsunami ravaged Indonesia, the US quickly sent troops to help distribute humanitarian aid, Japan contributed money and medical supplies, European governments and companies signed up to help, and China did virtually nothing. In 2020, as COVID killed

Europeans, then Americans, then many others, China saw a space that the US and its allies seemed no longer willing or able to fill—and jumped in with both feet.

The strategy worked. In June 2020, a study conducted by the European Council on Foreign Relations found that the experience of COVID-19 had further damaged European public attitudes toward the United States. It also reported that when asked whom they considered their most useful ally in battling coronavirus, just 4 percent of Italians cited the EU, while 25 percent named China. China took its share of criticism in 2020 over heavy-handed politics in Hong Kong, massive human rights violations in its Xinjiang region, and the poor quality of some of the relief supplies it offered. But the country's determination to bring about Xi's "new era" in international politics was on display as leadership during a global crisis—a display like nothing Beijing had attempted before.

During the worst days of the pandemic, relations between the US and China reached their lowest point in decades. While Donald Trump was blaming China for what he defiantly called "kung flu," Chinese officials encouraged a rumor that a US soldier had brought the coronavirus to Wuhan. They also pushed a sharp increase in broader anti-US content in the Chinese media. In particular, many stories appeared on social media in 2020 highlighting the incompetent American response to the virus, particularly in comparison with the dramatic and effective lockdown that China's government had ordered. At the same time, state media was playing up the story of Chinese entrepreneur Jack Ma offering the US five hundred thousand COVID test kits.

Across the Pacific, attitudes hardened in the US. In a survey from Pew Research conducted in March 2020, 66 percent of Americans expressed an unfavorable view of China, a 20 percentage point jump since Trump became president in 2016 and the highest number Pew had recorded since first asking the question in 2005. Just 26 percent indicated a favorable view. That gave both Democrats and Republicans even more reason to prove they could "get tough" with China. Joe Biden has picked up where Donald Trump left off, by keeping tariffs in place, criticizing China's secrecy, and adding new condemnations of China's human rights abuses. US vaccine diplomacy soon outpaced China's, but the competition between them intensified. In May 2021, Kurt Campbell, Biden's lead Asia adviser, declared publicly that the era of engagement with China "has come to an end . . . the dominant paradigm is going to be competition."

In short, the idea of a "rivalry partnership" between the US and China has receded into the distance. The rivalry is intensifying. The partnership, not so much.

FLASHPOINTS

Any one of many triggers might bring these two countries to blows in coming years. Let's start with one of the most dangerous. In 1996, China fired ballistic missiles into the sea to intimidate Taiwan. In response, President Clinton ordered two aircraft carriers into the Taiwan Strait to send Beijing a message. China backed down. That was a quarter century ago. In the ensuing years, China has spent trillions on modern missiles, air defenses, submarines, cyberweapons, and other twenty-first-century weapons of war. In March 2021, *People's Daily*, the Communist Party newspaper, reported that President Xi had called on China's military and police to become "combat ready" to defend the country's sovereignty, and a noted Chinese scholar predicted that Xi wanted to "[speed] up a resolution of the Taiwan issue during [his] third term as president." That means sometime between 2022 and 2027. A top US admiral warned in March 2021 that China might well invade Taiwan "in the next six years." If China fired missiles toward Taiwan today, how would President Biden respond? If he followed Clinton's example, would Beijing again back down? What if they didn't? What about five years from now?

In Asia more broadly, the balance of military power has changed. The US has defense treaties with dozens of countries, while China is committed only to defending North Korea. But would the US really go to war with nuclear-armed China on behalf of Vietnam and the Philippines to prevent China's domination of the South China Sea? If it did, how many allies would rally to its side?

A US-China confrontation would be more dangerous than the Cold War between the US and the USSR, because it would be waged with cyber- and other weapons that, as discussed, largely prevent either side from seeing the true balance of power, making escalation more likely. And the fight will be less about communist or capitalist ideology than about economic and technological power. Unlike the Soviet Union, China isn't exporting an ideology, however much Xi Jinping talks about Marxist-Leninist principles at home. Instead, it is asking the world to see it as strong, capable, wise, benevolent, and whole. ("Whole," by the way, means that Taiwan is part of China.)

The most disruptive issue isn't centered on a particular island or body of water, and it has nothing to do with tariffs. It's a battle over the future of technology—next-generation communications tools, machine learning, surveillance software, artificial intelligence—the subject of its own chapter later in the book. China is already a technology superpower, and there is already a bipolar Cold War structure to the US-China technology relationship that will affect every region of the world. In the markets for commodities, goods, and services, the US and China are both competitors and (potential) partners. Each wants more market share, but all benefit from an open trading system. Trade wars may be launched to achieve specific goals, but trade itself isn't a zero-sum competition. "Business as usual" on trade promises something for everyone. It's a critical support for global peace and prosperity.

But the global market for data and information is now breaking in two. At first, the internet—the World Wide Web—was driven by a single set of standards and rules. With very few exceptions, one consumer had virtually the same access as another. No longer. China and the United States are now building two distinct online ecosystems. This applies to the transformation of today's internet but also to the Internet of Things (IoT), the network created by the connection to the internet of devices as diverse as appliances, automobiles, wearable medical devices, and satellites. The American tech ecosystem, with all its strengths and shortcomings, is built by the private sector and (loosely) regulated by the government. The Chinese system is dominated by the state; so too is the collection of big data, the development of AI, the rollout of 5G technology, and defense and retaliation against cyberattacks.

We don't yet know where the virtual Berlin Wall will stand. Or whether the EU will align with the United States or fragment into a patchwork of decisions by individual European countries. It's likewise too soon to confidently predict where India, South Korea, Brazil, or even Japan will position themselves. We do know that on technology, the US wants China to fail or fall in line, because China's technological development, combined with its authoritarian and state capitalist political model, poses a foundational challenge to the values on which democracy, individual freedoms, and global stability and prosperity depend. This is the rare subject on which Democrats and Republicans agree.

Through its Belt and Road Initiative, China has already invested more than $100 billion in other countries' infrastructure. This process boosts Beijing's influence within these countries, but once these projects are built, anyone can use them. The technology competition is different. Splitting the global tech ecosystem in two creates different information and data spaces. In this way, a technology Cold War will tribalize humanity in new ways. If Americans who watch different cable channels see very different versions of their country, imagine the US-China disconnect in a *world* divided by differing rules and standards. It's "us vs. them" on a global scale. A "splinternet," the creation of parallel technology ecosystems, isn't just a threat to globalization. It's a competition that those who believe in political freedoms might lose. Each side's ideal outcome is eliminating the other system. This is a zero-sum game, and the biggest challenge to hopes for a future US-China rivalry partnership.

CHINA'S RISE OFFERS OPPORTUNITIES

To build the partnership needed to avoid Cold War and work together on the world's most pressing problems, Americans must recognize the value in China's rise. First, anyone who claims that Western values and leadership are the essential foundation for a secure, fair, and prosperous future must reckon with the reality that Western leadership helped drive us into today's chaotic, crisis-prone global state of play. Divisions between Europe and the United States—and the increasingly bitter polarization within so many Western countries—are plain to see.

The global financial crisis didn't begin in China. The United States is responsible for that, because Washington's failure to properly regulate lending set off the chain reaction in global banking that inflicted so much damage worldwide. Those who believe in the power of cross-border commerce to create a broad prosperity have to admit that China, not the United States, has become a champion of global trade. Nor did Western powers contain the coronavirus as effectively as China did. Western countries don't agree with one another on how to fight climate change, how to regulate new technologies, how to manage borders, how to engage Russia, or how to respond to China's rise.

And let's not pretend that US military intervention always produces stability. China's leaders, fearful of foreign intervention in their own country, and with plenty of history to justify their fears, insist that no nation has the right to preemptively invade another or to interfere in its internal affairs. Most Americans disagree, and the US military has intervened repeatedly in other countries, including militarily, sometimes with NATO or other allies, since the Cold War's end. The most obvious examples are Panama, Haiti, Somalia, the former Yugoslavia, Iraq (twice), and Afghanistan. The stated goals have differed in each case: to arrest a criminal, halt a humanitarian catastrophe, prevent ethnic cleansing, punish one country's invasion of its neighbor, block the production of dangerous weapons, or fight terrorism.

Some of these ventures—in Panama and the former Yugoslavia; the first Iraq war—achieved their stated goals, at least in part. Others—intervention in Somalia and in Haiti; the second Iraq war; Afghanistan—ended as fiascoes. China would not have invaded Iraq in 2003 to capture nonexistent weapons of mass destruction, creating the political vacuum that spawned a new generation of terrorists. The war in Afghanistan achieved little lasting benefit for the United States and cost US taxpayers trillions of dollars. Some of the last American soldiers to leave Kabul in August 2021 hadn't even been born when Al Qaeda attacked the United States on 9/11. The costs of these adventures, measured in long-term care for US combat veterans, will grow for decades to come. China's American critics charge that Beijing will refuse the costs and risks that come with intervening in foreign countries to prevent humanitarian disasters. But there are millions of people in Rwanda ready to remind the world that the United States and its allies don't always show up, either.

Further, China can help solve many of the world's development problems. The first obvious example: poorer countries badly need better infrastructure. As mentioned above, Beijing created the Asian Infrastructure Investment Bank, a multilateral lender that includes seventy-eight member countries, including, despite Washington's best efforts, many traditional US allies: the United Kingdom, France, Germany, South Korea, Australia, and Israel. The AIIB aims to help finance Belt and Road projects in Asia. It has invested billions in everything from roads, bridges, ports, and airports to controlling COVID-19. Though it has been criticized for serving Beijing's political objectives, in June 2020 the AIIB approved a $750 million loan to help China's rival India cope with the coronavirus in the same week that Chinese and Indian troops were locked in a deadly skirmish in disputed territory along their shared northern border.

China is often accused of creating the AIIB as an alternative to the International Monetary Fund (IMF) and other regional lenders in order to impose new lending rules that serve Chinese political goals. Yet it remains a major contributor to the IMF, and the AIIB has partnered with the World Bank, the Asian Development Bank, the Islamic Development Bank, the African

Development Bank, and the European Bank for Reconstruction and Development. The developing world, and many wealthier countries too, badly need investment in physical infrastructure. China is meeting some of those needs.

US policymakers warn that China is extending its influence across Asia by forming economic ties that entangle unsuspecting partners. Some fear that China will use the Belt and Road Initiative to saddle recipient countries with debts they can't repay, allowing China to strip those countries of strategically valuable assets. What happens, critics ask, when China finances construction of an Indian Ocean port in Pakistan as part of a plan to spend tens of billions on dams, power plants, roads, and railways? Economic troubles force Pakistan to default on its debt. China then claims this valuable port, gaining another foothold in waters traditionally dominated by rival India. But borrowing nations should be allowed to decide for themselves which loans they can afford to pay back, without an approving nod from Washington. The United States certainly has strategic goals in mind when loaning its allies large sums of money. Even the justly heralded Marshall Plan was designed in part to create markets for US exports and keep European governments from aligning with the Soviet Union.

The other problem with Washington's complaints about China's expanding commercial influence in Asia is that the Trump administration backed away from the Trans-Pacific Partnership, which aligned members with the United States rather than with non-member China. When Trump withdrew from negotiations, referring to the deal with characteristic subtlety as "a rape of our country," he left the remaining members to finish the deal on their own. China then reached out to most of these countries with an invitation to join its Regional Comprehensive Economic Partnership, a deal that included favorable terms for China.

That deal, arguably the largest in history in terms of trade volume, was signed in November 2020. Asian countries, many of which are now members of both pacts, are left to wonder if America can or will give them anything better than what China has on offer.

As China's economy grows, its leaders are using the country's new wealth to increase its power and prestige in the world—as all great powers have always done. There's no Chinese master plan to "make the world safe for autocracy," and there is no evidence that China means to "replace" the United States. For the foreseeable future, that will remain far beyond China's means. The world needs China closer to center stage. It needs Chinese investment. It needs China to remain stable and predictable—and to grow. And if Washington wants to build a pragmatic partnership with Beijing, it should join the rest of the world in recognizing that reality.

CHINA'S RISE IS ALSO DANGEROUS

But partnership on big challenges does not demand that Americans or anyone else ignore the dangers that China poses.

There is sometimes a price to be paid for China's "nonintervention." If NATO hadn't used force to halt the war in the former Yugoslavia, many more innocents would have been murdered. No, a superpower China wouldn't have invaded Iraq in 2003, but nor would it have repelled the Iraqi army from Kuwait in 1991, freeing Iraqi strongman Saddam Hussein to extend his unprovoked land grab deep into Saudi Arabia and allowing him to steal large volumes of crude oil and manipulate energy-importing countries. Successful multilateral foreign interventions don't justify the failures of others; nor should the failures obscure the need for multilateral action in the most urgent cases.

The risks associated with China's enormous investment projects aren't just hypothetical. In 2017, Sri Lanka *did* default on Chinese loans and *was* forced to give Beijing control of a major seaport for ninety-nine years. Malaysia's prime minister warned in 2018 that BRI loans from China could enable "debt-trap diplomacy" and a "new form of colonialism" (though he backtracked a few months later), and activists in Africa and Latin America have complained that Chinese-financed infrastructure projects often come with Chinese construction crews, depriving local workers of opportunities for good jobs. Others say too many BRI projects are designed to generate cash for investors rather than provide needed infrastructure, and that too many projects build roads that few will travel and bridges few will cross. While even the Soviets wanted to win hearts and minds in developing countries, Chinese investors often don't seem interested in the locals at all.

Every government acts in its own self-interest. But effective leadership requires risk-taking. To protect the free flow of commerce by working with allies to guard tanker traffic through a choke point like the Strait of Hormuz requires a willingness to put sailors at risk. During the 1990s, though very few US and European voters considered peace in the Balkans a national priority, American and European troops were put in harm's way to halt the civil war in Yugoslavia. Even under the assertive and self-confident leadership of Xi Jinping, China's Communist Party still has negligible interest in taking on risks for the common good. Beijing will loan large sums and contribute peacekeepers. But it won't deploy the People's Liberation Army to end the killing in a war in which China has no direct stake, whatever the humanitarian cost.

Leadership also means helping those who desperately need

it—for example, by granting sanctuary to refugees. The US has accepted more than three million refugees since 1980. EU member states and countries like Turkey, Jordan, and even Iran accepted millions of refugees during the war in Afghanistan and the migrant crisis of 2015–2016, and asylum seekers keep coming. China won't accept refugees even from North Korea, an ally and one of the poorest countries on earth. It has arrested and forcibly returned an unknown number of fleeing North Koreans over the years, defying its obligations under the 1951 Refugee Convention. The Trump administration's immigration policy was the subject of intense criticism, but the US still issued about one million green cards in 2019, while China reportedly granted permanent residency to some ten thousand foreigners from 2004 to 2017. Less than one-tenth of 1 percent of the people living in China were born in another country.

Western democracy has no monopoly on truth, and it's not the only path to a better life. Some insist, with strong arguments to back them up, that China offers a legitimate alternative to what passes today for US leadership, and that Westerners are morally obtuse (or maybe racist) when they refuse to acknowledge China's successes and the legitimacy of its political and economic system.

But China is no role model for anyone who believes that law exists mainly to safeguard the rights of the individual. In his 2004 book *The Case for Democracy: The Power of Freedom to Overcome Tyranny and Terror*, former Soviet dissident Natan Sharansky described what he called the "town square test": "If a person cannot walk into the middle of the town square and express his or her views without fear of arrest, imprisonment, or physical harm, then that person is living in a fear society, not a free society."

Walk into the middle of Tiananmen Square or any other

public gathering place in China, start passing out leaflets that challenge the Communist Party's right to hold power, and you won't spend that night in your own bed.

In 2013, Xi Jinping's Communist Party banned all discussion of universal values, freedom of the press, and the party's past mistakes. In 2018, teachers from kindergarten through university were ordered to adhere to "Xi Jinping thought" and to defend the Communist Party at all times. Teachers and professors seen to wander off the official path are spied on, attacked online by their students, stripped of privileges like internet access and the right to travel, publicly shamed, fired, and even arrested.

In short, China is a police state. On that score, nothing has changed since tanks crushed peaceful demonstrators in Tiananmen Square on June 4, 1989. For those who believe that all people in all nations should live in a free society, no amount of economic growth or technological accomplishment can justify single-party authoritarian rule or the brutality it can unleash on people who want to think and speak freely.

There are many ways to tell the story of state repression in today's China, but none as dramatic as the treatment of Uighur Muslims in its far west Xinjiang region. The Uighurs once made up a majority of Xinjiang's population, but over the years, the Chinese government has moved millions of Han Chinese into the area to dilute the Uighur advantage. To extend its control of the region's demographics, state officials have taken an active interest in "birth control." Xi Jinping has moved China away from the "one-child policy" for Han Chinese, but, according to a 2020 report from the Associated Press, the Chinese state has regularly forced pregnancy checks, implantation of intrauterine devices, abortion, and even sterilization on hundreds of thousands of ethnic minority women.

Uighurs have responded to discrimination and repression with protests, and sometimes violence. Xi Jinping has countered with systematic repression on a scale the world has rarely seen. China has imprisoned as many as one million Uighur Muslims in indoctrination camps. China's government refers to these prisons as "vocational training centers" and insists that their purpose is to teach Uighurs to reject terrorism and teach them job skills. It also insists that it's nobody's business but China's what happens within the country's borders. Human rights groups have uncovered evidence, including hundreds of pages of leaked Chinese state documents, that inmates have been raped and tortured. The plight of the Uighurs illustrates just how hollow China's principles of noninterference really are. In essence, China will ignore crimes within, and aggression from, other countries in order to defend the right to abuse human rights on a colossal scale within its borders. This is one of the most obvious reasons that finding common ground with China won't be easy.

A strategic partnership with China doesn't require the world to ignore these crimes. In fact, it can provide the only leverage outsiders have to nudge China toward change.

Cyber-Sovereignty

To surveil and control its citizens China has imposed a policy called "cyber-sovereignty," a lofty term meant to describe control of what people inside a particular country can access on the internet. China's cybersecurity law, established in 2017, requires all those using the internet to register using their real names, making it easier for the state to monitor viewing habits and discussion. The state has also given itself the right to access personal data "affecting national security, the national economy, and people's livelihood"—and the state, of course, gets to define these terms. Regulators have used this principle to ban companies like Google, Twitter, Facebook, Wikipedia, and YouTube in order to keep tighter control over what people see, hear, and read. And as more of its companies compete with Western giants in the developing world, China can try to write rules on privacy and censorship for governments that want to follow its lead on information control.

China is also using its enormous market power, in the form of access to its hundreds of millions of middle-class consumers, to change how Western tech companies act inside the country. In 2019, just one day after Chinese state media criticized its use, Apple removed an app called HKmap.live from its online store that protesters in Hong Kong were using to track the movement of police around the city. Apple explained the move by accepting Chinese complaints that demonstrators were using it to attack police, while critics charge the company was simply bowing to commercial pressure from Beijing. In this way, China threatens the ideal of an open internet everywhere, and autocrats in other countries are taking notes.

State intrusion on privacy is becoming increasingly absolute. In 2020, reports emerged that Chinese police had spent three years collecting blood samples from males across the country as part of a project to build a "genetic map" of China's seven hundred million men and boys, according to a report from the Australian Strategic Policy Institute. (The focus on males is premised on the idea that men and boys are more likely to commit crimes—and perhaps to protest against their government.) These seven hundred million people are not criminals. They're citizens. Many are children. And they have no idea how this information will be used. In the name of public safety, all citizens are treated as potential criminals. It's one more step toward a surveillance society supported by ubiquitous state-of-the-art cameras, facial recognition technologies, and artificial intelligence.

Social Credit

Chinese authorities also rely increasingly on the country's still-in-development "social credit system." Consumers in wealthier countries know that private companies create scores that tell creditors and potential creditors how much debt they have and whether they pay their bills on time. We also know that consumers can score each other on how well they fulfill the terms of commercial transactions—think ratings on Amazon, eBay, and Uber. But though there is not yet a single social credit system in China, state and local officials have expanded the possible uses of this concept to include penalties for petty crimes like jaywalking, public drunkenness, and disturbing the peace.

The system might one day go much further. According to state officials, its goal is to prevent "conduct that seriously undermines . . . the normal social order" and to "allow the trustworthy to roam everywhere under heaven while making it hard for the discredited to take a single step." Have you ever missed an alimony payment? Have you been fired from a job? Signed a petition? Attended a protest? Have any of your friends or relatives done any of these things? The state isn't yet asking these questions, but as it develops this system, the remaining obstacles to this sort of control are not legal but technological.

A good social credit score might get you a higher salary, a better apartment, the right to travel, and a higher pension. A bad score can ensure that you're permanently denied access to all those things, unless you can persuade a judge that you've mended your ways. The system can be used to punish people who cheat, steal, and commit violent acts, but it can also be used to control political dissent.

Selling the Tools of Repression

How China treats its own people should arouse our concern, even our anger. But we should also worry that China is exporting its surveillance technologies to other countries. All citizens want police to catch criminals, and many of us have learned to live with surveillance cameras looming overhead. But there is a growing debate about the use of facial recognition technologies on the general population. In China, home to many companies that are pioneers in this area, the state has invested heavily in these new tools, and tech firms have gathered huge amounts of data to make them more effective. China is, of course, developing its own rules and standards for how these technologies are designed and used—and they're selling them to foreign governments.

Xinjiang is a testing ground for instruments of repression that can be exported. An April 2019 investigation by the *New York Times* found that Chinese security officials have used surveillance cameras and state-of-the-art facial recognition technology to monitor the entire Uighur population. In essence, it's the first known use of artificial intelligence to automate racism. Successfully tested, similar tools can be used in all parts of China—and sold to foreign governments too.

As when CloudWalk, an AI company, reportedly sold facial recognition software to the government of Zimbabwe, which has one of the world's most repressive regimes, presumably as part of a project to develop secure banking technologies. That deal was backed by the Belt and Road Initiative. In the process, CloudWalk helped Zimbabwe develop a national facial recognition database, according to a report by *Science and Technology Daily*, a Chinese state-run newspaper. The deal with Zimbabwe served another, less obvious purpose: the database of Zimbabwean faces that the government then shared with CloudWalk has helped the company's AI technologists become much more accurate in identifying black faces, which will enhance the appeal of its software in other African countries and stunt the growth of African startups working on similar technologies.

A 2018 report from Freedom House, a pro-democracy nongovernmental organization, or NGO, found that seventeen other countries—from the United Arab Emirates, Venezuela, and Uzbekistan to Pakistan, Kenya, and even Germany—are now using Chinese-made "intelligent monitoring systems." China has provided training for three dozen more countries on topics like "public opinion guidance," a term we don't need George Orwell to explain for us. Western countries can sell these tech tools too. American big data firms like Palantir have come under international scrutiny, particularly for their relationships with the US Central Intelligence Agency and Immigration and Customs Enforcement. But there is a free press in the US and other democracies with license to investigate and to call both governments and companies to account. Not so in China, where secrecy is part of both the political culture and the sales pitch to foreign governments with which many democracies won't do business. It's not as though a pro-democracy activist or opposition lawmaker in Zimbabwe can force China to reveal what surveillance products it has sold to her government. Citizens exhausted by violent crime often welcome cameras and high-tech monitoring in their countries. But in a dictatorship, tools that police use to catch criminals are also weapons that secret police can use to monitor and crack down on dissent. What's true for cameras and facial recognition will also be true for artificial intelligence that tracks criminally (and politically) suspicious behavior online.

The invention of disruptive new tools (and weapons) is as old as humankind. They can't be un-invented. And as users surrender more and more of their privacy and fears for personal security grow, new information technologies might ultimately make America more like China rather than the other way around. Either way, suspicion, an obstacle to any form of China-US partnership, continues to grow.

CONFRONTATION IS NOT INEVITABLE

While acknowledging the differences between the US-Soviet conflict of the twentieth century and the US-China confrontation today, experts increasingly agree that we have entered a new Cold War. Historian and journalist Niall Ferguson calls it Cold War II: "We find ourselves once again with a peace that is no peace. That is the definition of Cold War."

"A new Cold War has begun," agrees Robert Kaplan, writing in *Foreign Policy* in 2019. "[D]ifferences between the United States and China are stark and fundamental. They can barely be managed by negotiations and can never really be assuaged." Peter Beyer, the German official charged with his country's relations with the United States and Canada, warned in 2020 that the "new Cold War between the United States and China has already begun and will shape this century."

I disagree. Despite their many differences, some of which cannot be resolved, Washington and Beijing are not yet locked in a new Cold War. And they need to stop behaving as if they are, because such a conflict would be a strategic failure of the highest order for both countries. A new great-power confrontation would undermine the interdependence that grows our economies, protects our security, and gives us the best means of addressing the impending global crises this book details.

The United States and China will find themselves nose-to-nose in many areas. In some, competition between them will be zero-sum: the US and Chinese governments will never agree on the future of Taiwan, Hong Kong, or the South China Sea. In others, like trade and investment, both competition and cooperation for mutual benefit is possible. In still other areas, like those I'll describe over the next three chapters, collaboration is essential . . . or we all fail. It's in the interest of both governments to clearly define, frankly and realistically, which issues fall into which categories.

For now, the greatest threats to America arise from its own failings—its hyper-polarized politics, widening inequity, and deepening mistrust of political institutions and the media. But over time, China will pose a unique challenge for America and for democracies everywhere, because it's a kind of rival none of us has ever seen before. The Soviet Union posed a military and ideological challenge, but it was never a commercial rival. In the 1980s, Japan proved a dynamic commercial competitor for the United States, but it remained a political and military ally. Twenty-first-century China is a military, political, and commercial rival—and in the realm of new technologies, the boundaries between these categories quickly become blurred. The US and China are the two great powers in a world that can't be neatly divided by a wall made from cheap East German cement.

F. Scott Fitzgerald famously wrote that "the test of a first-rate intelligence is the ability to hold two opposed ideas in the mind at the same time, and still retain the ability to function." In that spirit, the United States must work with China to meet the biggest challenges facing both countries and the world, even as they compete and come into conflict in other areas. Yes, the US and its allies should work to protect the principles of democracy, the rule of law, and human rights everywhere. (That work starts at home, of course, though it doesn't end there.) But China's ascent can't, and should not, be contained. Its rise is natural, and its people want and deserve a better life. Former US secretary of state Mike Pompeo once argued that the US and its allies should ensure "China retains only its proper place in the world"; but it's not up to Americans to define China's "proper place." Statements like Pompeo's bolster the arguments of those in China who say that America is determined to keep their country down.

There *are* ways in which China's contributions are good for the world. In those areas, Americans and others should welcome those contributions and even take part in them, for instance by joining Chinese-led trade and financial institutions. It will be much harder for China's nationalists to argue that the US wants to stunt its growth if the US actually supports China's development.

———

The crises detailed in later chapters don't care about walls or borders, and they can't be addressed if the United States and China launch a Cold War and demand that other nations choose sides. Without some level of shared cost, shared risk, shared sacrifice, and shared imagination between China and America, these challenges will not be met. The true US-China fight is not between the two governments but rather within each country— between those who believe that America and China must work together for the good of all and those who don't.

As I'll detail in the conclusion, there's ample common ground on which to build a constructive, cooperative, well-coordinated competition—if the two sides believe they can trust each other on the threats that both face. This is the important point: governments, business, civil society, and individuals must come to consensus on the fact that public health crises, climate change, and the advent of life-altering new technologies pose a threat to every nation and every human. That consensus must then become the foundation on which all these parties work to build real solutions and invest in our common future.

Now we turn to the first of these great tests and opportunities.

CHAPTER 2

PANDEMIC POLITICS

We need a crisis to forge new international cooperation and build a better international system. COVID gave us a crisis, and there are lessons in that story that can help us meet the bigger challenges ahead.

To learn these lessons, we must remember the speed at which this crisis unfolded. In less than three months, we went from the first COVID death in China to more than one million people infected worldwide. The true number will never be known—because tests weren't widely available, because many countries saw their health systems quickly overwhelmed, and because many people in developing countries never made it to hospitals at all. That speed makes it all the more crucial that governments do much more to prepare for the next health crisis well in advance. Cross-border communication and cooperation are central to that planning.

CATASTROPHE FORETOLD

Some crises are hard to foresee and prepare for. COVID was not one of them. As President George W. Bush said in November 2005:

> *A pandemic is a lot like a forest fire: if caught early, it might be extinguished with limited damage. If allowed to smolder, undetected, it can grow to an inferno that can spread quickly beyond our ability to control it. . . . To respond to a pandemic, we need medical personnel and adequate supplies of equipment. In a pandemic, everything from syringes to hospital beds, respirators, masks and protective equipment would be in short supply.*
>
> *If a pandemic strikes, our country must have a surge capacity in place that will allow us to bring a new vaccine on line quickly.*

And as President Obama said in December 2014:

> *There may and likely will come a time in which we have an airborne disease that is deadly. And in order for us to deal with that effectively, we have to put in place an infrastructure—not just here at home, but globally—that allows us to see it quickly, isolate it quickly, respond to it quickly. . . . So that if and when a new strain of flu, like the Spanish flu, crops up five years from now or a decade from now, we've made the investment, and we're further*

along to be able to catch it. It is a smart investment for us to make. It's not just insurance; it is knowing that down the road we're going to continue to have problems like this—particularly in a globalized world where you move from one side of the world to the other in a day.

Almost exactly five years later, COVID erupted in China.

Bill Gates warned us, too. While the Trump administration heeded no public health warnings and did nothing to prepare for an emergency that experts told us was coming, the Bill & Melinda Gates Foundation invested hundreds of millions of dollars in vaccine development research and systems that track disease. Gates himself called on world leaders to prepare for the inevitable. In November 2014, in response to an Ebola outbreak in West Africa, he warned: "The world as a whole doesn't have the preparedness for epidemics, and we've had a few flu scares that got us to do some minor things, but not enough. . . . With new tools, doing broad disease surveillance that's better than we have been doing is a very doable thing," he said. "You can do a pretty good job literally for hundreds of millions, not billions of dollars a year."

Scientists who've been raising pandemic alarms for decades admit that we can never completely contain every deadly virus. What's needed is a global effort to build new systems of disease surveillance, new means of tracking and understanding each virus, rapid response mechanisms to address outbreaks at their source, and new systems to quickly, efficiently, and effectively treat the diseases that a sudden outbreak can create for people around the world. This effort demands investment. But it also requires moral imagination and political will. It demands a new willingness among governments to compromise, cooperate, and coordinate for the good of all.

THE G-ZERO RESPONSE

The early COVID global response was not promising. The most damaging pandemic-related fights emerged inside the world's two most powerful countries. In the United States, COVID proved that even a $1 surgical mask could become a "culture war" wedge issue. A more substantive debate raged across the US, as in many other countries, over how best to strike a balance between containing the virus and keeping economies humming while avoiding the damage to mental and emotional health inflicted by extended isolation. That debate also descended into political warfare. Legitimate differences of opinion were pushed to extremes by politicians and the media, as left and right chose to believe only the information they saw confirmed on their cable news channels and social media feeds.

Some crises produce a rally-round-the-flag effect. After the 9/11 attacks, President George W. Bush saw his approval rating surge to 86 percent as Americans united in horror at the murder of more than three thousand people. Donald Trump, who began 2020 with an approval rating of 42.6 percent, never saw that number climb higher than 45.8 percent as Americans divided sharply over what was really happening, why it was happening, and what should be done about it. COVID gave both left and right new reasons to throw punches at each other, and the fight itself made the war against the virus much more difficult and costly to win.

And in China, a country without elections and culture wars, COVID also created plenty of trouble for politicians. Hundreds of millions of Chinese people now know how their government silenced doctors who tried to share vital early information about the virus. As the outbreak became a pandemic, other governments blamed Beijing for failing to contain it. It's no accident that, to divert attention from China's early mishandling of the COVID crisis and the economic damage it wrought, President Xi Jinping took an increasingly hard-line stance on democracy activism in Hong Kong, US support for Taiwan, border skirmishes with India, trade frictions and diplomatic dustups with Australia, and territorial disputes in the South China Sea.

China recovered more quickly and more completely from the initial coronavirus outbreak than any of its democratic rivals. It was the only major economy in the world that grew in 2020. Its leaders used this success to offer China as an alternative to Western leadership, including by developing and marketing an affordable vaccine that made its way across much of the developing world months before US and European vaccines won approval, and by stepping into the vacuum left by declining US leadership. Still, mistrust of China, on the rise long before the pandemic, has only deepened following Beijing's coverup of the original outbreak. In June 2020, the European Commission accused China (and Russia) of running "targeted influence operations and disinformation campaigns in the EU, its neighborhood, and globally." In one egregious example of disinformation, a Chinese embassy website posted a false story at the height of Europe's outbreak that workers at a care facility in France had abandoned their jobs, leaving residents to die.

In response to all this, China has faced an international backlash. A report from Pew Research published in October 2020 found that most respondents in fourteen countries in Europe, North America, and Australasia did not trust President Xi Jinping to "do the right thing in world affairs." It also found that more respondents now consider China the world's lead economic power. All in all, the pandemic has simultaneously increased China's self-confidence in the face of political dysfunction and bitter polarization in the US and increased other countries' dependence on economic ties with China and their suspicion of its larger goals.

In other words, COVID has deepened our geopolitical recession. A truly global crisis with both a public health and economic dimension produced far more finger-pointing than cooperation. There was little sharing of information or emergency supplies across international borders. Leaders of the world's two most powerful countries resisted cooperation with the World Health Organization—the international body best positioned to save lives and limit damage. Angry, often violent, protests erupted in country after country about what was really happening, how best to respond, and who to blame.

The COVID response failure spanned the entire political spectrum. Brazil and Britain (right-wing governments) and Mexico and Spain (left-wing governments) have all featured near the top of the list of per capita COVID deaths at various points. There is *so much* blame to go around that we must recognize this failure for what it was: the inevitable breakdown in international governance created by a fragmented world order. The system itself failed all of us because it offered no possibility that governments and international organizations would work together effectively. This is the problem that must be solved if future pandemics—and any of the (even larger) challenges described later in this book—can be addressed for the good of all.

A DEVELOPING WORLD THROWN INTO REVERSE

The great accomplishment of globalization over the past fifty years is the dramatic narrowing of the wealth gap between rich and poor countries and the creation of a single global middle class (even as inequality grew within many of the world's wealthy countries). COVID has thrown that historic process into reverse. The pandemic's deadliest legacy is the lasting damage it has done to many poorer countries, those with the most fragile health-care systems, the least effective bureaucracies, the rustiest infrastructure, and the least cash in reserve. These countries will also be last to reach herd immunity through a combination of infection and vaccination, and their economies will take many years to recover.

As the graph below shows, COVID recovery has been a three-stage process. China was first to recover, because its authoritarian government had the technological means and the domestic political authority it needed to track and isolate infected people and to enforce lockdowns. The United States and Europe had the vaccine access and money to cushion the economic blow, allowing them to lead the second stage of recovery. The lack of vaccines and cash leave poorer countries still wrestling with the pandemic and its economic aftershocks.

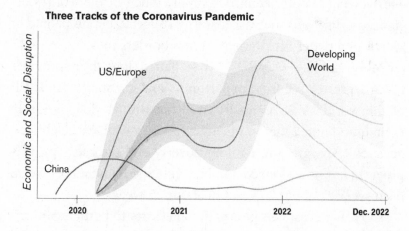

Three Tracks of the Coronavirus Pandemic

If people in wealthier countries feel inclined to shrug off widening inequality among nations as the natural order of things and persuade themselves that poor countries' distress won't affect their own lives, they should perhaps remember a few facts about communicable disease. If the virus is active anywhere, it's potentially active *everywhere*. Many of us have now heard this message hundreds of times, and yet there's little evidence that we have taken it to heart. Viruses cross borders; they mutate in places where they're left uncontained and create dangerous new variants that threaten all of us.

Economic slowdowns are also contagious. While wealthier countries saw quicker economic recovery from COVID-19's worst effects, people in developing countries have been forced to "live with the virus." Many in these countries don't have reliable internet access to help them work and learn remotely when workplaces and schools are shuttered. There is less tourism in poorer countries whose governments depend on the revenue it generates. There's also less money for families in poorer countries when fewer remittances arrive from relatives and friends who work abroad. Economic hardship creates political turmoil and violence. Poorer countries supply much of the world's organized crime and the vast majority of its desperate people in search of a better life. Refugees cross borders too.

More broadly, COVID-19 has halted long-term progress toward greater security, opportunity, and prosperity in much of the world. A 2020 report from the Bill & Melinda Gates Foundation noted that in previous reports "we have celebrated decades of progress in fighting poverty and disease. . . . This progress has now stopped." In fact, said the foundation, "we've been set back about 25 years in about 25 weeks."

COVID devastated international efforts to battle malnutrition and HIV. Health-care systems were overwhelmed. Educational opportunities evaporated as children were kept from school to help families scrape by financially. And global poverty has expanded. The World Bank predicted in October 2020 that the pandemic would push as many as 150 million people back into extreme poverty by 2021. That was the first recorded rise in that category in more than twenty years. Women, employed more often than men in the informal economy, have been hit especially hard. According to the Gates report, "data from the Ebola epidemic in West Africa suggests that, when schools open again, girls are less likely to return, thereby closing off opportunities for themselves and for their future children." COVID pushed more women than men into extreme poverty around the world. A report from the independent nonprofit foundation the Global Fund found sharply rising risk of much higher rates of HIV, tuberculosis, and malaria for both men and women.

Poorer countries will need a lot more help from wealthier countries in coming years, because debt crises are everybody's problem. Governments that can't borrow can no longer maintain order, and instability in one country spills across borders. Unfortunately, the idea of "bailouts" for the world's neediest was becoming less popular in the US and Europe even before COVID arrived. Millions of Americans still support former president Trump's stance on immigration from, and financial support for, poor countries. It will be hard for President Biden to change enough minds on this subject, whatever his intentions and policy goals.

Europe has its own struggles over immigration. Both the sovereign debt crisis and the waves of refugees from North Africa and the Middle East during Syria's civil war generated intense animosity between southern EU countries that called for financial help and northern EU countries that considered them irresponsible. The idea of international "debt forgiveness" isn't popular among taxpayers on either side of the Atlantic. China's investments and credit extension in the Belt and Road program have also decreased dramatically since its peak in 2015. China's economy and long-term growth prospects remain under pressure as well, as its population ages and the state is forced to spend more to strengthen its social safety net.

THE NEXT PANDEMIC

We might not have as much time as we think before the next pandemic strikes. The number of people traveling across borders over the past half century—whether business travelers, tourists, or refugees—has surged to new heights. Remember that it took days for COVID-19 to spread beyond China but weeks for scientists to retrace its path.

Scientists have discovered more than forty new lethal pathogens in the past half century that leapt from animals to humans; and the pace of new discoveries is rising as animals more often come into direct contact with ever-larger numbers of people in both developing and rich countries, where expanding suburbs and exurbs are encroaching on the animals' habitats. That's especially true of birds, whose flyways are now more often paved over to boost land development and who are more likely to land in populated areas or on farms at a time when viruses are moving back and forth at a growing pace among birds, other animals, and humans. Unsanitary factory farming also creates greater risks for the emergence of new viruses. Genetic analysis has shown that a 2009 swine flu outbreak that infected tens of millions of people and killed thousands in more than 120 countries originated on a factory farm in North Carolina.

More worrisome, COVID-19 was highly infectious, but it surely wasn't the deadliest virus that scientists will see in coming years. It's far from the deadliest we've faced in the past twenty years. Severe acute respiratory syndrome (2003), avian influenza strains like H7N9 (2013) and H5N1 (2014), and Middle East respiratory syndrome (2019) were all less infectious than COVID but more lethal. Given how much we don't know about the mutation of coronaviruses, it would be foolish to assume that the next strain won't be more transmissible and more deadly. Yet outbreaks are becoming more politicized as national leaders who mismanage efforts to contain outbreaks look for scapegoats across their borders or in the institutions that are supposed to coordinate responses. Bitter arguments over COVID-19, particularly between Washington and Beijing, have compounded that problem and encourage more secrecy when the next pathogen appears.

This pandemic was the biggest crisis of our lives. But it wasn't, by itself, frightening enough to make us forge a new system of international cooperation or, even at home, force Republicans and Democrats to work together. Few leaders recognized that COVID was a global threat that could never be effectively addressed without a global solution—and even fewer actually tried to engineer such a solution.

But COVID *has* taught us useful lessons for containing future pandemics. These could form the basis for future cooperation on other issues. Here are the three most important.

Invest—Right Now

The first COVID lesson is the most basic: prepare on sunny days for stormy weather—or reap the whirlwind. Governments are well advised to invest in national and local readiness, because disasters like COVID inflict much more human and economic damage when:

- scientists and doctors can't test large numbers of people for infection and track the movement of a virus through society;
- hospitals lack the medicine and equipment they need to treat a surge of infected patients;
- officials are left to improvise containment strategies in a moment of panic;
- state and local government can't access emergency funds from national or international sources; and
- governments at every level of society have no credible plan to respond to emergencies we know will eventually come.

No two disasters are identical, but intelligent planning for something as predictable as a novel coronavirus will reduce damage. Maybe if government thought of it less as a question of prudence and generosity and more as a crucial competitive advantage (as COVID response has been for China), officials would take the actions needed to limit the damage for all.

In particular, it's crucial to invest in redundancy. The demands of global economic competition force business (and governments) to maximize efficiency by cutting costs. This has created one of globalization's dominant features: the "just-in-time supply chain." Why pay for millions of extra umbrellas when it isn't raining? Why fill hospital space with ventilators that would only be needed in the kind of public health crisis no one has seen in decades? The answer is clear: one day, it's going to rain hard, and critical supplies will be needed to avoid catastrophe.

Yes, the need for preparation and investment is obvious. But it's a message worth repeating, because COVID-19 has proven that common sense does not mean common practice.

National governments must invest locally. Every government needs a clear chain of command and a distribution of responsibilities in place when a public health crisis emerges, and national governments have the financial reserves needed to stockpile critical supplies. But local governments are at ground zero in this kind of emergency, and they need investment before the critical hour comes. COVID has proven that the decentralized decision-making common in the United States can make an emergency far worse than it should be. A patchwork crisis response and bidding wars among states over access to scarce resources cost lives. Decades of underfunding for local public health agencies severely curtailed America's virus response.

It's not enough for governments to invest only within their borders. As noted, infectious diseases do not respect man-made boundaries and barriers. There is no effective national strategy to prevent or end a global pandemic. Only an *international* strategy can do that. When the storm breaks, everyone will need protective gear, testing equipment, effective treatments, and vaccines in order to avoid a national problem that can go global within weeks. COVID-19 has shown us the importance of investing in the manufacturing capacity of poorer countries to speed their responses to a health emergency in ways that help protect everyone else, particularly from viral variants.

In a world where governments are more likely to build walls than bridges, over-reliance on critical supplies from countries with potentially unfriendly governments creates new emergencies when supply chains are broken. Investment in "shock absorption" means investing in redundancies of both supplies and suppliers. Greater international cooperation doesn't imply *universal* sharing. Some governments will resist cooperation that they believe undermines their independence. But if enough governments work together to build resilience into the international system, holdouts will have better incentives to join them.

The investment in shock absorption can't come only from governments. Private companies create the tests, treatments, protective equipment, and vaccines that societies need to survive. COVID-19 illustrated how a few companies can become central to solutions—and earn windfall profits from government contracts—by working closely with policymakers as they've done in the wartime past. There's also a crucial place for the private sector in national and international planning for future crises as part of lines of communication and chains of command. Policymakers and universities take on the responsibility during the basic research phase, an area in which they excel. The private sector then brings that research to market by transforming it into new tools that can be quickly mass-produced.

The pandemic reminded political leaders that they depend in emergencies on the innovative capacity of the private sector, and it reminded businesses that those same emergencies expose their own vulnerabilities to politicians' poor decisions. COVID-19 inflicted enormous harm on both governments and businesses—reason enough to plan future emergency responses together. Companies and individuals can also support private philanthropic organizations that have the time and resources to understand, and help prepare us for, threats just beyond the horizon.

Finally, it's not enough for our leaders to have a plan; families and individuals must invest in one, too. That means learning how best to respond to the threat of communicable disease. Asian countries including Singapore, Vietnam, and Taiwan, hit hard by past viral outbreaks, responded more effectively than others to COVID-19, in part because people in those countries knew what to do and what not to do. It's not just about mask-wearing, handwashing, and distancing. They also knew where to turn for accurate information and good advice. In a world like ours, where hostile governments, partisan politicians and journalists, and political vandals inject disinformation into polarized societies, finding and sharing accurate information can be the difference between life and death.

Share Information

It's easier to contain a virus and save a million lives if you identify the virus and take effective action before it infects millions of people. Share information with your citizens and the rest of the world. China's leaders want to control the flow of information available to the country's citizens. But COVID-19 proved that some information can't be controlled.

If Chinese authorities had listened to doctors in Wuhan and invited the World Health Organization to listen to them, too, rather than trying to process and respond to information before sharing it, they would have spared themselves, their people, and the rest of the world enormous pain. If those doctors had felt freer to share accounts of what they had seen, China and the rest of the world would have had a crucial head start on containment. The international image of the Chinese Communist Party would be stronger, not weaker. More openness from China's leadership would have boosted public confidence in state information and the ruling party, making future crises easier to manage, with less effort.

In Iran, the government downplayed the health risks of COVID-19 both to keep turnout high for parliamentary elections in February 2020 and to avoid having to shut down an economy already reeling from the impact of international sanctions and low oil prices. Had they not, the country might not have become the first major COVID hot spot outside China.

Authoritarian secrecy isn't the only obstacle to the free flow of accurate information. Following an outbreak of bird flu in 2005, the Bush administration created a project to track, research, and organize responses to viruses that can be passed from animals to humans. Under the supervision of the US Agency for International Development (USAID), a project called Predict discovered nearly one thousand novel viruses. It trained thousands of people in thirty African and Asian countries, and it built or bolstered sixty medical research labs, mostly in developing countries. Then, in October 2019, the Trump administration announced that the project would be shut down, presumably because someone considered it a waste of money. "Predict was an approach to heading off pandemics, instead of sitting there waiting for them to emerge and then mobilizing. That's expensive," a project participant told the *New York Times* when news broke of the cancellation. COVID-19 appeared six weeks later.

More research and funding are needed on how animal-to-human viruses become deadly. Beyond monitoring viral leaps from animals to humans on the ground and researching why they happen, the world also needs more investment in global information sharing and coordination systems to shorten response times. This includes strengthening agreements to share samples and more cross-border cooperation among scientists. Of course, it's one thing to sign on to agreements that demand the sharing of information on large-scale public health threats; it's another to actually share. China is hardly the only country where officials are trained to worry more about spreading politically sensitive news than about spreading an infectious disease.

The information that scientists and doctors need comes from effective testing, because you can't fight what you can't see. In the early days of COVID-19, there was no scientific consensus on basic facts about the dangers it posed. Was it airborne?

What role did surfaces play in its transmission? Would masks make a difference? Did it affect people of different ages differently? The first major step toward answering these questions and finding lifesaving answers to them was taken with large-scale testing.

Positive tests provide vital information that saves lives and jobs—and political reputations. From the earliest days of COVID, political leaders were aware of a pandemic paradox: you'll get no credit for preventing a disaster that few people experience, and you'll be blamed for the economic fallout of lockdowns and other aggressive containment strategies. That dilemma feeds politicians' tendencies to hide bad news.

But when leaders treat test results as a political report card, with positive results lowering the grade, many of them will discourage testing. That leaves scientists in the dark and everyone in danger. More people die. More economic damage is done. The countries with the fewest deaths per capita and the least economic damage ramped up wide-scale testing as quickly as possible. The coronavirus crisis showed that success in fighting the virus doesn't depend on your form of government, the ideology of the governing party, the size of your economy, or the size of your population. Democratic South Korea, authoritarian Vietnam, rich Singapore, poor Greece, conservative Germany, liberal Canada, large Japan, and small New Zealand all managed the crisis much more effectively than the United States, Brazil, India, Mexico, and the United Kingdom, where leaders too often challenged or ignored the best scientific advice on how to respond.

The seventeenth-century French philosopher Blaise Pascal argued that it's entirely rational for an agnostic to believe in God. If he's right that God exists, he gains eternal life. If he's wrong, he loses nothing. By similar logic, if Donald Trump and other COVID-skeptic world leaders had taken the COVID threat more seriously from the beginning of the outbreak, they would have been better prepared to prove their leadership in a worst-case scenario and lost little if fears had proved to be overblown. We'll never know whether a more forceful pandemic response might have reelected Trump, but it's hard to imagine it would have hurt him in a closer race.

In South Korea, there was aggressive early testing. President Moon Jae-in didn't downplay the dangers that COVID posed. He didn't peddle fake herbal remedies like Madagascar's president, Andry Rajoelina. Unlike Belarus's president, Alexander Lukashenko, he didn't pretend that saunas and vodka could keep the population safe. Unlike Trump, he didn't deliberately attack the integrity and credibility of his country's most important public health institutions. Moon's government paid a short-term political price for the bad-news headlines that the tests generated, but South Korean authorities got their outbreak under control much more quickly than in countries with governments that pretended the dangers of COVID were exaggerated, and Moon's Democratic Party was rewarded with a landslide victory in April 2020, even as the pandemic raged elsewhere.

It isn't just governments that must share information. Drug companies depend on profits to finance research and development, and there's nothing wrong with a pharmaceutical firm protecting its intellectual property. But when millions are becoming infected with a virus that produces a deadly disease, sharing intellectual property and real-time information about trials and testing saves lives. These companies receive billions of taxpayer dollars to develop treatment and vaccines. And because the virus isn't fully contained in one country until it's contained in every country, that information should be shared much more effectively than it was during COVID, when private companies and state-backed national champions in countries like China and Russia competed with one another rather than sharing information for the good of all.

Share Burdens

International lenders must provide the money to help vulnerable governments weather future pandemics. The International Monetary Fund, in particular, did what it could to help during COVID. But the IMF has limited resources. Wealthier countries should boost its lending power. They should ensure that lending rates are designed to help poorer countries survive the repayment schedule, create incentives for NGOs to help, and forgive those debts that can't be repaid without creating political and economic turmoil inside struggling countries.

Here the US and China can collaborate to great effect, proving the system can work for both countries and for those who need help. We've already seen real progress with the IMF's commitment to organize lending according to UN "sustainable development goals," metrics endorsed by 193 countries in 2015. Investments in reducing poverty, hunger, and inequality, in part through more funding for education, especially for girls, will produce tangible benefits for people everywhere.

Throughout the pandemic, the World Health Organization was buffeted by criticism, some of it fair, that it had moved too slowly to understand and respond to the scale of the problem. By the time the WHO issued its 2021 report on the origins of the virus, the games China played with access for WHO investigators critically undermined the report's credibility. The WHO, like the United Nations itself, was created and financed by all, for the good of all. When governments attack the organization, they're attacking a tool they designed together for their own protection. But COVID has taught us that member states must redefine the WHO's mandate. Its budget is far too small to carry out all the responsibilities it oversees—from investment in nutrition and primary care, to environmental standards and product safety, to managing chronic disease and limiting contagion. This institution either needs much more funding or it needs to be broken up so its responsibilities can be divided among multiple organizations that have enough funding to take on the challenges most relevant to its current work.

COVAX (a global project that brought together governments and vaccine manufacturers to ensure equal vaccine access worldwide) faces similar hurdles. More than 170 countries joined talks on this project, along with the WHO and other NGOs and vaccine manufacturers in developed and developing countries. The Trump administration refused to participate in COVAX because it didn't want to be "constrained by multilateral organizations influenced by the corrupt World Health Organization and China," according to a White House spokesman at the time. In early 2021, President Biden recommitted the US to COVAX and pledged billions of dollars in additional support for the organization's work, but much time and many lives had already been lost.

In 2022, COVAX is helping distribute vaccines to people in places that might not otherwise get them. But as with the WHO, COVAX carries too heavy a burden. COVID-19 has proven that it's both wise and cost-effective to fund COVAX, or a COVAX-like organization, adequately. Invest the money now or pay a much steeper price later. Donor countries themselves have much to gain from greater generosity. Eurasia Group, the firm I established, has found that help for lower- and lower-middle-income countries can lay the groundwork for a much quicker world economic recovery in coming years. This means that bigger contributions now will pay for themselves many times over by boosting global growth. And sooner rather than later.

LEARNING FROM COVID-19

Every crisis contains the seeds of opportunity. COVID laid bare many failings of political leadership, but there were successes as well. What did we learn?

In the past, vaccines contained fragments of actual virus protein that "taught" people's immune systems how to recognize and subdue a dangerous invader. But the pandemic inspired scientists to test a new concept. Two COVID vaccines use "messenger RNA" (mRNA) technologies that teach the body how to produce its own virus fragments to target. This revolutionary new approach dramatically sped up the development and mass distribution of safe and effective vaccines. In the United States, these innovations were the product of government money, research from the National Institutes of Health, the Defense Department, and federally funded academic laboratories, with expertise and innovation provided by private-sector companies.

This invention saved jobs and lives. It limited the political damage for federal, state, and local governments. Drug companies made huge profits and boosted their brands. Every individual who contributed to that effort can take pride in knowing that they were part of a historic achievement. By itself, the COVID-19 pandemic will not force world leaders to confront today's geopolitical recession and tackle the even bigger challenges to come. But as with mRNA vaccination, it will create new opportunities for cooperation for those ready to seize them.

The economic damage the pandemic caused *will* help speed the transition from remnants of the twentieth-century economy toward the most dynamic elements of the twenty-first century by shifting power toward the world's most innovative companies, those that can change the way we produce, distribute, and consume food and energy. Think about climate change, the subject of the next chapter. Without question, the pandemic diverted national and international attention away from the bold action needed to limit the warming of the planet. But the economic damage inflicted by COVID has sharply reduced demand for the fossil fuels that pump so much carbon into the atmosphere, and it has already given oil and gas companies new reasons and greater urgency to boost their investment in renewable energy. And, more importantly, by forcing people around the world to gather, work, shop, and learn online—and by providing indispensable new tools that helped with everything from testing and contact tracing to the development of treatments and vaccines—the pandemic has empowered the digital-age companies that already have the deepest commitment to climate-friendly action.

For governments, the most positive geopolitical consequence of COVID is that European leaders stepped up to show American and Chinese leaders how to cooperate. The virus rolled across Europe more than once. In response to the first wave, most European countries locked down more effectively than the United States did, and without the lasting damage to personal privacy that we saw in China. The financial and sovereign debt crises (2008–2012), the migrant crisis (2015–2016), and Brexit (2016) all helped persuade EU leaders that inequality breeds resentment that stokes populism. If all member states are to commit themselves to closer EU integration, they need to believe that crises won't always pit rich countries against poor ones. With the support of all twenty-seven EU member states, European governments agreed in 2020 on a recovery package worth more than €2,364.3 billion, including €750 billion for COVID recovery, €540 billion to reinforce safety nets for workers, businesses, and member states, and a €1,074.3 billion EU budget for 2021–2027. This was the most important example of international compromise, cooperation, and coordination the world has seen in a generation.

To accomplish this, German chancellor Angela Merkel and French president Emmanuel Macron aggressively pushed a pro-European integrationist agenda, the same project that had infuriated taxpayers in wealthier countries, fed resentment in poorer ones, alienated former Communist members of the EU, and helped enable Brexit. In the process, Merkel and Macron weakened Euro-skeptic arguments across the EU, and many member states got help they badly needed. It will be years before all the money is distributed, but the unanimous emergency response showed the value of shared sacrifice at a time when country-first populism had thrown the EU's future into question.

These financial packages also include stimulus for investment in green technologies and regulations that require non-EU countries that want to trade with Europe to align with European technology standards or face higher taxes. That will strengthen European influence in global regulation of new technologies and environmental protection.

European governments were slower than the US to vaccinate their citizens, in part because member states don't always work well with bureaucrats in Brussels. "We were late to authorize [vaccines]. We were too optimistic when it came to massive production and perhaps too confident that what we ordered would actually be delivered on time," said European Commission president Ursula von der Leyen in February 2021. Yet in many ways Europe's action in 2020 provided a blueprint for crisis cooperation among governments that don't want to share costs and burdens.

Europe, the world's largest common market, lacks game-changing technology firms, a strong military, strong banks, abundant natural resources, and a global reserve currency. And consensus among members on anything requiring sacrifice and compromise will never come easy. But it does have the world's most capable rule makers, and the US and Chinese governments in particular should learn from Europe's lead on climate, technology, and construction of a social safety net that protects citizens in an evolving world of work. That's why, for all the focus in this book on America and China, we'll need European leadership to help us all escape from global disorder and create a sustainable international system for handling the crises we will soon face.

The COVID experience had better prepare us to work across borders before the next pandemic hits. The near total inability of the US and China to agree on anything doesn't encourage optimism, but other governments are offering leadership of their own. In March 2021, the leaders of twenty-three countries joined the WHO to propose an international treaty for pandemic preparedness to protect us all from the next global health crisis. This is precisely what the world needs for greater cooperation, collaboration, and coordination on pandemic preparedness—and a model for a post–G-Zero approach to all the other challenges in this book. Unfortunately, neither China nor the US signed on. Without them, this treaty is no more than a blueprint.

No, COVID was not the crisis we needed. But it offers direction and hope, both of which can help us respond more effectively to the next deadly virus and tackle the more dangerous emergencies to come. We now turn to a crisis we don't have to anticipate. It's well underway. Its effects on our lives and livelihoods—and on global peace and security—will be far broader and deeper than any damage done by COVID-19.

CHAPTER 3

CLIMATE EMERGENCY

Beginning in 2007, a devastating two-year drought swept across the fertile farmland of northern Syria. Three-quarters of the region's farmers lost their crops, and a cash-strapped government in Damascus offered little help. Hundreds of thousands of desperate people flooded into Syria's largest cities in search of jobs to feed their families, and they weren't welcomed when they got there. Anger over endemic corruption and a lack of economic opportunity was already stirring up trouble in city streets, and the new arrivals from the countryside added to overcrowding and tension.

Then in 2011 came the Arab Spring, regional unrest that began in Tunisia, pushed through Egypt, upended Libya, and triggered panic in governments across North Africa and the

Middle East. For Syria, the result was civil war. Half the people who lived there in 2011 have since been killed or forced from their homes. Fleeing the violence, millions of refugees began crossing borders, and many of them managed to reach Europe. They weren't welcomed when they got there, either.

The European Union was coping with economic and political fallout from the financial crisis of 2008–2009. Taxpayers in wealthier EU countries were angry over bailouts for buckling economies in southern Europe, and residents of the latter soon found themselves on the front lines of a historic refugee crisis. From the Balkans to the United Kingdom, people afraid that refugees would take their jobs and soak up state-provided services, people angry about periodic terrorist attacks by Islamic fundamentalists, revolted against the new arrivals. Millions of Syrian refugees who never reached Europe still live in Turkey, Jordan, Lebanon, and neighboring countries—and many of them still hope to make it out.

Now . . . travel 7,500 miles west from Damascus to Central America. Beginning in 2014, an intense multiyear drought scorched El Salvador, Guatemala, and Honduras. Over time, farmers in these countries lost faith that they could navigate fast-changing weather patterns to deliver decent harvests. Corruption and a lack of good jobs had long kept families poor, but devastated crops wiped out entire villages. Add heavily armed criminal gangs to the mix, and Central Americans began to decide there was no future in their native countries.

In 2018, hundreds of thousands of people fled the region in hopes of reaching the US to apply for asylum—at a time when President Trump had made plans for a "big, beautiful" border wall a central part of his political brand. Caravans of Central Americans found themselves trapped in Mexico, upending the politics of that country, too. When Joe Biden became president in 2021, tens of thousands more refugees, urged on by smugglers, headed for the border.

Civil war and traumatized refugees might seem a surprising place to start the story of climate change, which many people still see as mainly a matter of melting ice and rising seas; saving whales and hugging trees. But the warming planet creates erratic weather patterns that trigger droughts in some places and floods in others, ruining lives and livelihoods, particularly in the world's poorest countries with fast-growing populations of young people. As warming continues, climate disasters will push *hundreds of millions* onto the road—most without a clear destination. In the process, it will provoke economic and political upheaval everywhere. As familiar as we are with the phenomenon, few of us—and hardly any of our leaders—have properly assessed its vast toll in geopolitical terms. That's the aim of this chapter.

Climate change didn't create all the miseries in Syria and Central America, of course. The Arab Spring was the result of decades of frustration across the Middle East and North Africa. Syria's civil war had many causes. Crime and corruption have plagued El Salvador, Guatemala, and Honduras throughout their histories. But disasters that suddenly evict large numbers of hungry people within a poor country can ignite violent political turmoil. This is an inferno that, like a coronavirus, blazes across borders and capsizes the lives of people around the world.

Catastrophes in Syria and Central America are just the beginning. Populations will surge in Africa (+55 percent by 2040), South Asia (+18.4 percent), and Central America (+18.8 percent). The working-age population of sub-Saharan Africa alone will rise by nearly a billion people between 2020 and 2060. These people will be hit hardest by climate change. According to the UN, the number of undernourished people in drought-prone sub-Saharan African countries increased by 45.6 percent between 2012 and 2020. Climate change played a central role in that surge.

The United States is further removed from these refugee challenges than most. But we now face our own crises. As Americans saw in 2021, climate change can create overlapping disasters, as unprecedented wildfires on the West Coast and floods on the East Coast destroyed lives and homes, and released dangerous chemicals into groundwater. Studies show that by 2050, heat and humidity levels in parts of the Midwest and Louisiana could make it hard for the human body to cool itself for as many as eighteen days per year. It will become more difficult to grow food across large parts of the United States.

Droughts will be longer and hotter. Increasingly violent storms will produce more frequent floods. World leaders have done extraordinarily little to prepare for the inevitable consequences—more economic stress, more political upheaval, and more migrants. When civil war struck, Syria was home to about 22 million people. Soon, disaster will strike a country of 100 million.

Now for a sense of scale: we'll be wrestling with COVID and its impact for years, but climate will occupy us for decades, and it will disrupt far more lives. Much damage is already irreversible, and managing the fallout will be a central priority for the next generation of global leaders.

We all now have a clear idea of where climate change comes from. Over the past fifty years, human ingenuity and cross-border connection have empowered more people and unleashed more economic potential than any force in history. Globalization has lifted billions from poverty, helped people live longer and healthier lives, and created unprecedented opportunities for learning and upward mobility. But we can't ignore the trade-off: that these achievements come at the cost of unprecedented exploitation of the world's natural resources, which has changed the chemistry of our oceans and our atmosphere.

For the vast majority of the world's people, the trade-off has so far been worthwhile, though we can't say the same for the untold number of species we've pushed into extinction. Since 1970, the accelerating scale of human consumption of food and other resources has wiped out 60 percent of mammals, birds, fish, and reptiles, as well as 83 percent of the animals that live in rivers and lakes. This is the impact of the Anthropocene, the first period in Earth's history in which the dominant source of environmental change comes from choices made by humans.

We know the world is getting warmer. That's easy to measure and understand. The sun projects heat toward Earth. Our atmosphere deflects some of that heat into space, preventing the planet from becoming too hot to sustain life. At the same time, carbon dioxide in the atmosphere captures enough of that heat to prevent our planet from becoming a giant ball of ice. Not too hot, not too cold. This "natural greenhouse effect" sustains all life on earth. But the oil, gas, and coal we've been using to produce energy and power our economies has pumped a lot more carbon dioxide into the atmosphere. One-sixth of all the carbon emissions in human history occurred in the ten-year period between 2010 and 2020. It's a staggering reality. And it's meant more of the sun's rays are trapped, capturing more heat.

Destruction of the world's forests makes matters worse, because trees, and the soils they grow in, store carbon. The Amazon lost more forest cover in 2019 than at any point in the previous decade, and Bolsonaro's government in Brazil looks determined to make matters worse. The damage in Brazil was even more devastating in 2020. In 2019, more than one-third of all destruction of the world's tropical forests took place in Brazil, but forests are also under attack in Central Africa, Southeast Asia, and elsewhere. The total global loss of old-growth tropical forest in 2019 alone would cover an area nearly the size of Switzerland.

In geological time, this has all happened in an instant. During the industrial age, which began about 260 years ago, the amount of carbon dioxide in the atmosphere has increased by 30 percent, raising the earth's temperature by 1.2 degrees Celsius. This change is gaining speed; the twenty warmest years ever recorded have all come within the past twenty-two years.

Melting ice around the poles has raised sea levels by about 7.5 inches during the twentieth century and could raise them another three feet by the end of the twenty-first, according to the United Nations. Today, about 1 percent of the earth's surface is almost too hot to support life of any kind. (Think the Sahara.) By 2070, that portion is expected to be nearly 20 percent. Even more animals and plants will face extinction, because they don't have time to adapt to changes this drastic, and health risks to humans will follow.

More heat means more moisture in the air, with effects on temperature, humidity, air pressure, and atmospheric instability that dramatically alter weather patterns. It means more intense storms more often, more floods, more wildfires, more droughts.

As Tanya Steele, head of the World Wildlife Fund, said in 2018, "We are the first generation to know we are destroying our planet and the last one that can do anything about it."

POLITICS IN THE WAY

The solutions to these problems are enormously disruptive—politically, economically, and socially—making it easier for some to deny the scientific consensus or simply drag their feet. The leaders who signed on to the Paris climate accord committed their governments to limit global temperature increases to below 2 degrees Celsius, and the UN's Intergovernmental Panel on Climate Change has called for a more ambitious limit of 1.5 degrees. To reach these goals, CO2 emissions must quickly fall to *net zero*. By 2040 (for 1.5 degrees) or 2050 (for 2), we can no longer pump more carbon into the atmosphere than we remove from it. To reach the desired goal, governments must invest radically more in energy use and production that emits less carbon, and in new technologies that suck carbon out of the air.

Limiting the use of fossil fuels is the center of any climate strategy. However, those who profit most from them—the OPEC countries, Russia, and other nations, including the US, now the world's number one oil producer—have strong financial incentives to slow the process. Many governments in oil-producing countries will feel the pain directly, because 65 percent of global oil reserves are now held by state-owned companies, not by the private-sector multinationals we're more familiar with.

Coal has been a cheap and abundant source of energy for decades, and many countries have invested heavily in coal-fired power plants. Though renewables are now cheaper than coal in much of the world, the construction of brand-new infrastructure—and the upheaval it will create in job markets—will make this transition complicated and extremely expensive, particularly for developing countries. China and India, the two most populous countries on earth, still rely heavily on coal for domestic power generation.

Small, wealthier countries may have an easier time. Saudi Arabia's Vision 2030 plan, for example, is an ultra-ambitious strategy to diversify the Saudi economy away from increasingly dangerous dependence on oil exports. The United Arab Emirates has already made substantial progress in that direction.

Other countries, unable to function without fossil fuel revenues, will collapse. The most notable example is Venezuela, home to the world's largest reserves of crude oil and already a deeply unstable country that must import just about every other consumer product. As decarbonization strategies advance, these countries will export less oil and more turmoil. Even resource giant Russia has made little progress toward economic diversification, setting itself up for economic stagnation and political upheaval in the coming decades. The shift toward cleaner energy will also transform geopolitics as old fossil fuel–based partnerships—Europe and Russia, the United States and Saudi Arabia—become less relevant. That trend will create more geopolitical uncertainty by shifting the balance of power across entire regions.

Fossil fuel–dependent governments aren't the only ones that will resist the new world order. Companies and workers whose livelihoods depend on energy extraction, refining, and transport won't support plans to reach the net-zero target. The world's largest energy companies have invested hundreds of billions of dollars in long-term projects that won't produce profits for years or decades to come. They know that large-scale moves away from fossil fuels will "strand" enough of their core assets to force many of them out of business. And this isn't just a story about big Western oil companies. The ten companies responsible for the biggest surges in CO_2 emissions over the past five years were Indian, Chinese, Australian, Russian, Korean, and Swiss (a single cement supplier). They aren't crazy about net zero, either.

Other industries will be deeply disrupted, too. Think about the world's big automakers. Over the next twenty years, electric vehicles will conquer the internal combustion engine. That's why Tesla's market capitalization is already bigger than that of Ford, General Motors, Volkswagen, and Fiat combined. But US auto-makers aren't moving in this direction as quickly as rivals in Germany, Japan, South Korea, and China. Autoworkers will pay a heavy price. A 2019 study conducted by Germany's IG Metall union and the Fraunhofer Institute for Industrial Engineering found that though electrification will create twenty-five thousand new jobs in Germany by 2030, it will kill three times that many in engines and transmission production over the same period. The many losers in this disruptive transition can't stop the process, but they'll use their influence with policymakers to slow its progress.

Another obstacle to reaching net zero is the reality that the domestic politics around climate change and decarbonization will be ugly around the world. Few elected leaders are eager to take responsibility for policies that impose near-term pain, especially knowing that future leaders will claim the credit when positive results emerge. Leaders also know that they get more credit for addressing local problems than global ones. It's easier to kick the carbon can down the road and make it someone else's problem. But it of course makes the problem worse and the solutions more expensive.

One of the best ways to speed the transition away from fossil fuels is to raise the cost of using them. But countries as poor as Ecuador and as rich as France have already discovered that any hike in fuel taxes or reduction in fuel subsidies can quickly pull citizens into the streets. In some countries, voters, persuaded that climate change poses deadly dangers, will demand action from officials who have limited ability to bring it about on their own, since so much depends on what other governments do. In others, voters will prioritize the economic needs of today over the climate needs of tomorrow, limiting support for the investment needed to address climate change. Some will back candidates who publicly doubt whether climate change exists, especially if those candidates can convince them that their jobs and lifestyles are at stake.

And in countries with major national oil companies—Russia, Venezuela, Nigeria—governments have a tried-and-tested formula for using natural resources to create jobs. They don't know yet how to do that with renewables. Over the longer term, green energy will produce more growth and more (and better-paying) jobs than fossil fuels, but the energy transition from black to green will be economically—and therefore politically—painful.

NET ZERO MEETS G-ZERO

Here's the point where net zero meets G-Zero. There is still no agreement on how the burden of emissions cuts should be shared among countries. *Don't ask us for sacrifice*, say China and India. *Don't ask us to pay the price for damage inflicted on the planet by centuries of industrialization in Europe and America. Wealthy Western countries created this problem and got rich doing it. We aren't going to scale back our development to clean up your mess.*

You're right, Americans and Europeans respond, *but you're already pushing much more carbon into the atmosphere than we are, and the difference is only going to increase.* In 2018, well before the pandemic slowed economic activity everywhere, the United States and Europe combined for 8.9 gigatons of carbon emissions. By itself, China produced 10.1 gigatons. India and the rest of the world were responsible for the remaining 17.9 gigatons.

Fair or not, if we're going to solve this problem, we all have to cut emissions toward a sustainable target.

Of course, this ignores the fact that President Trump threw the commitment of the world's largest economy into question by pulling the US out of the Paris climate accord, the landmark agreement on emissions-cutting and burden-sharing. Trump is no longer in the White House, and President Biden has committed to a comparatively ambitious climate agenda. Yet other governments know that a US commitment might be all too temporary, depending on who occupies the White House. In all these ways, politics creates huge obstacles to action, and progress on climate change faces constant risk of stalling.

A less irresponsible motive for political can-kicking: many new technologies, still in development, are designed to limit the harm done by warming temperatures. Technologies become less expensive as they improve. Governments hesitate to invest large sums of money in unproven new inventions when better, cheaper versions might become available later. Especially when that means some future official will have to authorize payment.

THE RISKS

Despite all these obstacles, world leaders are starting to take action because it's increasingly obvious that they have little choice. Here are a few of the catastrophic risks that make climate action essential and inevitable.

Water—Too Much and Too Little

Thanks to all that carbon we've pumped into the atmosphere, millions of people will have much less water than they need, while millions of others will have more than they can handle. The changing weather patterns and droughts that created upheaval in Syria and Central America will hit every region of the world, including places with much larger populations living close to the economic brink. By some estimates, by 2050 half the people on earth will be living in places where there isn't enough water to meet their basic needs. The problem of too much water in other places is a result of melting ice and rising seas but also of more frequent severe storms. Experts estimate that by 2050 rising sea levels will push average annual coastal floods higher, above ground that is now home to three hundred million people.

Sometimes the problems are related—as in Jakarta, Indonesia's capital, home to nearly eleven million people. As a result of both higher sea levels caused by warming and the overbuilding that comes with sudden economic success, Jakarta is now the fastest-sinking major city in the world. A shortage of water in some areas is making the problem worse. Nearly half the city's residents have no access to piped-in water, and as people and businesses survive by illegally pumping water from aquifers, the ground sinks faster. In some northern neighborhoods, the ground has fallen eight feet in ten years. Almost half of Jakarta now sits below sea level, and the city has become so prone to such intense flooding that it can no longer serve as the nation's capital. Indonesia's new capital will be built on higher ground, on the island of Borneo. The cost of transfer will be staggering, particularly for a middle-income country with the world's fourth-largest population, and it's unclear how they'll pay for it.

Developing countries aren't the only ones facing such a nightmare. More than ninety American cities, most of them on the Atlantic or Gulf Coast, already face chronic flooding—and that number will double by 2030. New York and Miami appear the most vulnerable. About three-quarters of all cities in Europe, particularly in Italy, Spain, and the Netherlands, will suffer from floods created by rising sea levels. Fighting back will be enormously costly. The weather effects themselves are just the beginning.

Climate change will transform the global order. Its geopolitical impact will come from competition, migration, security, and inequality.

Competition

In coming years, atmospheric changes will make it impossible for farmers in many regions to grow the same crops that have been grown there for centuries. There will be tougher competition for increasingly scarce arable land, fish stocks, fresh water, and clean air, generating conflicts both within and among poorer countries. This kind of competition has been a constant throughout history, but the speed of change and the scale of scarcity combined with population growth in developing countries will create a fundamentally new kind of crisis. In the United States and Europe and in many wealthy countries, technological breakthroughs are already increasing crop yields and can help with the transitions forced by climate change, but in developing countries, particularly in Asia and Africa, the shock will be harder to absorb.

In February 2019, India and Pakistan offered a preview of what we can expect. About one in six of the world's people live in India, yet Indians have access to just 4 percent of the world's water. Scarcity is also an ever-present threat in Pakistan. Hundreds of millions of people on both sides of the border between the two countries depend on water from the Indus River and its tributaries for farming, hydropower, and drinking. In all, 235 million people in India, Pakistan, and Nepal are served by the Indus River. After a suicide car bomb killed forty Indian troops in the Indian-controlled sector of Kashmir in February 2019, India's transport minister announced plans to "stop our share of water which used to flow to Pakistan." Pakistan immediately warned that any diversion of water would be an "act of war." Had it followed through on this threat, India would have violated the Indus River Treaty—brokered by the World Bank and signed by Pakistan's prime minister and India's president in 1960—which provides for sharing this vital resource.

India didn't pull the trigger in 2019, but the risk of cutoff and conflict will become much more dangerous over time. When India's government accuses Pakistan of support for a deadly terrorist attack, as it has done, it has few good military options for retaliation. Both countries have nuclear arsenals that make conventional war too risky. Water is already a powerful weapon for India, because there's not much to prevent the country from tearing up a treaty that no one can enforce. And climate change will make that water much more valuable. Warming is expected to shrink the Himalayan glaciers that feed these rivers by at least a third in coming decades, and the rainfall that sustains crops is becoming less reliable, while populations are growing on both sides of the border.

About 2,500 miles to the west, a long-simmering dispute among Egypt, Sudan, and Ethiopia over the waters of the Nile has provoked similar fears and threats. All three countries depend on the Nile for agriculture and electricity generation. In 2011, a time when Egypt was distracted by Arab Spring unrest, engineers and workers in Ethiopia began construction of the now-finished Grand Ethiopian Renaissance Dam, Africa's largest hydroelectric power plant. This project has already diverted enormous volumes of water from the Blue Nile, the source of 85 percent of the Nile's water, to fill the dam's reservoir, which is larger than the entire city of London. Ethiopia announced plans to quickly fill the reservoir to capacity. Egypt, which relies on the Nile for 90 percent of its water, demanded that the fill advance more slowly to avoid the shock of a sudden loss of water downstream. Here, as in South Asia, increasingly volatile weather patterns and heightened risk of drought will intensify competition for control of the river.

In much the same way, climate change will politicize the production and export of food. Wealthy states that depend on access to imported crops will have more incentive to buy up arable land in poorer countries, and more locals will go hungry as a result. In 2020, with COVID disrupting the world's supply chains, many governments moved to protect national food supplies. Jordan built up record wheat reserves, and fear of shortages then drove Egypt, the world's largest buyer of wheat, to increase its purchases by more than 50 percent. China and Taiwan also announced plans for strategic food stockpiles. Trade in food will become more politicized between calorie-surplus places, those that produce more calories than they consume, like the United States, the EU, and Brazil, and calorie-deficit areas like China and much of Africa. (India will join this importing club as it passes China to become the most populous country on earth by about 2026.)

Migration

As we've seen in Syria and Central America, climate change has already advanced far enough to force millions of desperate people onto the road. Europe's proximity to Africa and the Middle East leaves it much more vulnerable than the United States to tidal waves of humanity. (That said, some worst-case estimates warn that as many as thirty million people might head for the US border over the next thirty years.) The twenty-six-country open border zone in Europe known as the Schengen Area will face its greatest test, and there will again be conflict between poorer countries in southern Europe on the front lines of future refugee crises and the wealthier northern countries whose citizens don't want to help them pay to manage them.

Climate change will have a multiplier effect on this trend, not just because rising waters or changing weather conditions will force people off their land, but also because the places where many of the displaced arrive will be hot, poor, and often as politically fragile as the countries they're fleeing. Developing countries host 85 percent of the world's migrants. Turkey hosts about 3.6 million migrants within its borders, and Jordan has accepted 2.9 million. Perennially unstable Lebanon hosts 1.4 million. The crisis in next-door Venezuela has pushed 1.7 million migrants into Colombia. These nations were vulnerable to political turmoil even before the migrants arrived.

The first country that climate change will completely destroy, the first "refugee nation," will be Kiribati, a collection of thirty-three islands in the Pacific Ocean that are home to about one hundred thousand people. The country's current average elevation is just six feet above sea level. Those who govern Kiribati know exactly what they're up against. Rising seas will erode the shore, drop salt into groundwater, degrade the coral reefs that serve as barriers against storm surges, and ravage the food supply for islanders who fish to live. Rising temperatures and changes in rainfall will also heighten disease outbreaks.

That's why in 2014 the country's government purchased land some fourteen hundred miles to the south, in Fiji. The current plan is to relocate Kiribatians to this higher ground. But these displaced people will no longer be living in their own country. They will live under the jurisdiction of Fiji's government, which will decide for itself how to assimilate them, and the land they've bought isn't exactly prime real estate. It's a combination of steep forested hills unsuitable for building and mangrove swamps unsuitable for farming. The current draft of the plan gives the refugees no fishing rights. These are serious problems, but the population of Kiribati probably won't expand much beyond one hundred thousand, and there is enough land for them. Few refugees outside Kiribati will be as fortunate as these Pacific Islanders are.

One day soon, Bangladesh (population 161 million) will face a similar crisis. More than forty-five million Bangladeshis live in coastal areas already prone to flooding. The frequency and severity of tropical storms affecting Bangladesh is on the rise, and the country will likely lose more than 10 percent of its land over the next three decades. Rising sea levels alone will force as many as eighteen million from their homes.

Where will they go, and how will they be greeted when they get there?

This is a global problem. A 2019 report from the US National Academy of Sciences found that if global carbon emissions continue along their current trajectory, the world will warm by about 5 degrees Celsius by the end of this century, melting enough Arctic and Antarctic ice to submerge food-growing areas of the Nile Delta and much of Bangladesh. Coastal cities like New York, Shanghai, and London would also be in danger. More recent studies indicate that enough progress has now been made on reduction of carbon emissions to help us avoid these worst-case scenarios, but even a much smaller temperature increase will upend hundreds of millions of lives.

Climate change will drive surges of migration in the coming decades in four major regions. First, there is Central America, particularly in the dry corridor that spans El Salvador, Guatemala, Honduras, Nicaragua, and Panama. Second is the Sahel, the zone of transition from the Sahara desert toward the humid savannas to the south, where drought and desertification create the kinds of economic disaster and poverty that can become fertile recruiting ground for terrorist groups. This area includes Burkina Faso, Chad, Mali, Eritrea, Mauritania, Niger, and parts of Nigeria, Senegal, and Sudan. Third, there is South Asia—India, Pakistan, Bangladesh, Sri Lanka, and Nepal—where rising temperatures and sea levels, more intense and frequent cyclones, and river flooding caused by melting glaciers will displace the greatest number of people. Finally, there are the Pacific island states, like Vanuatu, Tuvalu, and Fiji, which face all the same risks that doom Kiribati. At the height of the migrant crisis in 2015, there were about 1.5 million people moving from North Africa and the Middle East into Europe. Scientists have warned that rising sea levels could create *tens of millions of* "climate refugees" in coming decades.

Not all of these people will want to leave their countries, at least not at first. Many will turn to family nearby. But some will discover that the scarcity that forced them from their homes is more widespread than they had perhaps thought. They'll continue on in search of shelter and work in overcrowded cities that are liable to become tinderboxes of protest. As in Syria, many will then be forced to move on toward wealthier and more stable countries that may not welcome them.

There is no institutional framework to prepare for a global emergency of this scale—and little political will to create one. In 1951, the United Nations established the conditions under which its member states must give refugees asylum. War and political persecution topped the list. Not surprisingly, climate change didn't make the cut . . . and it hasn't yet been added.

This isn't a theoretical problem for future decades. Riverbank erosion now destroys the homes of about two hundred thousand Bangladeshis every year, and there are no accepted international rules to help these people find new homes and start new lives. There is nothing to prevent them from setting off on their own to join the two thousand migrants per day entering Dhaka, an already overcrowded city whose sewers frequently burst. Others will try to cross the border to India, where foreign Muslims are increasingly unwelcome. They can't expect much help from the United Nations Refugee Agency, which relies on voluntary contributions from member states for 90 percent of its funding. In a world recovering from the economic impact of COVID-19, few countries are willing to make large contributions. The Trump administration made clear it had no interest in this question, and whatever his preferences, President Biden will face resistance from Congress to any large-scale refugee spending plan. For now, climate refugees are on their own. In coming years, their numbers will become much too large to ignore.

Unrest and Conflict

Climate refugees will face public unrest and conflict wherever they land. We've already seen weather events and water shortages trigger political strife and violent uprising. It happened in the Bolivian town of Cochabamba. In 1999, arguing that private-sector discipline was needed to ensure that water be used efficiently, the Bolivian government auctioned off the Cochabamba water system to a consortium of foreign companies, which then began charging locals for their water supply. The government ignored the first round of protests, which began soon after the arrival of the first water bills. In February 2000, the demonstrations grew larger. In response, the government ordered a reversal of the price increases, but the protesters refused to go home and demanded an end to the contract with the consortium. The arrival of troops triggered bloodshed.

In sympathy with protesters, peasant groups in other parts of the country began blocking highways. The Bolivian army created a state of siege in Cochabamba, but the killing of demonstrators only stiffened the resolve of the swelling crowds. Bolivia's "Water War" was on. The consortium withdrew, foreign investors backed away from Bolivia, and the resulting economic slowdown and public resentment led to the election of Evo Morales, the country's first indigenous president. A fight over management of an increasingly precious resource—in this case, water—helped topple a government, but a generation later, erratic weather continues, droughts have intensified, and Bolivia's water shortages persist.

In 2011, unprecedented flooding in Thailand provoked protests and fighting over the distribution of emergency supplies. This unrest intensified until the military restored order in 2014 by seizing power. There were many factors that pushed democracy past the breaking point, but it was a natural disaster that moved citizens, and then soldiers, toward direct confrontation. Climate change will make the problems of "not enough water here and too much water there" much worse, and the resulting political and economic fallout will topple governments.

According to a 2019 report from the World Resources Institute, seventeen countries that are home to one-quarter of the world's population face "extremely high" levels of water stress, a measure of the degree of competition for fresh water. Cities, agriculture, and industry withdraw an average of more than 80 percent of the available water supply in those countries every year. A total of forty-four countries must manage "high stress."

No region will be more vulnerable than North Africa and the Middle East, an area that by 2030 will include twelve of the abovementioned seventeen water-stressed countries. Resource-related conflicts are already underway. In Yemen, nearly twenty million people lack access to clean water, and by 2025, Sana'a will probably become the first major city in the modern world to run out of water. (Cape Town came perilously close in 2019, but as a wealthy city with stronger institutions, it was able to respond to the crisis more effectively.) Yemen's catastrophic civil war has made water problems worse, as many of the millions of internally displaced Yemenis have descended on the highlands of Ibb, the country's most fertile area. This overflow of people has exacerbated the violence by intensifying competition in the country's last resource-rich area. Climate change didn't create all these problems, but it is an accelerant poured on existing ethnic, political, and economic wildfires.

Even more powerful countries will face new forms of competition and conflict. Climate change will create a race to control new sea lanes and the abundant resources of the Arctic made accessible by melting ice sheets. The United States, Russia, and China are ramping up plans to access fossil fuel, diamond, nickel, and platinum reserves that were once beyond reach, a process that will bring commercial and military infrastructure created by these countries to the region. Other countries with Arctic territory already face considerable pressure to accommodate such expansion.

The unprecedented availability of large oil and gas deposits in the Arctic will lower the price of fossil fuels and persuade some countries to slow the transition toward renewable energy.

In particular, Russia, the world's fourth-largest emitter of greenhouse gases, will own and develop many new oil and gas fields and operate many of the ships that transport fuel through the Northern Sea Route, the most heavily trafficked Arctic transport path. The Russian government, already resistant to a global move away from fossil fuels, will have even more reason to drag its feet on aggressive climate action.

More broadly, increased tanker traffic in the Arctic will accelerate environmental damage and quicken the pace of warming. The melting will release massive amounts of carbon now trapped in the ice. Parts of the Siberian tundra and Canada alone are estimated to store 1,700 gigatons of carbon, twice the amount now in the atmosphere. The release of large amounts of that gas will make it much harder to contain warming.

Climate Apartheid

Just as the refugee crisis of 2015–2016 pitted wealthy northern European countries against indebted southern European countries, and just as COVID-19 hit poorer countries and people hardest, so climate change will drive a wedge between developed and developing states—and between rich and poor within countries. UN experts have warned that poorer countries will bear at least 75 percent of the cost of restoring infrastructure damaged by climate change, and of managing refugees and feeding increased numbers of those left hungry, even though the poorer half of the world's people generate just 10 percent of global emissions. The result will be "climate apartheid," a term coined by Philip Alston, UN special rapporteur on extreme poverty and human rights, as richer countries—and richer people within poorer countries—build new sorts of barriers to protect their wealth. A half century of poverty reduction and the growth of a global middle class could evaporate in just a few years as climate further widens the gap between rich and poor worldwide.

The Dangers of Geo-Engineering

In a world where political leaders tell voters that walls can protect them from outside threats, some governments will turn to new technologies that offer miracle cures without sacrifice. Citizens, happy to hear about quick, cheap solutions, will be eager to try them.

A process known as "geo-engineering" or "climate engineering" is designed to address the problem of carbon in the atmosphere through climate manipulation. The process of "cloud whitening" (or "cloud brightening") involves spraying pressurized seawater droplets and dissolved salts high in the air above both land and sea to create salt crystals and new water droplets, increasing cloud cover over oceans to reflect incoming solar radiation back into space. Other projects are designed to release sulfur into the stratosphere to produce an effect similar to cloud whitening but much farther from the earth's surface. But scientists are now debating both the viability and the ethics of these plans, particularly those that are planned within individual countries. Spraying sulfate aerosols into the upper atmosphere to cool the earth by reflecting solar radiation back into space is risky. It's a lot less expensive than sharply cutting carbon emissions (to cut emissions abruptly would be to slow growth and likely kill jobs). But we don't know the potential dangers or whether it could actually work.

Or maybe we can continue to churn out CO_2 but develop tools to "capture" much of it before it reaches the atmosphere. We'll then need a safe place to store it all. This procedure is like collecting garbage and then burying it in a landfill. The downside, beyond the cost, is that this carbon will probably be stored in poor countries that need the money they'll be paid for housing it; and poor people are most likely to suffer if the carbon ever leaks. Or maybe we can dump a lot of iron-rich dust into the oceans in order to grow plankton that can then absorb all that carbon. The downside here, say some scientists, is that it might kill a lot of ocean life by removing oxygen from the water without absorbing much carbon.

No one knows the long-term effects of these technologies or how using them in one country will affect neighbors. We don't understand the adaptability of the earth's atmosphere well enough to let individual governments test theories that might have global (and permanent) effects. There is good reason to use computer modeling to research and invest in such ideas (especially so that we better understand the consequences if some countries decide to move forward on their own). But in a G-Zero world, with countries left to manage global challenges unilaterally, we might not have answers before irreversible damage has already been done.

And since we're on the subject of an every-nation-for-itself approach to the future, what happens if one government weaponizes these new tools? If researchers discover that they can create a healthier ecosystem in one country, they might also find ways to harm that of another. And if they believe that they *can* destroy a country in this way, with undetermined impact on yet more neighboring countries and the entire global ecosystem, nothing prevents them from doing so. The threat alone is enough to trigger a dangerous climate arms race.

CAN CLIMATE BE THE CRISIS WE NEED?

Success in the fight against climate change will depend on a deep respect for the rule of law—in this case, the laws of physics and chemistry. But no single tech fix will make the difference between life and death for the millions who will contend with the worst effects of the monster we've all created. To limit climate change and the catastrophes it can generate, and do it in a way that shares burdens fairly among rich and poor nations, the world's major carbon emitters—the United States, the European Union, China, India, Brazil, and others—must put aside their differences in other areas to work together. They must share information freely and coordinate their plans. They must also share responsibility for the costs and risks involved in getting this right. They *must* do these things, because if they don't, everyone will pay the price.

There's reason for optimism on this front. The so-called European Green Deal has boosted Europe as a leader on climate by committing unprecedented amounts of money toward the net-zero goal. EU governments and the European Parliament agreed in 2020 on a €1.8 trillion budget package that includes a commitment that 30 percent of that money will be spent on minimizing climate change. More than 115 other countries have pledged carbon neutrality by 2050, and China has now promised to get there before 2060. Even without the US, those countries account for more than half the world's carbon emissions and half its GDP. International lenders have announced targets as well. Multinational development banks have collectively pledged loans of at least $65 billion by 2025 for climate change containment and adaptation, with $50 billion targeted to low- and middle-income countries.

Another big change this decade has come from the US itself.

Donald Trump's decision to withdraw the US from the Paris climate accord didn't kill the agreement, and President Biden quickly reversed Trump's decision. Climate policy is the single biggest difference between the Trump and Biden presidencies. Trump, oscillating between indifference and denial, prioritized deregulation for the fossil fuel industry. Even as a candidate, Biden risked the ire of voters in oil-producing states to make climate a signature issue. As president, he's prioritized supporting international lending to reach sustainability targets. Rejoining the Paris Agreement commits the United States to reaching net-zero emissions by 2050. The commitment will bring major new investment in green industries, infrastructure, energy, and technologies.

There is even room for optimism regarding China. The Communist Party leadership recognizes that the drive for net-zero emissions offers big opportunities for the country, which has a decades-long dependence on imported fossil fuels. Many of those imports come from the Middle East, a region that is always at risk of turmoil and whose major players still mostly look to the United States for security guarantees. China has a strong commercial relationship with energy-exporting Russia, but the ties are transactional, and the world's largest oil producer today is the United States. There's much for China to like about a post–fossil fuel world in which its lack of natural resources no longer makes it vulnerable to foreign governments and geopolitical instability.

China is trying to become an industry leader and standards-setter for solar and wind technologies and the electric vehicle supply chain. And its state-driven economy lets it direct massive amounts of investment toward companies that can help achieve these goals. Its recognition of this opportunity can heighten competition with Western governments and companies. Or cooperation. Or both. Whatever choices its leaders make on working directly with other governments, at least China has a clear interest in pulling in the same direction as the world's other leading economies.

Some of the world's largest companies have made carbon pledges of their own. Amazon promises to be carbon-neutral by 2040. Apple pledges to become carbon-neutral across its entire business and manufacturing supply chain by 2030, and requires that all its suppliers commit to be "100 percent renewable for their Apple production" within ten years. Microsoft promises to be carbon-negative by 2030 and says that by 2050 it will have removed from the environment an amount of carbon equal to its total lifetime emissions. Google has committed to extend carbon-neutral status to encompass its supply chain. In September 2020, the Business Roundtable, a lobbying organization that represents more than two hundred major US corporations, not only endorsed a plan to cut US greenhouse gas emissions by 80 percent below 2005 levels by 2050, in line with the Paris Agreement, but declared its support for market-based carbon pricing, a process to limit carbon emissions by forcing emitters to pay for them. That's a dramatic change from the US business community's previous positions on this topic.

In addition, the cost of renewable energy is falling much faster than experts predicted even five years ago. Renewables are a crucial part of any credible strategy to reach net-zero emissions. Not only do they help reduce carbon emission and clean polluted air, they've also become cheaper than fossil fuels in many parts of the world.

Together, here's what world leaders can do next . . .

First, leaders of the countries that can contribute most to meeting this common challenge must accept that climate change threatens humans in every country on Earth, and that only through cooperation, compromise, and coordination can we avoid disasters that will destroy the lives of hundreds of millions of people. Promises and targets aren't enough. Leaders have to find the courage and imagination to work together across borders and over decades to limit the collective damage our past will inflict on our common future.

Smaller countries also have a role to play. The leaders of imperiled island nations—from Fiji to the Bahamas and the Marshall Islands to the Maldives—have banded together to shape the climate debate. Collectively, they helped craft the Paris climate accord and kept the United States, China, India, and Brazil at the table when talks threatened to veer off track. In 2017, Fiji hosted an international gathering of world leaders to discuss climate change, a move that helped these leaders see with their own eyes the shape of things to come.

Setting Rules

New rules can't just come from government—and here there is good news. Much of the momentum toward policies that limit climate change has come from outside governments, as heat waves, droughts, wildfires, and other local emergencies boost public support for bolder action. Unfortunately, magazine articles about island nations disappearing beneath the waves have not been enough to change millions of minds. But as citizens of wealthier countries begin to see the impact on their own lives, companies that sell to them see some advantage in appearing to lead the charge on climate action. Banks and investment houses, many of which focus on longer-term trends, have begun to direct money away from fossil fuels toward so-called ESG (environmental, social, and governance) investment targets, both for reputational reasons and because they're a likely source of future profits. In response, publicly traded companies face unprecedented pressure to become "ESG-compliant." By taking these kinds of actions, the private sector makes it politically safer for governments to adopt bolder climate policies. After all, when investors say they're no longer going to finance coal, it's easier for political leaders to stop issuing coal licenses.

Then came the pandemic and an extraordinary global economic shock, which dealt the brick-and-mortar economy a historic blow. The tech companies that allow us to work, socialize, shop, and gather information online, already more oriented toward the use of renewable energy, reaped the benefits. To manage COVID's economic fallout, governments shoveled massive amounts of money toward relief and recovery, speeding the transition toward a renewable economy. We can't ignore the power of innovation and markets in the West to unleash as yet unimagined technologies to move the needle. After all, in 1991, few would have imagined that the most valuable auto manufacturer in the world in 2022 would be a new entrant that makes only electric cars, a company run by a CEO who named his son X Æ A-12 Musk.

Joint R&D

International cooperation on COVID-19 included the beginnings of cross-border coordination on vaccine research and a global supply chain to distribute the vaccine. The world needs coordinated research and development work on climate technologies. Just as with the COVID vaccine, this need not be a single project. Competition among groups racing to be first with game-changing innovations in carbon capture, a green energy breakthrough, new food-production technologies, and other inventions can be positive—as long as they give us universally beneficial results. Investment in these projects can be internationally funded to ensure that costs are shared as well as benefits. Collaboration among governments can also minimize the risk that any of these innovations are weaponized to benefit one country at the expense of another.

Breakthroughs in green technology and climate management must be shared with the developing world, for the same reason that vaccines should be shared: as refugee flows show, a crisis in one country can quickly trigger an emergency in others. As with the pandemic, we can't meet the challenge of climate change anywhere until we meet it everywhere.

Managing Carbon

To establish a new architecture of international cooperation on climate, we'll need a World Carbon Organization, somewhat analogous to the World Trade Organization—an agency that regulates and oversees international trade in carbon credits and provides an accurate accounting of carbon emissions and carbon removal when these technologies become viable on a much larger scale. That's the only way to give governments confidence that all are playing fair as we advance toward a world of zero-net emissions.

The fight against climate change will also demand a joint international effort to discourage carbon emissions by making them more expensive. The shortest path to that goal involves carbon prices. This is not a new idea, and carbon-pricing plans, whether in the form of carbon taxes or emissions trading, have failed for many reasons. In the past, the industries that would be most affected by them have used financial and political muscle to defeat them. Their work has been made easier by the lack of cost-effective carbon alternatives. Another problem: some governments refuse to tax carbon because they want to give their local industries a competitive edge against those paying higher taxes in other countries.

Airlines, automakers, and others that rely on affordable fossil fuels are still recovering from the devastating blows dealt by COVID-19. These industries need financial help, not higher taxes. That said, they can be induced to accept future higher taxes in order to pay for a bailout today, particularly if the tax levels rise only after the proceeds of initial taxes go toward development of affordable hydrocarbon alternatives. After all, the ultimate goal of a carbon tax is not to make it more expensive to do business. It's to encourage industry to switch to cleaner forms of energy. Businesses can't do that until those new forms of energy are at least as cheap as their current energy bills.

This too must be a coordinated international effort. Otherwise we'll create a system in which governments that care less about climate change can drum up business at the expense of those that care more—with no reduction in the amount of carbon pumped into the atmosphere. Europe, once again, is leading the way on carbon pricing—with an Emissions Trading Scheme and an EU border carbon tax plan that can encourage European coordination with the Biden administration on a joint strategy to overcome Chinese opposition to these and other useful ideas. South Korea, South Africa, Mexico, and the state of California have similar projects in place. China has announced plans for a nationwide carbon market for its famously inefficient power industry. COVID delayed expansion of these projects, but they can regain momentum as economies continue to recover. In many countries, carbon taxes will become more popular with lawmakers looking to raise revenue for COVID recovery without raising taxes on voters.

The private sector will have a crucial role to play. The world's largest oil companies have the resources, the expertise, and the scale to move into green energy development and carbon capture. That may be the only way they can stay in business. They also face unprecedented pressure from governments and courts to do more. In 2021, a Dutch court ordered that by 2030, Shell must cut its carbon emissions by 45 percent from 2019 levels. That was the first time a court had ordered a private company to comply with the Paris climate accord. Shareholders have used voting power to force ExxonMobil and Chevron to take bolder climate action.

Companies can lobby governments for stronger climate legislation, as some US business groups have done through support for carbon pricing. By getting in front of the issue, companies give themselves the best chance to shape legislation and boost their public image. Most importantly, by pushing governments to set prices on carbon, they can create a much more predictable investment environment for themselves. It's better for them to know sooner rather than later what their costs and opportunities will be.

Just as many companies flipped production to focus on personal protective equipment or jumped into the vaccine distribution business, and tech companies created tools that help scientists test new drugs and trace infections around the world, so oil and gas companies can engineer new biofuels and chemicals that help reduce emissions. The most enterprising can expect big profits and future competitive advantages.

Companies have their own climate-based risks to manage. Those with real market power can help bring about positive change on their own. Retail giant Walmart pledged in 2020 not only to reduce its own carbon emissions to zero by 2040 but to require everyone in its supply chain to decarbonize too. Multinational consumer goods company Unilever is using satellite imagery and geolocation data to "achieve a deforestation-free supply chain by 2023." These and hundreds of other large companies can also exert peer pressure on their partners and competitors to keep pace, which relieves pressure on each individual company to maximize quarterly profits at the expense of a smart long-term investment.

Software giant Salesforce announced in early 2020 that it would "support and mobilize the conservation and restoration of 100 million trees over the next decade" as part of the 1t.org initiative, the World Economic Forum's plan to conserve, restore, and plant one trillion trees by 2030. Salesforce is also contributing its formidable logistics technology to the organizational challenge this plan represents, which will create future opportunities for the company while earning credit with the public and the civil society groups that grade companies on their corporate social responsibility.

Trees

People and trees live in harmony: we inhale oxygen and exhale carbon dioxide, while trees suck in carbon dioxide and produce oxygen. That helps explain why climate change is made worse by clear-cutting trees for agriculture or logging in the Amazon, in the Democratic Republic of Congo, in Indonesia, and elsewhere. Fewer trees take in less carbon dioxide, and trees that are cut down and burned release the carbon they've been storing into the air. Climate change is making this problem worse by generating droughts in some areas that make wildfires more likely. Researchers at Global Forest Watch, an NGO, estimated that the loss of tropical forest during 2019 released more than two billion tons of carbon dioxide. That's more than the emissions from all vehicles in the United States that year.

Brazil was responsible for about one-third of all the world's deforestation in 2019. President Jair Bolsonaro has aggressively removed legal protections for the land for the benefit of investors in mining and large-scale farming. When world leac..s point to the climate implications and criticize his actions, he tells them to mind their own business—after all, these much wealthier countries failed to act when it was their companies doing the environmental damage that brought us to this point. The country's Amazon territory and what happens there are, he insists, the concern of Brazil alone. But just as India and Pakistan or Ethiopia, Egypt, and Sudan trade threats over access to the waters that flow across their borders, so does the Amazon rainforest impact the climate of the entire planet.

If the world's most powerful countries see the problem with these terms, they can persuade Brazil's president to change his tune. While respecting Brazil's sovereignty, they can invest in protecting the remaining rainforest and in reforesting areas that have been destroyed. Brazil (and Bolivia) can reap rewards as stewards of this irreplaceable global resource. In poorer countries, such as the Democratic Republic of Congo, loggers and logging companies have become a law unto themselves. They literally outgun those who would enforce the law. Wealthier countries, particularly resource-hungry China, benefit from some of these illegal activities. Just as international peacekeepers preserve order in many of the world's conflict zones, a similar contingent can enforce laws designed to prevent deforestation, and to plant and protect new trees.

Who Pays?

Of course, all these plans will cost a lot of money, and the smartest way to finance them is through cost-sharing among the world's wealthiest countries. Easier said than done, as always, but these are the governments that will have to spend trillions to clean up and repair the damage that climate change inflicts over time. It's cheaper to share the cost of investment in a global strategy to limit climate change now than to bear the cost alone of bailing out cities, companies, industries, workers, and displaced citizens after climate change has done its worst.

Think of it this way: if a government could invest a large amount of money to change a Category 5 into a Category 1 hurricane instead of spending an even larger amount on the devastation associated with the superstorm, shouldn't they do it? Unfortunately, some people refuse to believe the storm exists, or don't understand how powerful it is, or think it will be a problem only for people unlucky enough to live in the future. And, of course, some still profit, economically and politically, by ignoring the storm. But as the warning signs become even more blindingly obvious, it will be harder for most governments to deny the undeniable. And more and more companies and investors are recognizing that business models will have to change for companies to remain profitable. There is already much more international cooperation than there was a decade ago at both the government and grassroots level, but it isn't yet clear whether either will move far enough or fast enough.

National and local governments can spend to prepare their cities for rising sea levels and their coastal communities for more frequent and violent storms. They can invest to protect other parts of their territory from the impact of erratic weather patterns. But international funding will be critical for joint research and development projects on carbon capture, new sources of energy, and multinational protections for forests, water, and other natural resources. It will also be needed to help people in countries whose governments lack the resources to protect them.

Refugee Rights

In 2013, a man named Ioane Teitiota applied for asylum for himself and his family in New Zealand. He claimed that climate change made it impossible for him to continue to live in Kiribati. When New Zealand rejected his application, he appealed to the UN Human Rights Committee and asked to be classified as a climate refugee. He explained that the island where he lived had become overcrowded, as rising seas made it impossible to live on nearby islands. The overcrowding, he said, created social tensions, violent crime, water shortages, and a variety of health problems. He cited studies that predicted that all of Kiribati would be uninhabitable within ten to fifteen years and asked the committee whether he really had to wait until he was waist-deep in water before he could have a refugee's rights and protections.

In January 2020, the UN committee ruled against Teitiota. It argued that Kiribati, with help from the international community, could still relocate displaced people in an orderly way. But, crucially, the committee also ruled that, though this particular case didn't yet meet the standard, governments cannot return people to countries where their lives might be threatened by climate change. This ruling didn't help Teitiota (or at least has not helped him yet), but it recognized that climate change will impose dangerous hardships on many more people, and that countries will have responsibilities under international law to protect climate refugees.

The risk of two hundred million climate refugees in 2050 is a worst-case scenario, but even best-case scenarios will still force millions from their homes. If European leaders could have planned in advance for Syria's civil war and the migrant crisis of 2015–2016, that disaster would have killed far fewer people and imposed much less human, economic, and political pain in dozens of countries. The world's leaders must start planning now for the larger crisis to come.

These preparations must do more than protect the fortunate from the unfortunate. That approach is both immoral and unworkable. It's immoral because the world's poorest people didn't create this problem that will affect them disproportionately. It's unworkable because their presence as long-term refugees inside the borders of other countries will create economic and political turmoil in the countries that host them and spillover effects for nearly everybody else within.

That's why the world's governments must forge an international agreement on the rights of climate refugees. The United Nations has no power to force countries to respect international human rights law or the ruling of its committee in the Teitiota case. If there is to be the kind of burden-sharing that can help avoid chaos for all, a new multilateral compact is the only way forward, but this is an area where it's hard to be optimistic.

A Green Marshall Plan

In 2019, Representative Alexandria Ocasio-Cortez and Senator Edward Markey proposed a plan known as the Green New Deal, an ambitious response to climate change that reduces greenhouse gas emissions, shifts US energy use from oil and gas toward renewable sources, creates large numbers of jobs in the growing clean energy industry, and even tackles problems of wealth inequality and racial injustice. This is a serious piece of legislation designed to solve serious problems—though unless it's funded almost entirely by debt, the middle-class tax increases it would demand make it a nonstarter in Washington.

But the Green New Deal's more significant limitation is that it's a national approach to a global problem. And as we've seen, climate change isn't just a threat to the United States.

We need a Green Marshall Plan, a global, government-funded project that commits to enacting similar principles worldwide. The United States and China don't have to agree on how Hong Kong should be governed, how maritime boundaries in the South China Sea should be drawn, or how democracy should be defined. But they need to agree on the urgency to invest in energy plans that limit the damage climate change will inflict on all of us.

The big obstacle to achieving a Green Marshall Plan is creating a mechanism that gives countries "climate credit" for the investments they make under it. To create incentives for public and private investors to fund green development in other countries, they need credit that allows them higher emissions in return. (The atmosphere doesn't care whether a ton of CO_2 comes from Boston or Bangalore.) This isn't a new idea. The 1997 Kyoto Protocol tried but failed to accomplish this because too few countries had faith in the score-keeping system. But as the sense of urgency on warming increases and the specifics of the plan are refined, many governments are ready to revisit this idea, which is the principle behind the World Carbon Organization, mentioned above. A growing number of private-sector companies aren't waiting. They calculate that by helping to move the planet toward zero emissions, they can improve their standing with the public and with government regulators. In the meantime, Mark Carney, UN special envoy for climate action, is trying to jump-start the effort by creating "voluntary carbon markets."

COVID-19 has boosted cross-border cooperation on climate change. It presented an immediate, crippling global problem that forced many governments, the private sector, and civil society organizations to work together. Without the COVAX project, for example, the problems of vaccine hoarding and inequality between rich and poor nations would have been even worse than they were. The willingness of some countries to export excess supplies of vaccines—as the US did for neighbors Mexico and Canada and as the US, Japan, India, and Australia did for other Asian countries—created a blueprint for shared sacrifice at a time of serious political and economic stress for all these countries.

The pandemic also underscored the value of science. Shocking numbers of people still see science as a scam used by phony experts to rob them of their freedom and dignity, but throughout the world it became evident during COVID that scientists, innovative companies, and resourceful individuals created solutions to unprecedented threats. That will matter as the impact of climate change becomes a lot more obvious to a lot more people.

Maybe the biggest boost that COVID provided the fight against climate change comes from the end of Donald Trump's presidency. Trump didn't care about warming, and that removed some of the incentive many other world leaders might have had to offer the compromises and sacrifices needed to reach net zero. In many ways, Washington and Beijing have avoided responsibility for leadership in this crisis. But before, during, and after the COP26 summit in Glasgow in November 2021, the increasingly unavoidable and ugly reality of the climate crisis, together with increased pressure from climate activists, has moved other governments and large corporations to take more aggressive action. That's not enough to solve the G-Zero–net-zero problem. The US remains politically dysfunctional. The US-China relationship is still headed in the wrong direction. Too many developing countries are still wrestling with COVID and waiting for promised vaccines. But maybe our limited success in boosting cooperation to fight COVID can prepare us to do much more on climate.

Climate change isn't an alien invasion. We did this to ourselves. Only a global effort can limit its damage. But if world leaders can rise to the challenge before it's too late, they will have created the foundation for cooperative work against the biggest and most insidious threat of all—the life-altering impact of disruptive new technologies.

CHAPTER 4

DISRUPTIVE TECHNOLOGIES

In the introduction, I wrote that COVID had started a war, and nobody won. Let me amend that. Technology won, specifically, the makers of disruptive new technologies and all those who benefit from them. Before the pandemic, American politicians were shaking their fists at the country's leading tech companies. Republicans insisted that new media was as hopelessly biased against them as traditional media, and they demanded action. Democrats warned that tech giants like Amazon, Facebook, Apple, Alphabet, and Netflix had amassed too much market (and therefore political) power, that citizens had lost control of how these companies use the data they generate, and that the companies should therefore be broken into smaller, less dangerous pieces. European governments led a so-called techlash against the American tech powerhouses, which they accused of violating their customers' privacy.

COVID didn't put an end to any of these criticisms, but it reminded policymakers and citizens alike just how indispensable digital technologies have become. Companies survived the pandemic only by allowing wired workers to log in from home. Consumers avoided possible infection by shopping online. Specially made drones helped deliver lifesaving medicine in rich and poor countries alike. Advances in telemedicine helped scientists and doctors understand and fight the virus. Artificial intelligence helped hospitals predict how many beds and ventilators they would need at any one time. A spike in Google searches using phrases that included specific symptoms helped health officials detect outbreaks in places where doctors and hospitals are few and far between. AI played a crucial role in vaccine development by absorbing all available medical literature to identify links between the genetic properties of the virus and the chemical composition and effects of existing drugs.

Contact tracing and smartphone apps that tracked whether people had come in contact with others who later tested positive for the virus helped contain its spread as researchers raced to develop vaccines. In China, apps helped fight COVID by providing detailed data on where to go for quarantine, by tracking where each person had been and assigning a color-coded status that defined the level of risk they posed for other people, and by limiting their movement based on that status. Authorities also used GPS and telecom data to prevent cheating. A person with a code that signaled low risk could move freely, while lockdowns in other countries confined nearly everyone, regardless of their health status. These technologies had been in development for years, but COVID and its variants hit the fast-forward button and sent us hurtling toward the future.

But it would be shortsighted to simply celebrate these new developments without scrutinizing the next generation of risks they will present. Some disruptive new technologies, those that fundamentally change the way we live, create *risks of dehumanization*—by transforming the nature of work at the expense of workers, by creating new forms of inequality within and among nations, and by inventing new ways to break traditional links among families, old and new friends, and people around the world. There are new *risks of outlaw tech*, as weapons of war and powerful cyber-tools increasingly fall into the hands of criminals and terrorists. There are *risks to the peace among powerful nations* that we've enjoyed since the end of World War II. In this chapter, we'll see how disruptive new technologies create all three of these forms of threat.

As humans have known for millennia, new technologies are simply tools that can boost our quality of life, destroy things, or (sometimes) do both at the same time. Let's start with the positive. The pandemic was only the latest showcase for the countless ways that new technologies can help us live safer, healthier, and more prosperous lives. For example, imagine you're one of the 124 million residents of Maharashtra, India's second most populous state and home to Mumbai, one of the world's biggest and fastest-growing cities. But you don't live in Mumbai. Your life unfolds in a one-room hut about 150 miles from the big city. Electricity has only arrived recently in your home. You still carry water from a nearby well, grow your own food, and cook outside. You need kerosene for the stove and fertilizer for the garden. You need a bank account, quality health care, and a decent education for your kids. Like many other developing countries, India offers subsidies and services to those who need them, but for most of your life, you couldn't access any of them, because nobody had ever recorded your birth. You have no piece of paper that proves you are who you say you are.

That's why you're so grateful for Aadhaar, a biometric identification system that has now established the identities of virtually everyone in India, one-sixth of the planet's population. You gave the government your thumbprint and an iris scan to match the photo taken of you at the Aadhaar office. You now have a unique twelve-digit number that proves who you are and opens a world of opportunity for you and your family by allowing you to access services provided by your government.

For the first time in history, people like you have a chance to get things that many others take for granted. More importantly, your son and daughter will live a completely different kind of life from you and your ancestors. You couldn't care less about warnings that you've surrendered your privacy to the government. Aadhaar brought life's essentials within your reach. It made you visible. It made you a citizen. In Hindi, the word *aadhaar* means "foundation," and this system creates a foundation upon which nearly 1.4 billion people can build their future.

In this case, what's good for you is good for your government. Those without a verifiable identity can't join the formal economy. Aadhaar brought an unprecedented number of people within the state's orbit, and in becoming true citizens, many of them have also become taxpayers for the first time. The more people who pay taxes, the more revenue the government can spend to lift still more people out of poverty. And by establishing the identity of everyone in India for the first time in history, the government has already saved billions by cutting into waste and fraud. One example: an Indian government investigation found that, before the rollout of Aadhaar, schools in three different states had inflated attendance rolls with 440,000 nonexistent students in order to draw more money from state-funded school lunch programs. Now there's no need to use corrupt local officials as middlemen between government and citizens. Aadhaar allows the treasury to transfer funds for state pensions, fuel subsidies, and other government help directly into new bank accounts which legitimate recipients can access with a thumbprint.

It isn't just those who live in the hinterlands who will benefit from the ongoing global digital revolution. Big changes are coming to the world's most dynamic cities. Cities power the global economy. Those who live in them, half the world's people, account for about 80 percent of global GDP and two-thirds of all energy consumption. By 2045, the earth's urban areas will be home to more than six billion people, two-thirds of all humanity, according to the World Bank.

Here's an example of how new technologies will dramatically improve city life. Traffic accidents kill more than one million people on the world's roads each year and injure millions more. Most of these accidents occur in cities. Multiple studies over decades have shown that human error contributes to the overwhelming majority of these tragedies. Enter driverless cars. Replacing human drivers with computers that obey speed limits, follow traffic rules, and don't drink and drive or fall asleep at the wheel will prevent the vast majority of these casualties. In the US, it could save $190 billion per year in health-care costs alone, according to consulting firm McKinsey & Company. That's not counting the value of the time and energy saved by liberating millions of commuters from the daily drudgery of driving to work. The world's urban traffic congestion has grown far worse as billions of people flock to cities, join the ranks of the middle class, and buy cars. Time behind the wheel in traffic is dead time. Freeing that time for work or leisure will boost both human happiness and economic productivity. Truly self-driving cars are still years away, but they will become a reality as advances in AI and 5G networks connect cars to each other and to other objects in the urban environment—like traffic signals—on a massive scale.

The potential financial gains haven't been lost on Big Tech companies and automakers, who are now locked in a high-stakes race to ease humans out of the driver's seat. Autonomous vehicles that combine high-resolution sensors, streaming data, and sophisticated algorithms to pilot themselves will one day change the way cities operate and citizens live. You won't need to own, drive, park, maintain, fuel, and insure an automobile. That's more money in your pocket. You'll hail a driverless electric car that can operate twenty-four hours a day with short breaks to recharge. That means far fewer cars on the street, less air pollution, fewer pollution-related health problems, and more green space.

Digitizing the guts of the world's mass transit systems will also ease rail and bus congestion, reduce delays, and cut travel times. Maintenance crews will spot problems with tracks, switch equipment, and railcars before they fail. Trains that navigate by computer will run more frequently and closer together than trains that rely on visual signals and human drivers. The more efficiently a city runs, the more productive its inhabitants will be, and the wealthier it will become.

The digital revolution is also helping cities address one of the fundamental problems of the twenty-first century: security. Take a short walk down the street from Eurasia Group's London offices and turn right onto Goswell Road. After a few minutes, you'll encounter a cast-iron statue of a dragon marking the northern boundary of the City of London, the British capital's ancient core and one of the world's most important financial centers.

A little farther on, past this symbolic guardian of London,

you'll make your way imperceptibly across the real thing—a security cordon known formally as the City of London Traffic and Environmental Zone and informally as the ring of steel. The ring is a dense network of traffic barriers, checkpoints, and surveillance cameras that safeguard the square-mile-sized financial and skyscraper district against terror attacks. Constructed in the 1990s to protect against Irish Republican Army bombs, the cordon was reinforced after the 9/11 attacks. Today, the City of London police, the small, elite force tasked with protecting the financial district, uses automatic license plate scanners cross-referenced against a national database to spot suspicious or stolen vehicles and potential terror threats.

Half a world away, in the smart-city development of Songdo, South Korea, police use automatic license plate scanning to spot rogue vehicles, too. They also use a network of AI-enhanced surveillance cameras to spot people who are fighting, collapsed on the ground, or walking erratically—and to alert nearby officers. Microphones can detect people shouting in distress and send police to help.

New technologies not only help police keep us safer, they can also help keep us safe from police. In 2016, film star Will Smith told interviewer Stephen Colbert that he didn't believe that racism in America was getting worse: "We are talking about race in this country more clearly and openly than we have almost ever in the history of this country," said Smith. "Racism is not getting worse, it's getting filmed." Police continue to commit unlawful acts of violence, and the smartphone camera in everyone's pocket broadcasts the reality of racial hatred, as the police killing of George Floyd dramatically demonstrated in 2020. These cameras, and their owners' ability to share images across social media, have made it easier to document human rights abuses in many countries.

More broadly, the separate but simultaneous revolutions now underway in AI, connected devices, and ultrafast data networks will bring tens of billions of new devices online—onto our wrists and into our homes, cars, factories, and everywhere else that human activity takes place. These innovations won't rely on humans to spot trends and find hidden efficiencies within the vast sea of data they produce. With the right mix of data and computing power, artificially intelligent computers, operating with inhuman speed and superhuman insight, will do that work instead.

RISKS

And yet . . . all revolutions produce unintended consequences, and not all destruction clears ground for something better. Badly designed AI can make our lives miserable. Biased data can produce unfair results that deprive citizens of all sorts of rights and opportunities, and it won't always be easy to appeal—or in some cases even recognize—the decisions that AI makes for us. Here's an example. In October 2019, researchers published a paper in the journal *Science* that presented compelling evidence that an algorithm used in the US to help decide when sick people should be eligible for more intensive health care unwittingly created bias based on race. They found that for patients who were equally sick, the algorithm was less likely to refer black patients for extra care because it used the historical cost of care as a proxy for health-care needs. The data failed to capture the fact that black patients, who tend to have lower incomes, may historically have spent less on health care or received lower-quality care than white patients who were similarly ill. Biased data produced biased results.

That's hardly an isolated instance. In 2018, Joy Buolamwini, a researcher at the MIT Media Lab, presented evidence that facial recognition algorithms sold by IBM, Microsoft, and Face++ (a Chinese facial recognition company) were better at recognizing light-skinned faces and worse at recognizing dark-skinned ones, particularly female. A study in 2019 by the US government's National Institute of Standards and Technology of 189 different facial recognition algorithms sold by 99 companies found that they made mistakes identifying Asian and black faces 10 to 100 times more often than they did Caucasian faces.

Even AI that works as planned can subvert the best intentions of those who designed it—and those who would use it to make things better. As twenty-first-century automation, machine learning, and AI change our lives, entire economic sectors will disintegrate, and many forms of human labor will disappear. There's nothing new about technological change and the "creative destruction" it brings, but even before the pandemic, digital-age changes were coming too fast for most societies and individuals to manage. Then COVID-19 took a wrecking ball to much of what remained of the twentieth-century economy and accelerated the transition toward new forms of work and commerce.

DEHUMANIZATION RISKS

Some of these disruptive technologies are stripping many people of the opportunities that make them citizens—the chance to earn a living and confidence that better government can create equality of opportunity. Neither of these values is an absolute, of course. It's always been easier for some than for others to find work, to earn a decent living, and to find and share accurate information about the world. But as machines change our lives faster than governments can understand, much less address, humans are left with much less confidence that government could help them even if it wanted to. The greatest dehumanizing risk of all comes from the ways in which a kind of "digital authoritarianism" undermines democracy itself.

The New Workplace

We can define "security" in many different ways. One of the most important is our ability to get and hold a job. Wages put food on the table and a roof over our heads. They help us educate ourselves and our children. For tens of millions of Americans, jobs provide health insurance and pensions. They give us an outlet for our energies and a sense of purpose. They give us self-respect.

More than a decade ago, the financial crisis forced millions out of work around the world, and because many companies seized the opportunity to scale back their labor costs while others went out of business, some of those jobs never came back. COVID-19 dealt workers another blow, and while the economic rebound has been much faster this time, we're still tallying the number of lockdown-related permanent job losses. But well beyond these unexpected emergencies is the (long-anticipated) long-term impact of technological change in the workplace.

Over the past twenty years, smart machines have begun to replace people on an ever-expanding array of job sites. As with almost all the technologies discussed in this chapter, the benefits of this development are real and wide-ranging. Automation of manufacturing makes production more efficient with each passing year. Goods can be made and delivered more cheaply. That means lower prices and more money in the pockets of consumers, who can then invest that extra cash or spend it in ways that boost production across the economy. Automation also means lower labor costs and higher profits for companies.

A generation ago, American companies moved factories overseas to Mexico, China, and other places where workers accept lower wages and fewer benefits. But machines have changed the game. Outsourcing is now yesterday's news. There's much less need to pay the cost of building new factories in countries with low-wage labor and the risks that come from dealing with foreign governments when machines are becoming more sophisticated and more productive much more quickly than we imagined even ten years ago. Robots don't miss work. They don't take vacations or demand health care and pensions. They don't go on strike. A 2018 study from McKinsey & Company found that intelligent machines could add as much as $5.8 trillion in annual value for the companies that deploy them.

This trend ensures that the manufacturing jobs lost to other countries will not return to American workers—and many more existing jobs will be automated. What's true for the US is true in all industrialized countries. In 2019, there were about 2.25 million robots in use worldwide, a threefold increase over the previous twenty years. Some forecast as many as twenty million robots on the job by 2030. Reports from Oxford Economics and McKinsey published in 2019 estimate that machines will eventually eliminate tens of millions of jobs worldwide. Robots offer another important advantage for producers and society as a whole: They don't catch and spread diseases. They don't need to be quarantined. That's why the pandemic has accelerated the pace of this transition more quickly than all these pre-COVID job studies had predicted.

There's nothing new about technological changes that kill jobs, and we know from past tech revolutions that new jobs, and new *types* of jobs, will be created. It's entirely possible, though not inevitable, that the trend toward automation will create more jobs than it destroys. But these transitions have never been smooth, and this one will be the rockiest ever because it's happening exponentially faster than any of its predecessors. Many workers will never be able to acquire the skill set to perform jobs that require experience in the use of advanced technology. For those who can adapt, the transition will be difficult; retraining costs time and money. In addition, many immigrants, including those who are well educated, put down roots in their adopted countries by first working in manual labor and service jobs. If there is less demand in the future for humans to do this kind of work, many immigrants won't be able to establish a foothold.

Those who profit from automation have given the process an exciting name: the "fourth industrial revolution." In 2016, the World Economic Forum described it as "a new era that builds and extends the impact of digitization in new and unanticipated ways." Though that report went into admirable detail on the ways in which these "unanticipated" changes would likely upend citizens and societies, a more accurate term for the state in which those on the wrong side of this trend may find themselves is "postindustrial shock." That phrase captures the ways ever-smarter machines will permanently deprive many people of a job.

It also points to the "shock" facing entire societies as this trend exacerbates the defining issue of our age: inequality. During the pandemic, the opportunity gap widened as some workers lost wages while others reported to work by opening a laptop. Postindustrial shock will hit lower-income workers first and in far greater numbers than it will anyone else. In 2016, President Obama's Council of Economic Advisers forecast that 83 percent of workers in jobs that paid less than twenty dollars an hour were at high risk of replacement by machines. Compare that with just 4 percent of those earning more than forty dollars an hour. The pandemic, and the premium it placed on digital connectivity, has magnified that trend and will further stoke anti-establishment anger in Western democracies that have already seen plenty of furious protests and surprising election results over the past five years.

The US and some European governments are gradually accepting the need to help those less fortunate—through strengthened social safety nets and guaranteed basic income and in other ways. Unfortunately, there is little urgency to actually enact these policies. Even in those countries where the pandemic led to direct payments to citizens, these policies remain temporary and highly controversial. Some argue that they slow production and allow unemployment to become chronic by paying workers to stay home and live off government checks.

Those who own capital, shareholders in companies that profit from automation, workers with twenty-first-century job skills, and the politicians who draw their support don't see the coming emergency. The so-called Great Resignation, the trend of US workers leaving the workforce in the later stages of the pandemic, has amplified this worry. But the fortunate and less fortunate live in the same societies, and there are no walls high or thick enough to always protect the haves from the have-nots. It will take a crisis to bring change. The news—good and bad— is that this crisis is coming.

THE DIGITAL DIVIDE

Automation is just one of the technological revolutions that will force us to remake the relationship between the individual and the state, and job security is not the only form of security at stake. Add access to quality health care. Here's an area where we already see revolutionary impact from emerging technologies.

Millions of people now wear watches that count their steps, track their heart rate, and monitor their sleep quality. One day soon, we'll monitor our blood flow and brain waves in real time by ourselves, without a doctor's help, and sensors connected to our bodies will detect early signs of cancer. These innovations can add decades to the lives of those who can afford them.

But billions of people won't have access to these technologies. Globalization has reduced but not eliminated differences in life expectancy from one country to another. The average person born today in Japan will live to age eighty-five; the average Nigerian will be lucky to see fifty-six. Differing access to the best health-care technologies is the single most important reason for this discrepancy, but even within countries, the disparities between haves and have-nots are growing. As people monitor their bodies for signs of disease, companies will develop products for, and target them to, those with the money to buy them. If technology renders the yearly medical checkup unnecessary, and face-to-face appointments with doctors become too expensive, more people will trade away their personal privacy for lower insurance premiums and longer, healthier lives. That's especially true for people with preexisting medical conditions, and technological advances that help detect them will sharply increase the number of people who know they have them. When the next global health crisis arrives, these new technologies can further divide rich from poor, and those that make it much easier to determine who is infected can leave people without quality health care even more isolated and more suspicious of a system that excludes them.

Some people will be able to afford personalized medicine via technologies that map and analyze our individual DNA. Using the information from these analyses, health-care providers can tailor an individual's treatment specifically to their genetic risks and advantages. Those who can afford these treatments will live longer, healthier lives. Those who can't afford them won't.

Humans can also derive various forms of security from their governments. But in the United States, costly failed wars in Afghanistan and Iraq, the financial crisis, deepening inequality of opportunity, political polarization, large-scale substance abuse, and racial bitterness leave citizens cynical about the government's ability to deliver positive change. In Europe, divides between northern and southern countries over debt, and between eastern and western EU members over political values like freedom of the press and institutional checks and balances, have stoked public resentment and mistrust of the institutions that govern the European Union. Inequality and insecurity in Latin America have increased antiestablishment sentiment, spurred growing mass protest and violence, and weakened political institutions across most of the region.

New communications technologies stoke antiestablishment fury within these countries by making have-nots more aware of what others have, intensifying political polarization. An essential component of any healthy democracy is a set of values that all citizens share, but voters and politicians in the world's democracies increasingly think and express themselves in tribal terms. They believe that the greatest threat to their nation's security comes not from foreign governments or terrorists or deadly viruses or damage to the planet but from those within their country who don't share their values. Health inequality will fuel that anger and bitterness on both sides of the divide.

Adding to that partisan grievance is the digital-age fragmentation of our sources of information. In the United States, many people blame the polarization of cable news for much of this strife, but a 2020 study from Pew Research found that only about one-third of Americans regularly watch cable news channels. According to Pew, nearly three-quarters of US adults use Facebook every day. We scroll through our news feed; we "like" the stories that gratify us. Facebook algorithms then add those data points to what the company already knows about our likes in order to send each of us more of the content it expects we want and less of what we might not.

This is the "filter bubble." Tens of millions of Americans are presented with completely different sets of facts and opinions about what's happening across the country and around the world. Some users are told that wildfires in California are the inevitable result of climate change. Others are encouraged to blame the blazes on poor forest management. Many Americans read that the fires may have deliberately been set by Black Lives Matter activists or antifa. Opportunistic politicians seize on the anger generated by differing versions of reality to win power. Social media companies didn't set out to erode democracy. But they have. The internet offers so many points of view that only the loudest and most provocative gain large-scale attention.

Finally, we're already witnessing a growing digital divide among countries. The dominant trend of the past fifty years in international politics and economics has been what Fareed Zakaria in 2008 called the "rise of the rest": the emergence of China, India, Brazil, and other fast-developing countries, and the creation of a global middle class as the free flow of ideas, information, people, money, goods, and services lifted billions out of poverty. Today's technology is throwing that process into reverse. Differing internet speeds create differences in economic growth, a trend that sets richer and poorer countries on diverging paths. The countries that benefited most from globalization in recent decades, particularly in Africa, will see many of their gains evaporate.

The other great difference among these countries is in the percentage of citizens with access to the digital tools that are more and more important for prosperity in today's world. In 2019, just 39.6 percent of Africans had internet access, compared with 62.7 percent of people in the rest of the world. The differences are also sharp within Africa. Before the pandemic, nearly 90 percent of Kenyans could surf the Web. Just 5.3 percent in Burundi could say the same. COVID forced the beginnings of change, but there's still far to go.

The digital divide takes so many forms that only a truly global investment in narrowing these gaps—and effective regulation of those companies unwilling to shift business models that profit by dividing opinion and people—can reverse a trend that will destabilize entire societies on an unprecedented scale. The risks of future public health crises and of climate change are at least now better understood and addressed, if not quickly enough. But on emerging new technologies, we're headed in exactly the wrong direction.

DIGITAL AUTHORITARIANISM

New technology changes power balances within countries as well as among them. From dictatorships to democracies, rulers have long used the newest media to boost their popularity and power. In the United States, President Franklin Roosevelt understood the reach of radio. Presidents John Kennedy and Ronald Reagan knew the power of television. Tyrants have transformed communications tools into political weapons.

Think of state control of television and newspapers. There's a reason why twentieth-century military coups usually began with a race to capture radio and TV stations.

Yet today's information tools are far more powerful and dangerous implements of state control than their forebears, because they reach much more deeply into the life of every individual.

We have advanced from the communications revolution, which empowered the individual at the expense of government, to the data revolution, which bolsters the power of government at the expense of the individual. In 2010, a young Egyptian computer engineer named Wael Ghonim created a Facebook page to honor a man who'd been beaten to death by police. Within months, several hundred thousand people had liked it. When news of unrest in neighboring Tunisia began making its way into Egypt via Facebook and Twitter in late 2010, alarm bells went off inside Egypt's government. To crack down on activism inside the country, police arrested a number of social media activists, including Ghonim, but the online backlash to his detention forced authorities to quickly release him. The uprising that followed toppled dictator Hosni Mubarak, who'd been in power for thirty years. At the time, it was easy to believe that the internet, social media, and smartphones would prove the worst thing that had ever happened to police states and the autocrats who run them. "If you want to liberate a society," Ghonim said, "all you need is the internet."

Yet today Egypt is again run by a military government. Current dictator Abdel Fattah Al-Sisi is more deeply entrenched in power than his ousted predecessor, in part because government now has the right under Egyptian law to "safeguard" society by removing anyone it chooses from social media. And because the government can now use the data generated by social media to find and punish its critics. The king is dead. Long live the king.

When Syria's Bashar al-Assad faced threats from opposition activists during his country's civil war, he turned to a small army of Russian engineers to help his security forces find and imprison them. Some ended up dead. Within months, Assad had eliminated many of his moderate critics. In the process, Assad and every other dictator and would-be dictator in the world learned the value of tech-savvy friends. Russia also helped Assad disseminate digital propaganda and disinformation to tens of millions in Syria and elsewhere.

Chinese leaders recognize the power of the internet and social media to amplify voices of dissent and organize protest. They also see that the old weapons of digital censorship—the famed Great Firewall—aren't comprehensive enough to meet the challenges posed by future generations of potential tech-smart malcontents. So the state has invented new ways to cut internet access across cities and to isolate entire provinces. The authorities have also found ways to use online media to their advantage. They've been helped by a shift in the ways that technology creates power.

The communications revolution gave millions and then billions of people access to the internet's bounty, first via computers and later through smartphones. The data revolution is different. The phone that gave you superpowers now records your decisions every day. It tracks what you're thinking about, what interests you, what you want, and what you buy. Multiply that amount of data by every wired device you come in contact with when the Internet of Things is embedded in our way of life, when even information about your body temperature and heart rate is available to tech companies—and potentially, therefore, to government.

You can still access information, connect with others, and broadcast your beliefs. But your anonymity is not protected, so the power conferred by tech has shifted away from individuals to institutions—specifically, the institutions that collect and control all the data you create. It's no exaggeration to say that tech companies already know much more about you than you know about yourself. And if companies have that information, governments can get it.

China's social credit system, which I detailed in chapter 1, is a crucial piece of the country's use of data. According to the People's Bank of China, the social credit system covered more than a billion people at the end of 2019. The economic planning commission reported in July 2019 that, as a result of poor scores, 2.56 million people had been barred from air travel, and 90,000 had been denied high-speed rail service. Chinese courts had declared about 300,000 people to be untrustworthy. Today, you need a satisfactory score to secure a loan. This system could one day determine whether you're allowed to graduate from school, use a dating site, buy a home, get a job, get a raise, see the best doctors, or help your children earn these advantages. A bad score might land you in jail. "Those who lose credibility will find it hard to take a tiny step," warned Premier Li Keqiang in 2018.

The data used to power China's social credit system comes mainly from financial, criminal, and government records, and the databases that store this information are managed by China's state economic planning commission, the central bank, and the country's judicial system. But when computers process unprecedented amounts of data and advanced facial recognition technologies allow cameras to identify individual faces within large crowds, the state will find new ways to monitor personal behavior, and citizens are unlikely to find ways around this system.

COVID-19 has accelerated state intrusion into people's lives across China. As the country returned to work after the worst of the outbreak had passed, officials required citizens to use software on their phones that determined their health status if they wanted access to public places and transport. At sign-up, a wallet app assigned users a color code that revealed their health status without explaining how that judgment was made. Users are not told that the state shares this data with law enforcement, which had joined with local governments and Chinese tech companies in developing the app. As the *New York Times* noted, an American version of this system would be "akin to the Centers for Disease Control and Prevention using apps from Amazon and Facebook to track the coronavirus, then quietly sharing user information with the local sheriff's office."

As I wrote in chapter 1, Chinese security officials have used surveillance cameras and facial recognition tools to surveil the entire Uighur population. As the tech is refined, these tools will be used in other parts of China—and sold to foreign governments. As part of the Digital Silk Road initiative, Chinese companies have already helped the governments of Uganda, Zambia, and Zimbabwe refine how they spy on political opponents. More on that later in the chapter.

Americans may be tempted to believe they'll never suffer authoritarian-style surveillance. Unlike China, the US government has no coherent national strategy to develop big data or AI. However, the biggest companies in American history are already reaping unprecedented profits by vacuuming up all the personal information they can. This is "surveillance capitalism." Every day, Americans generate about 2.5 quintillion bytes of data. (That's 2.5 followed by eighteen zeroes.) Summon Uber. Open Google Maps. Click a button to tell Facebook and Instagram what you like. Drop by Amazon to make a purchase. Pay with Venmo or PayPal. Add those apps that track our heart rate, blood pressure, and the number of steps we take. All that information is being gathered, organized, and monetized—and unless you're that rare individual willing to spend forty-five minutes reading a fine-print disclaimer, you'll click "Agree" to share your data without even thinking about it.

And even in democracies, the state is sharpening its surveillance capabilities. Cameras in public places have become a familiar sight in American and European cities, and rapidly advancing facial recognition technologies have become a hot political topic. A 2020 report from Safety.com, an advocacy group, found that the average American is caught on security cameras about 238 times per week. The *New York Times* reported in January 2020 that a tech company called Clearview AI had created an app that allows users to take a photo, upload it, and identify the person it captures via links to sites where that person's image has appeared before. The company says it has amassed more than three billion images from Facebook, YouTube, Venmo, and millions of other websites. Federal and state law enforcement officers admit they've used the app to catch murderers, sexual predators, shoplifters, identity thieves, and fraudsters. That's good. But it's easy to imagine the million possible abuses of a tool like that.

People who obey the law expect authorities to protect them from these kinds of crimes. If open societies become more dangerous—whether due to increased inequality or public anger and violence, or because new technologies make it easier to commit and get away with certain crimes—citizens may decide to trade privacy for security. The 9/11 terrorist attacks persuaded many Americans that these trade-offs are sometimes necessary. For example, the US government broadened its use of warrantless surveillance and created the Total Information Awareness program to find terrorists by sifting through mountains of digital data.

There hasn't been another large-scale attack on US soil since 9/11. In the event of one, law enforcement would turn to far more sophisticated and invasive tools than those available in 2001.

Remember India's Aadhaar system, which has helped hundreds of millions of people gain access to public services and subsidies? One of the ways Aadhaar reduces local corruption is by establishing bank accounts for all these people and wiring payments directly to them so that middlemen can't intercept the cash. The benefits of a biometric identification system like Aadhaar are real for unprecedented numbers of people, but a government that can wire money directly to your bank account might one day pull it directly *from* your account. If the state is wrong to do so and you have the law on your side, you might get a refund. However, we can't be sure that the law will always be on our side—even in a democracy like India's. And though participation in Aadhaar was once voluntary, it's now mandatory.

Aadhaar has expanded to include a database with information about citizens' cell phone contracts, train travel, and social media accounts. None of that was part of the plan when citizens began signing up. To quote Darth Vader, "I am altering the deal, pray I don't alter it any further." And even if you're a supporter of Prime Minister Modi and you trust him and today's Indian government to respect the rights of the individual, do you trust every future Indian government with the same capabilities? The questions looming in India are coming soon to a theater near you.

As we move from smartphones to the Internet of Things, from the communications revolution to the data revolution, humans will create more and more data, companies will find new ways to monetize this data, and the state will rely more heavily on it for national security. And because time is our most important asset, our toughest challenge will come from speed— innovations that happen too fast for us to understand and regulate them.

Here we arrive at the birth of 5G (fifth-generation) technologies. Back in the 1980s, 1G was the technology that allowed us to hoist that big, ugly mobile phone. Then 2G gave us the ability to wirelessly transmit a text. The first time you opened a web page on your smartphone, you were using 3G technology, the standard that became commonplace in the mid-2000s. At the time, 3G offered download speeds of about 4 megabits per second. The 4G networks still in wide use are several times faster and allow live video streaming. A few years from now, all these innovations, remarkable at their inception, will feel like the Stone Age.

Although 5G will be much faster than any previous network, that's not the best way to measure the force and scale of its impact, because it doesn't just connect our phones. It's the foundation on which developers will build the Internet of Things. It enables driverless cars and the smart cities described at the top of the chapter. It will provide the wireless guts of the next generation of US critical infrastructure. It's the technology that connects everything that contains a microchip.

It will even enable governments and companies to aggregate information about our genetic codes. It will create mountains of data made of personal information about every individual connected to it. This is the foundation of a true global central nervous system.

And 5G has become a primary arena of conflict between the United States and China, because unlike territorial disputes over Taiwan or the South China Sea, this is how the twenty-first-century global balance of power will be determined. US officials have warned that Beijing could ask the Chinese tech giant Huawei to use 5G technologies to undermine the security and privacy of all the devices connected to it—which in theory means anything that contains a computer chip. This means that one country could shut down another country's critical infrastructure—its national central nervous system.

OUTLAW RISK

On the first day of any political science class, students are taught that a nation remains stable only if the state can maintain virtual monopoly control of violence within its borders. But national security was much easier to establish when the most powerful weapons were too expensive and complex for criminals, terrorists, and destructive individuals to buy and use. In addition, the development of cyberspace makes it harder for states to defend boundaries and easier for outlaws to ignore them. The outlaw risks from disruptive technologies put increasingly deadly weapons in the hands of increasingly risky individuals and groups.

Autonomous Weapons

No technologies are more destabilizing than those that intensify the destructive power of war. Intelligent machines are now making their way onto battlefields real and potential. For those who use them, their appeal is obvious. Leading military powers like the United States, Russia, and China want to maximize their chances of military victory with minimal risk to their soldiers. Technology that increases the efficiency and lowers the risk of killing is hardly new. People have been pulling triggers and pushing buttons to destroy enemies, sometimes in vast numbers, for centuries. What's new is buttons that (figuratively) push themselves—machines that calculate how and when to strike without human oversight. Autonomous weapons are also highly profitable for those who make them. For example, the global market for drone aircraft is expected to grow from $27.4 billion in 2021 to $58.4 billion by 2026. There is also a fast-growing market for drones that target other drones. It's one thing to persuade governments to limit the use of weapons they find militarily valuable. It's another to regulate an industry that's churning out enormous profits, particularly when, as in so many other sectors, some of those profits find their way into the pockets of those with the power to regulate them. Few of us want to live in a world where robots decide whether to kill people. We've seen this movie. It doesn't end well.

Crucially, because governments are using autonomous weapons and the market for them is growing, outlaws—criminals and terrorists, in particular—are gaining access to them. Some of the problems these weapons pose—for those targeted by them and for governments trying to limit their proliferation—are practical ones. Terrorist groups will use autonomous weapons to anonymously attack large groups of innocent people at minimal expense. Automated weapons will be hacked to turn on those who made them. Armed aggression will become more common, as autonomous weapons lower the financial and human cost of military action and as they provide criminal gangs and terrorist organizations with unprecedented opportunities to inflict mass casualties on innocent people.

Cyberwar

Criminals and terrorists also pose cyber-threats. The total cost from ransomware attacks, the use of cyberspace to threaten or commit acts of destruction in order to extort money from targets, was probably close to $1 trillion in direct losses globally in 2020. That's double the cost in 2018. Some of this success comes from improvements in the sophistication of attacks, some from greater vulnerability, given the explosion of pandemic-driven work from home. And while much of the damage is direct costs of paying off the criminals, the impact from disrupted/lost data is also becoming more significant. Hospitals, in particular, have faced a spate of ransomware attacks, a significant danger during the pandemic and vaccine rollouts. The payment of ransom drives up all costs for companies and individuals, and while tourists can avoid dangerous places and ships can steer clear of pirate-ridden areas like the Horn of Africa, cyber-risk exists everywhere, all the time.

But to date, most of those attacks come from comparatively sophisticated cybercriminal networks, whose interest is to maximize (illegal) profit from their activities. They're not trying to destroy anything; indeed, some have even established help desks to ensure that it's easy for targeted companies to pay ransom and restore their systems. It's a market-clearing equilibrium—if you have a (comparatively) positive experience with your cyber-attackers, you're more likely to tell your friends to pay them off when they're attacked as well.

But what happens when those offensive cyber-capabilities get into the hands of rogue organizations and individuals with more destructive goals? Environmental terrorists, radical Islamic extremists, white supremacists? So far, the world hasn't faced off against any such groups that also had significant cyber-capabilities. At the height of its control of territory in Iraq and Syria, the Islamic State was the best-funded and best-organized terrorist organization in history, with a functioning government bureaucracy and more than a billion dollars in operating capital, much of it looted from Iraqi banks. All the same, its cyber-capabilities were remarkably undergraduate. But terrorists have now learned to code, and coders can become terrorists.

CATASTROPHIC RISK

At the Cold War's close, Americans breathed a sigh of relief. The great international conflict of the age had been resolved with the collapse of the Soviet empire. The shadow of nuclear Armageddon receded. America stood as the world's undisputed military colossus, because no other country could match US military firepower, the global reach of the country's military footprint, or the breadth of its alliances. Thirty years later, that's still true. The United States continues to spend more each year on its armed forces than all potential challengers combined (though Russian nuclear capabilities remain at rough parity with those of the US), and it remains the only country on earth that can project hard military power worldwide.

But new kinds of weapons are changing the game. Russia, China, and even Iran and North Korea have developed offensive cyber-capabilities that cut deeply into US advantages—and therefore into US security. That's why the next major war won't be fought with aircraft carriers, fighter planes, or long-range missiles alone. In all these areas, the US still reigns supreme. But cyberweapons, which will be an integral part of any future conflict, have leveled the playing field in profoundly disruptive ways.

Cyberweapons are much less destructive than Cold War–era nuclear weapons, which could kill millions in minutes, but that's where the good news ends. Atomic weapons haven't been detonated in war since the attack on Nagasaki in August

1945, but cyberweapons of various kinds have been deployed on countless occasions, and with increasingly disruptive effects, in recent years. They are used frequently against foreign targets because they're much cheaper to build than traditional weapons. It's easier to hide them, and they become obsolete quickly, creating incentives to use them or lose them. They can be calibrated to inflict a level of damage that's unlikely to provoke a massive response. They defeat distance, since anyone connected anywhere can attack anyone else connected anywhere else. The identities of those who use them can be kept hidden for a time, making it difficult to know where to strike back.

Nor should we take much comfort in the weapons' inability to deliver nuclear-level destruction, because their use can still lead to large-scale escalation of violence using other weapons—and because mutually assured destruction doesn't work the same way in cyberspace. Among the world's most powerful countries, each government knows that an attack on the critical infrastructure of another invites retaliation. China can attack the US, but its leaders know that the US has the means to hit back. That's why most of the action in cyberspace among well-armed countries is focused on stealing secrets and testing defenses rather than inflicting immediate large-scale damage. But there are no enforceable rules that limit a government's capacity to share its capabilities with outside actors. This stands in stark contrast to the days when nuclear weapons posed the greatest existential threat to our species. Then it was much harder for a great power to sell missiles to an ally. And rigorously enforced international agreements made it difficult to build more nuclear weapons than permitted. There are no such agreements today for cyberweapons. The United States can prevent Iran from developing a nuclear bomb. That's not true of cyberweapons.

Finally, history shows that war becomes more likely when the balance of power is unclear. If everyone knows who is most powerful, there's much less incentive to start a war. That's why Iran and North Korea dare not attack the US with conventional forces. But where relative strength is unclear, it's more likely to be tested. There are limits to what anyone can say with high confidence about the cyber-capabilities of any major power. There's too much iceberg hidden beneath the surface. And a cyberattack on one country can inadvertently inflict dramatic damage around the world, as when a Russian malware attack on Ukraine known as NotPetya accidentally hit systems in multiple other countries, including the United States.

There are also more subtle ways in which cyber-capabilities can be used to undermine another country's security and resilience. US intelligence agencies have found ample evidence that Russia interfered in the 2016 US presidential election—mainly by stealing and exposing secrets that helped Donald Trump by harming Hillary Clinton, and by planting false information on social media to undermine confidence in the nation's political institutions. There is no hard evidence that Russia changed the outcome of the election, but they did significant and lasting damage to Americans' faith in the security and legitimacy of their political system. That problem didn't leave the stage with Trump.

The pandemic created ample new opportunities to sow fear, doubt, and confusion via the internet. To combat what World Health Organization officials called an "infodemic," a plague of false information about COVID-19, the WHO worked with Facebook, Twitter, Google, and other sources of online information to contain the damage. Their success was limited, because it's so easy for bad actors to spread bad information at low cost with little fear of punishment. Some of them were state actors using COVID as part of their larger bid to undermine other nations' confidence in information of all kinds.

This threat will become more insidious as more of the objects in our lives are connected to the internet. The Internet of Things will create new opportunities for hacking and new streams of data that governments and companies can use to compromise our privacy. Hackers can commandeer large numbers of connected devices and use them as a kind of zombie army to launch distributed denial-of-service (DDoS) attacks. In 2016, a twenty-one-year old hacker from New Jersey and a couple of associates created the Mirai botnet, which targeted IoT devices like digital cameras and DVD players rather than computers to launch a massive attack on Dyn, a company that acts as a kind of "phone book for the internet." The attack briefly knocked dozens of heavily trafficked websites offline, among them Airbnb, the BBC, and Starbucks. At the time, it was believed to be by far the biggest DDoS attack in history. If a small group of hackers can do that, imagine what a deep-pocketed government security agency could do.

AI/MACHINE LEARNING

Artificial intelligence is a catchall term for the set of tools that allow humans to automate a process that requires "intelligence," like planning, learning, reasoning through problems, and predicting the future. Artificial general intelligence (AGI) could make complex calculations and decisions. The idea of AGI is to enable reasoning and learning—bringing machines to a much wider range of jobs than robots that are programmed to perform a small set of physical tasks well. Studies show that even if manual labor is disrupted first, white-collar professionals with college degrees are probably most vulnerable in the long run. A 2019 study from the Brookings Institution found that "workers with graduate or professional degrees will be almost four times as exposed to AI as workers with just a high school degree." If you're a lab scientist, a medical researcher or administrator, an engineer, a corporate lawyer, a financial analyst, an urban planner, or a transport administrator, you had better start watching your back.

Because of its vast impact on the workplace, AGI will transform the relationship between individual citizens and the state. Our leaders will have to expand social safety nets in unprecedented ways to avoid a surge in human misery—and the unrest that would surely follow. At the same time, we're entering a world in which machines will know far more about who we are and what we want than we ourselves know. And the governments and corporations that own those machines will use that knowledge in ways that threaten individual freedom and perhaps democracy itself. That means more inequality, more surveillance, and fewer freedoms.

AI is changing what it means to be human. There are already moments when we wonder whether a face we see or a voice we hear belongs to a person or a clever bit of software. A bot can help your kids with their homework, offer you advice, and even hear your confession. But machines will never learn to be "moral." They are capable of learning but not of empathy. They don't value human rights, privacy, or freedom of thought. They can't feel music, recognize beauty, or experience the thrill of discovery and innovation. The more we depend on them to make our daily decisions, from the mundane to the profound, the less likely changes in our society will reflect the value we attach to these essential human characteristics.

GETTING THERE FIRST

In managing catastrophic risk, it matters who develops technologies and writes the rules for their development and use. Russian president Vladimir Putin once predicted that whoever masters AI first will rule the world. The winner won't be Russia, but he's surely right. Whichever country first dominates artificial intelligence will seize a strategic advantage in writing the rules of the next global order. That country's economy will grow faster, its cities will run more efficiently, and its people will live longer. Its military will become much more powerful. It will be able to steal vital secrets, disrupt commerce on an unprecedented scale, and destabilize entire societies.

The greatest risk that AI presents is the possibility that one country will develop an insurmountable lead in its development, an achievement that would allow it monopolistic control over the world order.

The near-term disruptive technology that's most likely to upset the geopolitical order is quantum computing, a form of computation designed for problems of great scale and complexity. Quantum computing uses subatomic particles as the basis of information storage and analysis. That will sharply reduce the size of computers, while dramatically increasing their speed and power. Like every form of technology in this chapter, the disruption it creates can be both wondrous and deadly. Quantum computers will deliver breakthroughs in science, medicine, security, and economics. But if the benefits aren't widely shared, if advances lead to some level of "quantum supremacy," quantum computing can, for example, make it impossible for anyone to hide secrets via encryption, a process essential not only for maintaining personal privacy but for the security of a nation's infrastructure—from power grids and water systems to food security, public transportation systems, and a stable financial system.

This threat is so great that a suspicion the other side *might* be approaching AI mastery could be enough to trigger a war—a preemptive strike that seeks to prevent this mastery. Such a scenario is exactly the opposite of the mutually assured destruction that saw us through the US-Soviet arms race without a big bang.

The countries most likely to reach quantum supremacy—and induce mutually assured destruction—are China and the United States. A little history might help us see the dangers of their impending rivalry more clearly. In the nineteenth century, Western powers subjugated a technologically primitive China, which still remains a profound humiliation in a nation that had been a leading technological, cultural, and economic power for many centuries. In that sense, China's rise of recent decades is less an "emergence" than a restoration. To return to the tech pinnacle, President Xi knows that China must advance a national strategy to build its AI capabilities. In 2017, his government announced a Next Generation Artificial Intelligence Development Plan, a road map to lead China to global leadership in AI. The plan's explicit goal is to break the chains foreign powers have historically put on China.

China's leaders then tasked the country's tech companies with building new tools in image and voice recognition. Industries formed alliances, and cities announced ambitious plans to help achieve the national goals. To demonstrate the power and scope of China's national project, Beijing instructed tech giant Alibaba to design a "city brain," a kind of municipal AI central nervous system, for a new smart city about sixty miles southwest of Beijing. Then came Xi's speech to the Communist Party conference on plans to use the internet, big data, and AI to transform China into the world's leading industrial power by 2030. The state named Baidu, Alibaba, Tencent, and iFlyTek, a voice-recognition software startup, as inaugural members of an AI National Team charged with leading the way on autonomous vehicles, health care, voice recognition, and smart cities.

As part of an emerging plan to undermine fast-growing Chinese tech champions, the Trump administration responded in 2019 with a bid to drive Huawei out of global tech supply chains by threatening sanctions on companies that supplied the global leader in 5G technologies with critical components for certain products. But despite early breakthroughs that gave Silicon Valley a solid head start in AI development, Washington has yet to fully answer China's challenges with a comprehensive national plan of its own. This is likely to change as concern mounts in Congress and industry over the lack of a true national strategy.

In this race, China will have two big advantages. First, Chinese companies have much more data to power their AI engine, because there are many more Chinese people to produce the information that feeds the algorithms, and because each Chinese citizen produces much more of this information than Americans do. China has about three times more mobile phone users than the United States, and the average Chinese consumer makes fifty times the number of mobile payments as does the average American consumer. And it's easier to refine facial recognition tools when ubiquitous surveillance cameras provide so much raw material to work with. American (and, more so, European) tech companies know that consumers can call them to account for how they handle personal data and privacy. China's tech champions operate in a society in which citizens have no right to data privacy.

Second, Chinese companies are aligned much more closely than their American rivals with their government. During the

Cold War, the US government turned to private-sector companies like Lockheed, Northrop Grumman, and Raytheon for the innovations needed to tip the military balance in America's favor. Beijing has even bigger advantages. It can pressure leading tech champions to show how their development strategies serve national goals, and party committees within companies help maintain that alignment. The state subsidizes research, as well as venture capital and special development zones for experimentation. It rewards discipline and loyalty by using its political and economic muscle to back Chinese companies' commercial prospects around the world.

In contrast, many American companies breaking new ground in AI—Google, Facebook, Apple—face resistance from employees and shareholders to any attempt to coordinate policy with government or the military. In China, the state is powerful enough to offer itself as the force promoting the national interest and the well-being of its citizens. In the United States, where mistrust of government amounts to a defining national trait, there's a long history of Hollywood films in which heroes fight to keep state-of-the-art tech out of government hands. In other words, there's a lot more separating the Pentagon from Silicon Valley than 2,800 miles of highway—and much more separating US and Chinese values centered on the relationship between the citizen, the private company, and the state.

THE NEW WALL

About 850 million people explore the internet, shop online, and trade messages behind China's Great Firewall. That's more than the entire populations of the United States and the European Union combined. Every other country can see the digital Berlin

Wall going up, and they're wondering when they'll have to pick a side. They'll need to choose one or the other, because they'll be hobbled without access to new AI technologies, and the Chinese and American versions will be mutually exclusive. This is one way in which a new Cold War will mirror the old one—on tech, at least, countries will have no choice but to align themselves with one side or the other.

That's why most governments are already asking themselves which companies, Chinese or American, will build their digital infrastructure. Who will design the systems and set the standards that govern their Internet of Things? Whom will they trust? Chinese technologies will be cheaper, given the lower cost to make them and the state subsidies that boost their competitiveness. Once these governments borrow to finance these projects, they'll be more closely aligned with their new sponsors, Chinese or American, than they've ever been.

And that's how you get a twenty-first-century Cold War instead of the rivalry partnership we need.

WILL DISRUPTIVE TECHNOLOGY CREATE THE CRISIS WE NEED?

When two strangers meet in the street, they're more likely to treat each other with respect if they are walking rather than driving. The same logic applies online. People who know each other's name and something about each other's life are more likely to respect each other than if they recognize only screen names and avatars. Unfortunately, our online lives are increasingly isolated. We receive ideas and information within the filter bubbles described earlier. In the United States, those who believe that the 2020 election was stolen from Donald Trump see

THE POWER OF CRISIS

entirely different sets of news and images than those who believe that Trump supporters have deluded themselves. COVID only made that problem worse.

When we logged onto the internet in its infancy, we may have believed—if we thought about it at all—that every user had access to the same news, the same search tools, and the same opportunities. That there was only one internet, and you either had access or you didn't. That for the first time in history, we were all part of a single global conversation. Such freedom posed a direct challenge to authoritarian governments everywhere, because dictatorships die without control of citizens' access to information.

New technologies subsequently offered authoritarian governments the filters, firewalls, and kill switches that provided protection against "foreign influences" online. China, in particular, began creating alternate search engines and social media sites that answered to state censors. As a result, its internet and the West's are not the same. The most widely used applications are different, and so are the filters that determine what products you'll be nudged to buy, what information you'll be prompted to read, and which people you'll be able to connect with.

If the internet can become a splinternet, then the Metaverse will become a Splinterverse. Trade in hard goods and services will continue to globalize, but all the digital information that will be shared between devices implanted with chips—smart cars, phones, appliances, home sensors, medical monitoring devices—and the external environment will exist in separate ecosystems.

Dividing the world into two camps of human beings that have almost no digital connection and radically separate experiences of the world will create even more misunderstanding and mistrust than do the filter bubbles within individual countries.

We've already seen these divisions stoke tribal hatreds in America. Imagine that problem on a global scale.

That's why all of us—political leaders, business leaders, thought leaders, and individual citizens—must be willing to coordinate, collaborate, and compromise on how best to govern these changes. The first obvious step toward achieving this goal is to recognize the destructive futility of a new Cold War. As the computer says in the climactic scene of the Cold War–era movie *War Games*, "The only winning move is not to play." In 1983, when *War Games* first hit screens, US and Soviet leaders could hope for the collapse of the other side. We don't have that option now. The US and China need each other to succeed, and both sides have recognized that in the past. Neither side can thrive and address truly global challenges without the other. As more powerful AI tools come online, regulators in different countries will have to work together across borders to protect safety and privacy. Governments will also have to agree on how to keep dangerous technologies away from criminals and terrorists.

Government and business can work together to broaden and strengthen the social safety net by training people for new forms of work, subsidizing the transition they'll have to make, and offering financial protections to those who can't make the leap. The public and private sectors can invest to reduce the widening digital divides within countries and partner with multinational institutions to narrow the gap among countries for the good of all. Rules to limit the threat of autonomous weapons and cyberwarfare must be negotiated, with credible verification processes that include digital-era forms of international inspections. Unfortunately, it will take a crisis larger than any we've seen since World War II to force politicians and corporate leaders to look beyond self-interest and address rising inequality and the dangers of digital conflict. The pandemic didn't do it, and climate change is likely to get us only partway there. But we can learn lessons from these crises—and from history—that can help us meet the unprecedented challenges that weaponized new technologies pose for humanity.

Once upon a time there were no rules to govern the development of nuclear weapons and the missiles that deliver them. Then came the Cuban missile crisis, and governments that otherwise didn't trust one another forged a few early agreements that prevented another such crisis. Since then, more countries have gained nuclear capabilities in defiance of existing rules, but the weapons themselves have never been used in war since 1945. Americans and Soviets survived threats and close calls during the Cold War, but the common menace was clear enough to force the leaders of competing systems, men who despised each other's values, to sit together and cut deals. Their shared horror at the risk of nuclear annihilation made friends of Mikhail Gorbachev and Ronald Reagan, even as they disagreed on a thousand things of lesser importance.

All of today's threats can be addressed, too. Let's begin with "fake news," the deliberate disinformation and conspiracy theories now plaguing the internet and social media. Here's an area where one technology can be tamed by another. Beginning in early 2019, YouTube launched a project to refine the way its algorithms promote content. That experiment has been remarkably successful in teaching a machine to recognize a conspiracy theory or other malignant misinformation and to push it off the first pages that come up in searches. The content isn't deleted. It's simply no longer promoted. Behavioral science suggests that conspiracy theories create an appetite for more conspiracy theories. For instance, someone who believes that the world is flat is also more likely to adhere to the belief that vaccines cause autism. By burying misinformation, content providers can limit the demand for it by limiting the number of people exposed to it. This is a way of training the global central nervous system to identify and reject viral disinformation in much the same way our immune system, if it is functioning properly, protects us from infection.

Facebook hasn't yet followed YouTube's lead, at least on political fakery, but it did work during the worst of the COVID pandemic to rid its pages of dangerous lies about the virus and vaccines. It also banned political advertising for about four months following the 2020 US presidential election, but it has not fully addressed the related problems of filter-bubble echo chambers and the promotion of incendiary false information by its algorithms. Tech companies don't want to spend the money or forgo the revenue required to address this problem, but the tobacco industry didn't want health warnings on cigarette packaging, a ban on broadcast advertising, or greater regulation of their products. It took a cancer crisis to change that. Food companies didn't want to print a list of ingredients and detailed nutritional information on their packaging, but an epidemic of obesity boosted demand for bold action. Social media, like cigarettes and some food additives, is designed to be addictive. But machines can be taught that addictions aren't healthy. Systems designed to anticipate the human need to log off, exercise, and rest can become an integral part of all the technologies we'll rely on for our health. For online disinformation, as YouTube has shown, it's not technically difficult to program these settings into the technology. As the dissemination of fake news becomes more sophisticated, as AI makes it virtually impossible to distinguish between bots and humans, the AI that can bury it will become more sophisticated, too.

Government can mandate these changes, and government

must be pushed to take action, as with the tobacco and food industry changes, by public pressure, advocacy organizations, and legal action. Unlike in China, we can allow internet users to remain anonymous if we create a system of verified accounts, tied to actual humans, that hold people accountable for terms-of-service violations and prevent them from opening additional accounts to game the system. Today's internet algorithms can be regulated to penalize those who disseminate fake news, racism, and violent messages. We can't afford to wait until a terrorist attack kills hundreds or thousands of people. The twin threats of misinformation and incitement to violence are already clear online.

TOWARD A WORLD DATA ORGANIZATION

Beyond what happens within particular societies, the authoritarian model of tech-based surveillance and control poses a broader threat. To find the proper balance between the legitimate needs of the state and the rights of the individual, governments and tech companies will have to agree both on new international rules for how to manage vast oceans of personal data and on how to build a multinational institution capable of enforcing those rules. The most formidable obstacle to that goal is China's Communist Party, which has a very different conception than the world's democracies of the right relationship between state and citizen.

By attacking tech giants such as Huawei and trying to cut other firms out of the global supply chain, the Trump administration taught China's leaders that they should strive for self-sufficiency. They know they can't count on continuing access to state-of-the-art Western hardware, software, and intellectual property, particularly since the Biden administration hasn't sharply reversed course, and they've responded by throwing their deep financial and scientific resources at this challenge.

China's bid to develop cutting-edge tech on its own is the most significant geopolitical development since the Soviet Union detonated its first atom bomb in August 1949. In response, the world's democracies must build a comprehensive multilateral system to control the development and use of emerging technologies. To accomplish this, governments must understand the complexities of the problems they're trying to solve by drawing on the wisdom of unbiased observers who can see where the world's digital development is headed. This is the AI equivalent of the UN's Intergovernmental Panel on Climate Change, a body that provides objective information about and insight into the implications of global warming. Governments must also establish a multinational institution composed of like-minded allies who will write the rules and set the standards that dictate the use of data. The ultimate aim is to unleash human ingenuity and enable prosperity without compromising freedoms and undermining human rights. Here, we should emulate the World Trade Organization, which was founded in 1995 to facilitate trade, establish best commercial practices, and resolve disputes. It has done a very good job on those fronts overall.

First steps will likely involve an informal group of governments willing to coordinate some aspects of digital policy, starting with the easy ones. Members can share information on Chinese investments in critical infrastructure in their countries and then review any concerns these investments raise. This sort of coordination will create both carrots and sticks that nudge China toward a deeper technological interdependence in areas where cooperation is in everyone's interest. The US must forge enforceable agreements with allies and offer their companies greater access to US consumers (by, for example, easing tariffs) to encourage the largest number of partners to join over time. China is already a data superpower that can't be coerced to fall in line. So, as with the World Trade Organization, this new alliance must offer incentives that give China compelling reasons to align its rules more closely with others. It must also encourage compatibility, if not true integration, between China's internet and ours. The broader the alliance, the more China gains by being part of it and the more it gives up by not joining.

This is not unattainable; it's already underway. In early 2021, the Biden administration partnered with Japan, India, and Australia—fellow members of the Quadrilateral Security Dialogue (Quad), an informal bloc of democracies with a common interest in promoting democracy and openness in the Indo-Pacific region—to discuss tech policy issues. Coming years will see more of these discussions in existing forums like the D10—which includes the US, the UK, France, Germany, Italy, Japan, Canada, India, Australia, and South Korea and which comprises about 60 percent of world GDP—a powerful potential counterweight to China. Members will also debate whether and how to add concrete data rules to existing trade accords.

Building a World Data Organization (WDO) atop this foundation will be extraordinarily complicated and invariably contentious. The US and the European Union share democratic values but have very different views on data privacy and government surveillance. Europe has imposed new rules to limit the market power and risk to personal privacy created by the US firms that dominate social media, online search, e-commerce, and cloud computing. Its leaders differ with Washington on driverless cars, advanced factory automation, and AI. Many US officials see tough EU-style privacy rules, digital taxes, and updates to e-commerce legislation as protectionism that unfairly targets successful US tech companies. Countries like India may hesitate to fully align with a Western project that would limit their own tech development options by imposing rules that inhibit innovation. There are also conflicting views among and within these countries on controversial tech like facial recognition. In addition, a successful tech alliance will have to agree on how companies and governments should handle personal data. It must also set a common policy for granting law enforcement and intelligence agencies access to data. It must create effective policies on cybersecurity, machine data, and a common approach to the use of data that powers critical infrastructure. Overcoming differences among democracies will require shared recognition that China is now moving quickly to embed its political values in the technologies it's developing, deploying, and exporting.

Finally, this alliance would also have to agree on strategies for engaging China, Russia, and other countries that would use new technologies for authoritarian ends, and on how to entice those countries to work with the WDO. Here the experience of the World Trade Organization offers both positive and cautionary lessons, particularly on how an expanded organization's rules can be enforced. But even if China and Russia never agree to join, the authoritarian model of tech development would have a powerful foil, and we'd all have more reason for confidence that democracies will remain democracies and that individual rights and freedoms will endure.

The US remains at the center of tech innovation. Europe offers expertise in smart regulation. Japan and South Korea can provide tech talent and its willingness to embrace new technologies early. India has some of the world's finest information engineers, and the size of its population, soon to be the world's largest, will make it a world leader in data collection, and hence data innovations. Other democracies can make vital contributions.

Poorer countries eventually will be forced to choose among several competing "technology stacks," including Chinese systems that are far more likely than Western versions to undermine individual freedom. A World Data Organization that brings together the United States, the European Union, Japan, and other advanced democracies can offer an attractive alternative, a choice that comes with commercial and security connections to Western societies that China can't match.

The aim here is not to "defeat" China but rather to encourage it to work with the rest of the world. That doesn't mean that it must become a democracy. But its leaders know that their country will never achieve true national security without access to American and European markets, as these are a cornerstone of its prosperity. In short, a World Data Organization can offer an alternative to China's authoritarian vision for the internet, data, and artificial intelligence—an alternative that even China can adopt.

―――――――

More broadly, we need a global discussion on all the ways technology companies will play ever-larger roles in our lives. World leaders have been meeting every year since the mid-1990s to discuss climate change. The COP Climate Summit is now a global agenda–setting event—and one that helps build momentum for new agreements and progress. We need an annual UN Politics of Technology Summit that brings together public policy and private-sector leaders, engineers, social scientists, and activists. As with rising seas and increasingly erratic weather patterns, we must create a global community to drive this agenda to limit the harm that information technology companies can inflict on democracy and society. This is an urgent priority, because disruptive technologies and the companies that create them are changing our lives much more quickly and decisively than global warming can.

COVID-19 showed us how much each nation can benefit when governments and the private sector share information and resources—and the vast human, economic, and political damage that results when they don't. Climate change will give us a much larger opportunity to coordinate cross-border responses—or suffer the consequences of not doing so. The lightning-fast development of new technologies presents the biggest benefits if we collaborate across borders—and the biggest threats to our species if we don't. If governments don't keep cyberweapons out of the hands of unstable states and terrorists, the economy and security damage they inflict could be unprecedented. If governments don't share data on developments in quantum computing, one government will eventually gain the power to defeat encryption on a global scale, rendering every other country defenseless. Even the threat of such a breakthrough could trigger World War III, which would threaten the survival of the human race. That's why this moment is much more dangerous than the 1930s. A next world war will be fought with weapons far more destructive than tanks and fighter planes—or even atomic bombs—and the conflict won't be limited to "theaters of war." It will be universal.

CONCLUSION

Chance favors only the prepared mind.
—LOUIS PASTEUR

We live in a time of extraordinary opportunity. Never before have so many humans had a chance to survive childbirth, go to school, escape poverty, access higher education, meet people from other places, get a job, start a business, earn a living, invent something new, vote, receive quality medical care, cross borders, and offer their children these same advantages. Billions of people now have comforts and opportunities far beyond the reach of medieval kings. Human invention has reached heights unimaginable even a generation ago.

But as I've detailed throughout this book, we also face risks of catastrophe. The historic gains of the past fifty years— including the most important one, the emergence of the first worldwide middle class—are threatened by our leaders' failure to work together to protect us from contagious disease, rising seas, changing weather, tidal waves of toxic disinformation, the human disruptions created by job-killing technologies, digitally enhanced dictatorship, and new kinds of war.

And it's all coming so quickly. There was no intelligent life on our planet for billions of years. For millions, there was intelligence but there were no humans. For two million more, there were a few humans, but there was no cooperation, or even communication, to build societies and enable progress. Then came trade among people who hunted and fished to survive. Terms of trade became more complex, rules were written, and independent authorities were created to resolve disputes. Populations and complex relationships began to grow. In AD 1, there were 170 million people on Earth. Over the next thousand years, that number edged upward to 254 million. Thanks to the bubonic plague, there were still just 343 million humans in 1400. It took two million years to reach a global population of one billion people (in 1804) and just two hundred years more to reach seven billion.

The acceleration of human development is even more obvious in our technologies. At the dawn of the twentieth century, soldiers still fought on horseback, and in 1945, the United States dropped atomic bombs on two Japanese cities. Or think of advances in communication. The first handheld cellular telephone call was placed in 1973 with a device that weighed two and a half pounds. In 1989, Tim Berners-Lee invented the World Wide Web and the first browser. Today, more than 4.4 billion people explore cyberspace. Think how quickly flight took us to new heights. In 1903, Orville Wright piloted a biplane one hundred twenty feet and remained aloft for twelve seconds. Just fifty-eight years later, the Soviet Union launched Yuri Gagarin into space, and eight years after that, Neil Armstrong bounded across the surface of the moon. In 2021, NASA flew a drone aircraft carrying a thumbnail-sized piece of the Wright brothers' plane across the surface of Mars.

Now, imagine twenty-five years into the future. These are the perspectives we need in order to see where we are, where we're going, and how fast we're getting there. Our capacity for both creation and destruction is accelerating faster than we can track. We've unleashed forces that are changing the planet and slipping beyond our control, and if we can't agree on ways to intelligently manage the consequences, we can destroy everything humans have created.

We've reached a crossroads. As I hope this book has persuaded you, unprecedented global challenges aren't lurking somewhere in our future; they're here today. Climate change will intensify, no matter what we do, and its effects will be felt everywhere. Much of our planet is becoming hostile to life. The wealthiest countries and people will spend all they can to shield themselves from the worst effects of this unfolding calamity, but the upheaval and misery will continue. Only a global response can limit the damage. Our leaders in politics, business, and philanthropy must compromise, cooperate, and coordinate in new ways.

As climate change disrupts more lives and displaces more people, creating even deeper global inequality, millions of its victims will become desperate and angry. Some will express these emotions through violence, and history teaches us that violence can beget more violence. The damage to the privileged is limited when the disenfranchised have only sticks and stones. Or handguns. Or a fertilizer bomb. But when human invention gives them access to dangerous new technologies, weapons that can target the spaces we all share in the real and virtual worlds, they will kill more people—and destabilize entire societies.

The speed of technological change is the biggest risk of all. Companies are now using artificial intelligence to figure out the most efficient ways to change human behavior in ways that profit them—and without understanding what effect that technology actually has on the people who depend on it. Even in a time of pandemic, when tens of millions of lives hang in the balance, we don't use a new vaccine until we've tested it. We want to know how it will affect people, whether it will protect them, how long its effects will last, and whether it produces side effects. We regulate tobacco and alcohol. We try not to let children smoke cigarettes or use narcotics. But when we develop new algorithms that determine which ideas, information, and images we ingest, the products we'll consume, the way we'll spend money, how we'll interact with other people, we do no testing at all. We simply inject all of this into the bloodstream of the body politic. New technologies are already changing what it means to be human—and we have no idea where that might lead.

These are problems no nation can address alone. And that's precisely why they create the most important opportunity that humans have ever had to merge their practical and moral imaginations for the good of all.

PRACTICAL COOPERATION

People everywhere—in democracies and dictatorships, rich and poor countries, and all the places in between—share many of the same aspirations: security, dignity, prosperity. We want ready access to food and water. We want the law to protect us, our possessions, and our rights. We want a fair chance to earn a living. If we lose a job, we want to know that we can find another one. We want our children to have all these things, too.

Increasingly, all of this is contingent on what happens far beyond our borders. Boundaries shift, empires rise and fall, alliances form and fall apart, and political leaders come and go, but, more than ever before, other people's problems are becoming our problems. Panic spooks markets across continents. Storms sweep across seawalls. Diseases spread. Crime triggers more crime. Political upheavals remake societies. Wars change lives thousands of miles from the battlefield. Until the world's richest people shoot themselves into space and make new homes on Star-a-Lago, we'll all share a single ecosystem, metaphorically and literally.

This book is an argument for practical cooperation on a few important issues. We don't have to like each other, much less agree on a single set of political and economic values. We don't need everyone to work together. We don't need to solve every problem. We certainly don't need a single world government to save us from chaos. But never has it been more obvious that citizens of all countries had better cooperate, at least where near-universal benefit toward goals we can't achieve alone is concerned.

I'm a patriotic American. I'm truly grateful for everything my country has done for me and the people I love, and for every opportunity it has created for us. But I am not a nationalist. I don't believe that our values are naturally superior to others'. America is a community of people with diverse opinions and conflicting beliefs, an assembly of all races, of people who follow different faiths and no faith. Nor do I believe that "American values" offer the best solution to every problem. Representative democracy is the best form of government, in my opinion, but every nation ruled by a dictator would not be better off if it held free elections three months from today. Democracy takes time to build, and it's not the best form of government for every stage of a nation's development. It was tyrannical Soviet Communism that pushed Russia from czarist feudalism in 1917 and put Gagarin in orbit just forty-four years later. No democracy has lifted hundreds of millions people from poverty as the Chinese Communist Party has done. Soviet and Chinese Communists are responsible for some of history's worst crimes against innocent people. But it's also true that much of today's European democratic prosperity was built atop centuries of imperialism, and much of America's current wealth was accumulated on the backs of people brought here in chains. Because I'm not a nationalist, I can accept that all these things are true.

Nor do I believe in an inexorable march toward peace, equality, justice, or freedom. History shows us that none of these outcomes is inevitable. Yet for tens of thousands of years, even as we have expanded our ability to kill, we've also extended our capacity for cooperation. Archaeology reveals a progression in human history from the simple to the complex. Collaboration among people has formed the basis of that complexity. From the invention of the wheel, to the beginnings of a barter economy, to the development of democracy and the creation of the modern supply chain and social safety net, our achievements have come to depend ever more deeply not just on new technologies but on complex forms of social engagement, cooperation, and coordination. Our willingness to cooperate must progress faster than the destructive forces we've set in motion.

The processes we now call globalization have left too many have-nots living in hardship alongside the haves. By treating efficiency and profitability as the sole road to prosperity, we've created a brutal form of governance that poisons the soil in which societies grow by profiting owners and shareholders while discarding millions of people. Reducing this kind of dangerous inequality begins at home, by preparing workers to absorb the shocks and meet the challenges that inevitably accompany accelerating change. And a new international system of cooperation can't be built all at once. It will begin with collaboration among like-minded allies and peoples, with countries that share political values and people who already trust one another, before more skeptical governments will find advantage in joining such projects. To get there, allies will have to build a new bargain with their rivals.

Sound utopian? Before we give over to easy cynicism, let's remember the historical precedent for just such a grand vision— *a precedent that has allowed billions of humans to survive and thrive in the modern world.*

Following World War I, a conflict once optimistically dubbed "the war to end all wars," many Americans believed future presidents should keep US soldiers out of all future European wars. Attempts to build a League of Nations failed, in part because America refused to join and Germany, Italy, and Japan renounced it. In the 1920s and '30s, it was still possible to believe that the Atlantic and Pacific Oceans provided all the security Americans needed, and that events in Europe, Asia, Africa, and the Middle East were irrelevant to American life. Victorious European powers believed that post–World War I Germany should be ruined and humiliated. As if life could return fully to prewar normal once the shooting stopped and the boys came home. As if a powerful nation brought to its knees could never rise again to threaten the peace.

A generation later, World War II killed seventy-five million people, and when that conflict ended, the White House and the

Pentagon finally saw wisdom in investing taxpayer dollars in the futures of the very countries that had just done their best to end the American way of life. That wise and unprecedented investment made the world safer for democracy, in nations that were ready to build it, and enabled commerce in places where industries could be rebuilt.

The two world wars revealed our species' power to invent ever more effective means of destroying life, but they also expanded our capacity for cooperation—for both the individual and the common good. Fascism was defeated. Empires crumbled, and millions earned their independence. Humanity proved its resilience. Global trade and investment, enabled by new technologies, took great leaps forward. More countries became democracies. Crucially, the victorious Allies created a new system of international governance founded on the principle that the conflict could not end until each of us accepted responsibility for all of us. The United Nations was created in order to institutionalize a global commitment to security, dignity, and prosperity. The UN Charter commits the organization to "achieve international co-operation in solving international problems of an economic, social, cultural, or humanitarian character." Other institutions were created to help poor countries develop their political and economic systems for the good of their citizens, to provide financial help to those who needed it and could facilitate free and fair trade, to share resources to fight disease, and to promote respect for international law. World War II was the greatest catastrophe ever visited on the human race. It was also the crisis we needed to make the efforts necessary to ensure that our species would survive the twentieth century—and even thrive.

Countless books and articles have detailed the many failures of these organizations. Today, they reflect a balance of power and influence that existed in 1962, not 2022. But if we scrapped all of them tomorrow, we'd need to reinvent them the next day: the interdependent world they reflect plays a role in each of our lives that is exponentially larger than when these institutions were founded. The United Nations gives every nation a voice on the international stage, and it helps the world's most powerful nations limit the risk of war among themselves and with other countries. Its peacekeepers come from many nations, allowing member states to share the burdens, risks, and costs that come with keeping the peace and with easing the misery that follows conflicts. It has saved lives in many places and failed to save others, but its successes have benefited innumerable people, and it deserves considerable credit for staving off another world war.

Similarly, the World Trade Organization benefits all who participate. The rules it creates can't prevent every trade dispute, and enforcement is slow and incomplete. But, as in any arena of intense competition, it's far better to have imperfect rules and a fallible referee than no rules at all. The International Monetary Fund and other multinational lenders offer a financial lifeline to nations that need help, often as a last resort. Their lending terms sometimes generate controversy, suspicion, and bitterness, but they've helped many a developing nation and their citizens avoid catastrophe.

The European Union, which has evolved from a liberalized trade zone to the most ambitious multinational governing organization in history, has likewise generated its share of frustration, mistrust, and cynicism. Many member-state citizens accuse European political elites of using EU institutions to create rules that serve the most powerful governments at the expense of smaller states, that benefit multinational companies at the expense of small business, and that meet bureaucrats' needs at the expense of individual liberty. But the EU has helped eliminate wars on a continent responsible for the two most destructive conflicts in history. It has helped all member states punch above their economic weight in relations with the United States, Russia, and China. It has offered citizens the once unthinkable chance to cross national borders freely in search of better opportunities. It has cleaned the air and water in countries whose own governments might not be willing or able to spend on these projects. It has taken the lead on both climate and tech privacy standards. It has created a system in which wealthier countries can boost living standards of poorer members—and sometimes help rescue them from crisis. It has served as a model of cooperation for the rest of the world.

All these institutions are easy to criticize; it is especially easy for those who profit from the criticism. But all of them help safeguard the safety, dignity, and opportunities of people around the world. They protect human rights. They make war less likely. Crucially, they ease the burden on each individual government by creating a structure that supports collective responsibility. With each passing year, there are fewer people old enough to remember the horrors of World War II and the challenges of decolonization that inspired and necessitated these organizations.

We must not forget the lessons these institutions have taught us. If we do, we'll have to learn them again—with even more pain than accompanied the previous set of lessons.

THE COLLISION COURSE

In chapter 1, I detailed two risks of collision. The first is the fight between red and blue America that has badly damaged the political life and democratic integrity of the world's sole superpower. The second is the conflict between established power America and rising power China. The larger risk posed by both is that they divert the world's most powerful governments and institutions from meeting the true challenges ahead. We are all on a collision course with the inevitable next global health emergency, with climate change, and with the power of disruptive new technologies to destabilize our lives and societies. These are the risks to our common future. Every moment, every idea, every ounce of energy, and every dollar wasted on fighting one another, at home or in some potential war zone, increases the risk that we all suffer together when these global threats grow beyond our ability to control them.

I don't believe that America's poisoned politics will destroy its democracy. Threats to the integrity of US political institutions are real, but they've absorbed big shocks before. I don't underestimate the damage that poisonous partisanship can inflict on American life, but I still believe in the willingness of Americans to defend democracy when it's truly threatened and the ability of US institutions to place the law before cultural prejudices. I don't believe the United States and China will go to war over Taiwan or anything else. Both countries have too much to lose from catastrophic collision, and neither Washington nor Beijing should expect other governments to follow them down the road to disaster. But . . . I've written this book because I'm worried that red and blue Americans and US and Chinese leaders are so busy preparing for possible conflict with one another that they're failing to prepare for the true storms ahead. To do that, they will have to cooperate; instead their illusions about what matters most prevent them from doing that.

A GOLDILOCKS CRISIS

Humans function most effectively when crisis demands their attention and clarifies the challenge they must meet. But not just any emergency will do. We need a "Goldilocks crisis," one large enough to force our engagement but not so destructive that we can't respond effectively. We need a crisis frightening enough to force us to look squarely at the risks posed by a geopolitical breakdown, a future pandemic, climate change, and the vast impacts of technological revolution. A crisis that causes so much pain and creates so much risk for those in power that they finally accept that collaboration and compromise are the only protection against total defeat. A crisis big enough to bind us together in common projects to meet the challenges detailed in this book.

In the early days of COVID-19, it appeared the pandemic might create a true Goldilocks crisis. It was certainly big enough to touch billions of people. Every government on earth was forced to respond. The resulting economic damage was severe and will prove long-lasting. The virus undermined governments, political leaders, and companies that have resisted change, while empowering scientists and innovators who could help us understand the threat and cope with its fallout. We faced a common threat, one that was in some ways as foreign and insidious as Ronald Reagan's hypothetical alien invasion. Yet too many of our political leaders tried to use this crisis to stoke anger at others, at home and abroad.

As we saw in chapter 2, advances in testing, contact tracing, treatment, and vaccine development will help us weather the next viral storm. COVID's global economic fallout will speed the transition from the twentieth-century brick-and-mortar economy toward a digital future where most people work, shop, and learn online. The pandemic has also empowered the companies with the deepest commitment to climate-friendly commerce. But COVID didn't do nearly enough to convince governments that the future will demand new ways of thinking about how to provide security and enable prosperity. The COVAX project offered an excellent model for future cooperation on global health, but too few governments invested in it, and the Trump administration withheld its support altogether at the moment most critical to its potential success.

As in past crises, the pandemic persuaded central banks to begin printing money to help countries cope. That was necessary, but it did little to address the deepening inequities that plague us. Rather than inventing and investing in new institutions—for instance, a World Data Organization—our leaders seem content with treating symptoms, not the disease that threatens all of us. Climate change and disruptive new technologies represent bigger crises than COVID and can give rise to the domestic and international institutions we need. We must act now so we'll be ready to seize the opportunities these impending crises will create.

A POSITIVE VISION

To invent new forms of practical cooperation, however, humans need more than fear triggered by crisis. We need a positive vision for the future, plans we can set in motion when and as needed. Too many of our leaders, and too many of the rest of us, focus on what we can't do and what we don't believe others will do. We close doors before we've glimpsed what might be on the other side. Complacency allows cynicism and habit to prevail. We also focus far too much on satisfying near-term needs.

Consumers aren't the only ones who want immediate gratification. Politicians, business leaders, and shareholders want it. They, and we, fixate on the current leader's immediate term, on navigating this year, on meeting quarterly targets, or on the next news cycle. Perhaps our biggest failing of all: too few of us are willing to plant seeds we know others will harvest.

To survive the challenges ahead, we need our leaders to listen to one another and to people everywhere. They don't have to agree on questions of politics, economics, culture, or national values. But they must agree that great-power conflict, future public health crises, climate change, and new technologies pose global threats—and that our species' survival depends on cooperation. They need to agree on what to invest in and how to share costs and risks.

In preceding chapters, I've offered possible strategies that can form the basis for compromise, cooperation, and coordination among nations. Here they are again:

A Global COVAX

In response to COVID-19, 172 countries signed on to the COVAX project to partner with vaccine manufacturers to ensure equal access worldwide to a vaccine. China, Russia, and the United States were slow to join. Had the project won support and investment from all the world's leading governments, it would have been much more effective in fast and fair global distribution of vaccinations. It must be bolstered in preparation for the next pandemic. And COVAX might still provide the breakthrough in global imagination needed to create similar—and more effective—partnership projects to respond to future emergencies of all kinds.

CONCLUSION

A Binding Agreement on Reductions in Carbon Emissions

Climate change can't be contained unless the emission of carbon into the atmosphere is reduced to net zero by 2050. No one wants to make more than their fair share of sacrifice, and progress depends on trust that others will keep their promises. Any agreement on emissions must be binding, and it must be verified by independent international monitors. Credible solutions require both political will and scientific breakthroughs, and governments can share the costs of developing technologies that accelerate progress.

A Green Marshall Plan

A binding agreement on emissions can form part of a broader international compact to invest in and shift toward renewable energy, create green jobs, and resettle the many millions displaced by the damage that climate change will inflict even in best-case scenarios. It should include a global agreement on refugee rights that can help avert future conflicts and meet increasingly urgent humanitarian needs. Unlike the Marshall Plan that helped rebuild Europe after World War II with US funds alone, the success of a Green Marshall Plan will depend on globally shared costs and other burdens.

A World Data Organization

The world badly needs to manage, through an independent source, the data that humans are producing in ever-higher volume. We need rules and standards that apply to both governments and the companies that own and use the personal information we generate. Just as the UN Intergovernmental Panel on Climate Change offers independent insights on global warming, and the World Trade Organization creates rules that resolve disputes and facilitates trade for all its members, so a World Data Organization can govern artificial intelligence, privacy, intellectual property, and citizens' rights. China and other authoritarian states will be slow to join, because they won't agree with democracies on how best to balance security, privacy, property protections, and personal liberty. But if like-minded democracies create the organization and it sets standards that in turn create opportunities, future compromise for the good of all will become possible.

WHO WILL MEET THESE CHALLENGES?

As I wrote in chapter 1, America isn't on a path toward reconciliation of left and right. The 2024 presidential election is likely to be the ugliest and most dangerous in American history. That's no exaggeration. The coming years promise more left-right culture-war bitterness, particularly as Donald Trump continues to attack the institutions of American democracy. Fortunately, the world doesn't need American unity to meet global challenges. We just need the world's most powerful nation to prove its resilience yet again and continue to accept many of the costs and risks that come with leadership on complex issues like climate change and the AI revolution.

Nor does the world need the US and China to patch up all their differences. That isn't going to happen. But if US and Chinese leaders can avoid escalating hostility and ward off a new Cold War, they can work together on climate and disruptive technology questions that threaten them both—and everyone else.

Crucially, if worst-case scenarios inside the US and between Washington and Beijing can be avoided, there will still be enough space for other actors to play important roles.

The European Union must play a vital part in meeting climate and technology challenges, and if the US and China can avoid a conflict that forces Europe to align entirely with one side at the expense of the other, the EU can boost international cooperation on all these questions. There is good cause for optimism. When COVID struck Europe in early 2020 and oil prices plunged in response, some feared that even within the EU, a leader on climate change policy, momentum to cut carbon emissions would be lost. Past crises, including the financial crash of 2008–2010 and the migrant surge of 2015–2016, drove wedges between EU countries. But COVID offered the EU a chance to chart its own path not only on the pandemic and economic reconstruction but on climate change as well.

One of the most controversial questions within the EU is whether it should be allowed to tax member states in order to fund its larger goals. Many of northern Europe's more cost-conscious countries have pushed back against large-scale redistribution of wealth toward financially vulnerable southern members including Italy, Spain, and Greece, countries with governments that critics say spend too much and tax too little. But these same northern countries are the most sympathetic to an aggressive push to limit climate change. By making climate spending a central pillar of its €1.8 trillion budget package and its COVID-19 economic relief plans, the European Commission has boosted its own power to raise future funds for pandemic relief and climate change from historically reluctant member states. Only members that comply with EU standards on emissions and other climate-relevant policies can expect to get generous support for COVID recovery.

In addition, the EU's emissions trading system is kicking into high gear as Europe's best tool for achieving its 2030 emissions-reduction goals. The EU's latest plan would reduce total annual emissions allowances each year, create a separate system for transportation and building emissions, and phase out the "free allowances" that have been given to heavy industry, airlines, and shipping. There will be plenty of controversy and horse-trading as this plan comes together, but the emissions trading system will become stricter, and there will be higher carbon prices in the EU to speed up emissions reductions.

Some European leaders have conditioned bailouts of industries hard-hit by the COVID slowdown on a "reshoring" of production back to their home countries. That's good for local jobs, but in some industries, including the automotive sector, it also helps ensure that manufacturing processes and the final product comply with EU climate rules. Importantly, there are also moves underway to use tax breaks and tax penalties to nudge companies based outside the EU to meet European standards if they want to do business in Europe. The money raised by higher taxes on higher-polluting foreign products can then be directed toward EU-approved green technologies.

These are historic accomplishments—and a model for the kind of cooperation needed to tackle all the challenges discussed in this book. The EU has used COVID-19 to combat climate change by channeling recovery money into green projects, clarifying which projects qualify as green, mandating that any money that doesn't go toward green projects won't go toward anything that makes the warming problem worse, and making emissions targets more ambitious.

Europe is playing a crucial regulatory role on other pressing issues, too. On questions of data use and privacy, EU leaders are using the size of the European consumer market to set rules that US and Chinese tech companies can't afford to ignore. If the US and China can avoid a new Cold War, the EU can make rules and set standards that boost international coordination on the challenges profiled in this book while safeguarding the rights and liberties of the individual.

But we also have to think beyond government, because politicians can't create a new globalism by themselves. There are organizations with influence and interests that extend across borders in ways that government doesn't. And they will only become more important. That's good news, because global organizations' ability to bring about change is far less limited by artificial boundaries, and they can adapt to change much more quickly.

The most important of these by far are the world's largest technology companies. If there was any remaining doubt that Big Tech companies have accumulated plenty of geopolitical power, the aftermath of the January 6 riot at the US Capitol should have eliminated it once and for all. While Congress couldn't hold Donald Trump responsible for inciting the most serious assault on American democracy in living memory, Big Tech took decisive action. Within hours of the attack on Congress, Facebook, Twitter, Apple, Google, and Amazon had suspended the accounts of Trump and other politicians who had spread the lies of election fraud and encouraged the insurrection.

They temporarily banished Parler, a service through which many Trump supporters encouraged or coordinated the storming of the Capitol, cutting off its access to web-hosting services and leading app stores. Government and law enforcement played no role in this process. The deplatforming of Trump and his supporters was a decision made solely by companies that could exercise power over code, servers, and policies they alone controlled. By May, Facebook's Oversight Board—established in 2020—had issued a ruling affirming the company's decision to suspend Trump's account. The tech companies have also done much more than governments have, or can, to find and shut down other bad actors in cyberspace.

Facebook, Google, Amazon, Microsoft, and Apple have accumulated power that makes them arbiters of global affairs, not just bystanders. No other non-state actors today or arguably in history have come close to this kind of geopolitical influence—which creates both dangers and grounds for optimism. The lead US and Chinese tech companies are central players in the drama that will determine whether the world descends into a new Cold War or heads toward a much more hopeful future. Google, Facebook, Microsoft, Amazon, Alibaba, Tencent, and ByteDance aren't just responding to geopolitical trends. They're creating them.

Private power has played a significant role in geopolitics before. The East India Company and its own army ruled the Asian subcontinent on behalf of the Crown in the 1700s and 1800s. Big Oil wielded huge political influence during its heyday. But today's biggest tech firms differ from these forerunners in two critical ways. First, the tech giants don't wield power exclusively in physical space. They maintain and exercise deep influence over an entirely new dimension in geopolitics: the digital space they also created. People do business with these companies in order to learn, find love, shop, and store wealth—and sometimes to plot the overthrow of governments. Even China's Communist Party can't fully control this territory. Physical space is finite. Digital space is growing exponentially. In raw population terms, Facebook's nearly three billion monthly active users make it twice as big as the biggest countries on Earth. YouTube's two-billion-plus users span over one hundred countries. Google claims that over one billion hours of video are consumed on the platform each day. Industry watchers estimate that the total size of the "datasphere"—the amount of digital information created and stored around the world each year—hit nearly 60 zettabytes in 2020. The datasphere will expand dramatically as the next phase of the digital revolution sees cars, factories, and entire cities wired with internet-connected devices, compounding the complexity of the problem for politicians.

Politicians themselves are increasingly beholden to the digital realm. A candidate's ability to attract followers on Facebook and Twitter—more than their connections with political insiders—is what unlocks the money and votes they need to win elections in many democracies. For a new generation of entrepreneurs, Google's search engine, Facebook's ad-targeting tools, Amazon's marketplace and web-hosting services, and Apple's app store have become indispensable to launching a successful business. The more people turn to digital space to meet their basic needs, the bigger the task for governments, many of which already struggle to deliver for their citizens in the face of twenty-first-century challenges such as the pandemic, widening income inequality, the opioid epidemic, climate change, and the social and economic disruption sparked by rapid innovation.

Governments are pushing back against this usurpation of their power. China has targeted domestic tech firms like Alibaba, Ant Group, and other online companies. The EU has tried to regulate personal data, online content, and internet gatekeepers to protect its citizens' privacy. A slew of new antitrust bills introduced in Congress during 2021 and India's ongoing pressure on foreign social media companies like Twitter show how governments around the world are trying to impose their will on an unruly digital realm. Yet governments are generally slow to regulate an arena few lawmakers understand, and tech companies have proven adept at resisting government efforts to reverse their accumulation of power.

Tech companies also differ from private-sector power brokers of old in the depth and breadth of their reach. In the past, many private companies provided water, electricity, transport, and other essential services. Today, a few tech giants have vital roles in those areas and in many, many more. Start with the IT sector itself. Just four companies—Microsoft, Amazon, Google, and Alibaba—meet the bulk of the world's demand for cloud services. In the first year of the COVID-19 pandemic, it was this essential computing infrastructure that kept the global economy running, enabled people to work, and helped establish virtual classrooms in which kids could continue to learn. Very soon, the success of all industries and governments will depend almost entirely on how effectively they seize new opportunities created by 5G networks, AI, and the Internet of Things. All run on infrastructure built and managed by these cloud leaders.

The ability of tech companies to work with governments and one another to respond to future pandemics, limit the damage from climate change, and build a more rational approach to the introduction into our lives and societies of new technologies will depend on whether they're driven by goals that are *globalist, techno-utopian,* or *nationalist.*

All companies exist to make money. For companies that provide digital services, that's easiest when operating at a global scale. For decades, the most successful tech companies have followed a simple formula: create a killer app and sell it in as big a market as possible. Microsoft, Amazon, Google, Facebook, and Apple all built their empires by acting as *globalists.* They first worked to dominate an economically valuable niche and then began to sell their services worldwide. Chinese companies like Alibaba, Tencent, and ByteDance emerged at the top of

China's massive cutthroat domestic market before going global, but the principle behind their growth is the same: set up shop in as many countries as possible, localize content as needed, and compete like hell. The government relations departments of the world's leading tech companies—some of which employ hundreds of former diplomats, lobbyists, and lawyers with deep experience in government—reflect the priority that companies have historically placed on the globalist approach.

Globalism may be the tech sector's default mode, but it competes—and sometimes clashes—with a *techno-utopian* impulse that also holds significant sway in Silicon Valley, Seattle, Hangzhou, and Shenzhen. Some of the world's most powerful tech firms are led by founders with unique visions for their companies' role in the world. In the West, a few of them, like Mark Zuckerberg or Larry Page and Sergey Brin at Google, maintain outsized control of their companies through founders' shares or other financial structures. This makes them less susceptible to traditional forms of shareholder pressure than other founders or CEOs. They all share a vision of technology not just as a global business opportunity but as a potentially revolutionary force that can save humanity from itself. Elon Musk, CEO of Tesla and SpaceX, is probably the most recognizable example of the techno-utopian tendency, with his open ambition to remake energy markets to stave off global warming, design a high-bandwidth brain-computer interface, and make humanity a "multiplanetary species" by colonizing Mars.

Nationalism also exerts a pull on tech companies' business models. As the US-China technology confrontation has intensified since 2016, and as Europe has started to put political and legislative weight behind its mantra of "digital sovereignty," a growing number of Big Tech companies have responded by trying to position themselves as "national champions," partners with government in important technology domains like the cloud, AI, and cybersecurity. Along with Microsoft's increasingly vital role combating hacking by state-backed actors and criminal gangs, both it and Amazon are competing to provide cloud computing infrastructure to the US government.

These three categories don't capture the full complexity of tech companies or their leaders' intentions; tech firms are large, complex organizations, and the globalist, techno-utopian, and nationalist motivations mix inside each company. But the categories can still help us understand the choices facing tech firms as they navigate the shifting geopolitics of physical and digital space over the next decade. Do they fall in line with governments that pressure them to "choose sides" in the increasingly ideological struggle between the US and China? Do they try to resist becoming national champions, fend off regulation that threatens their business models, and maintain a more globalist approach? Or do they bet on a future in which states fade and tech companies help usher in a new social contract, or even new forms of human governance?

As competition between Washington and Beijing intensifies and companies and governments negotiate control over digital space, America's tech giants will operate in one of three scenarios: the state reigns supreme and national champions are rewarded; the corporation captures the state, handing globalists a historic victory; or the state fades away, empowering the techno-utopians. Here's how each might play out.

The State Reigns Supreme/National Champions Win

In this scenario, the US and its allies organize to offer governments cash and create policy that rewards "patriotic" companies whose business models and resources are aligned with national goals while punishing those that do not fall in line. Companies, confident that there is sustained political and financial capital behind this effort, finally forsake the fight for market share inside China and throw in their lot with the US and other Western governments in hopes that they can profit from a boom in public spending on new, digitally connected infrastructure and an array of tech-enabled social services backed by those governments. The state remains the dominant provider of security, law, and public goods in American life, with systemic shocks like the global financial crisis and the pandemic further cementing government's importance as the provider of last resort. In this scenario, a bipartisan push for greater regulation limits the powers of tech companies whose development plans aren't aligned with government. This depends on a coordinated push by the US with governments of other advanced industrial democracies to form alliances to contain the expansion of China's power and influence while also making big investments in pandemic recovery and a green transition.

Corporations Capture the State/Globalists Win

In this scenario, government continues to weaken as polarization intensifies and income and wealth inequality grow alongside automation and digitization. The backlash against major technology companies fails to deliver big reforms on privacy or antitrust that could upend business models, leaving Big Tech largely sovereign over digital space. Regulators can't keep pace with innovation. Companies put even more effort into lobbying politicians and preempting legislation that could limit their overseas operations, including in authoritarian countries like China and Russia. Unlike the national champions, the globalists will care less about supporting government than keeping it out of the way. The globalists need stability to succeed over the coming decade. They can survive the continuing erosion of America's democratic institutions, but not a surge in the power of the US state. They can manage periodic strains in the ᴜ ͻ-China relationship and even persistent distrust between the two countries, but not a new Cold War that forces them to choose between Washington and Beijing.

The State Fades/Techno-Utopians Win

In this scenario, growing public disillusionment with politicians dissolves the social contract. Americans and some developing countries embrace a digital economy that keeps government at arm's length, and confidence in the dollar as a global reserve currency collapses. The disintegration of centralized authority in the lone superpower leaves the world much less capable of addressing climate change, pandemics, nuclear proliferation, and other international challenges.

For tech visionaries with vaulting ambitions and deep pockets, patriotism becomes moot. Elon Musk plays a bigger role in transforming transportation, energy, and communications infrastructure—and in how we explore space. Mark Zuckerberg gets a much bigger voice in how we connect with one another personally, professionally, and politically. That said, the erosion of the US state would not give techno-utopians free rein worldwide. The Chinese state would also need to suffer a collapse in domestic credibility.

This globalist-nationalist-techno-utopian model doesn't apply as neatly to China, where the state has so much centralized power. Techno-utopians like Jack Ma are learning not to challenge the Chinese state directly, and even would-be globalists are forced to behave as if they're nationalists first. Alibaba, which hosts the world's largest consumer-to-consumer, consumer-to-business, and business-to-consumer websites, has to be careful, as does ByteDance, whose video-sharing app TikTok has helped it become the world's most valuable unicorn. So does Tencent, which cooperates more deeply with China's state security bureaucracy than Alibaba does.

If the Chinese economy begins to stagnate, and national champions prove less profitable or productivity-boosting than the globalist companies, the state could give the globalists more freedom to act within its borders. But for now, China continues to exert heavy pressure on its tech companies to line up behind state plans and strategies.

A world in which the state grows stronger would be the one most likely to produce a new Cold War and quash global cooperation. If Washington and Beijing continue to prioritize strategic competition over tech cooperation, there won't be much hope of using the solutions detailed in this book to strengthen the international system for the good of the US and China and everybody else. A scenario in which tech companies become more independent of (and competitive with) government in both countries is more likely to encourage cooperation during the biggest emergencies and innovation to meet new challenges. A world in which techno-utopians are calling more shots is hardest to predict, because that's a world in which power in concentrated in the fewest—and often the most eccentric—hands.

Governments must share costs and responsibilities for meeting these challenges with all who can help, because political officials and lawmakers neither understand nor control these areas. Those institutions, like banks and energy companies, that invest in projects that take years to produce profits must think longer-term than most governments do, and that makes their perspectives especially valuable. Energy companies, in particular, understand that future profits depend on renewable sources of fuel and electricity. Many of the world's most forward-looking NGOs have similarly long-term perspectives. Even within government, it isn't just *national* leaders and lawmakers who matter. When Donald Trump announced that the US would abandon the Paris climate accord, governors and mayors around the country declared that they would maintain their own climate targets. The importance of that becomes clear when we recall that California's economy is larger than that of India, Britain, or France. The New York metropolitan area has a larger economy than Canada or Russia. In the world of social media, even individuals—and not just the celebrity activists of the world—can mount campaigns that politicians and the private sector must reckon with.

We're also fortunate that the next wave of people to confront these problems have come of age in a globalized world. Generation Z, the 2.5 billion people born between 1996 and 2016, will see their impact on politics, culture, and the global economy surge over the next decade. Gen Z will be scarred by the pandemic and its lasting impact on education and jobs, but even in a world of fragmenting power and communications, this is the most globally interconnected generation in history. The overwhelming majority of them will come of age in developing countries, and fortunately for the rest of us, they will have their own expectations of government, of cross-border cultural engagement, and of what can and can't be done.

It's always easy to make "children are our future"–style arguments when calling for sweeping change, but in this case, the

Gen Z experience of the world is vastly different from that of my generation. I grew up in Boston in the 1970s with a kind of *National Geographic* image of kids in other parts of the world. I knew, and I think most of my friends knew, that our view of the world was heavily filtered by adults, but we didn't have much chance to see past the filter and interact directly with kids in other places. Today, young people in America and Europe are listening to and watching music and images created all over the world. They're playing games in real time with kids in Asia and Africa.

This isn't the globalization of twenty-five years ago. The children of this generation have a 360-degree view of the world that no other young people have ever had. They're aware, in a much more immediate way, of just how much they have in common with others. In particular, they're more aware than any previous generation that adults often have narrow minds and a limited imagination with respect to the problems they're leaving to the future. It's easy to be cynical about the immediate impact of young celebrity activists like Greta Thunberg, but, thankfully, younger people around the world have a perspective on these problems that very few adults have. Their ability to find new purposes for the tools that today's adults create—and to invent things that today's adults can't imagine—should boost our faith in the future.

Fear of an alien enemy has often inspired people, tribes, and nations to work together to conquer, or at least survive, a particular threat. Reagan and Gorbachev knew that. Today, the nations and peoples of the world don't face an alien menace; we confront common existential challenges we ourselves created. In that sense, we are interdependent—and that is the foundation for *the greatest opportunity in human history*.

Necessity must now become the mother of cooperation. We

must build a new international system that allows us to compete where we can and cooperate where we must. We are the first humans to recognize these global threats and the last that can defeat them.

Given the stakes, if we fail, we won't get another chance.

ADDENDUM

For three decades, the world didn't need to worry about the prospect of a nuclear conflict between major powers. But on February 21, 2022, as this book was about to go to press, President Vladimir Putin professed his unwillingness to further tolerate the European security status quo and the existence of a sovereign, independent Ukraine. Days later, he ordered Russian troops into Ukrainian territory, triggering economic sanctions from the United States and Europe and thrusting the world into a new Cold War.

This second Cold War is very different from the first. In a way it's less dangerous, because it's no longer a fight among equals. Russia doesn't have the global reach of the former Soviet Union. During the first Cold War, the Americans and Soviets fought for influence over every inch of the world, in Africa, Asia, Latin America . . . and, of course, with an Iron Curtain that divided the European continent in two. Today, Europe stands united and firmly (if not always completely) aligned with the United States, while Russian influence outside of the Middle

East and the more immediate former Soviet neighborhood is marginal at best.

But it's also more dangerous, because much of the institutional architecture that helped to reduce the risk of direct military confrontation—the Open Skies Agreements, the Intermediate-Range Nuclear Forces Treaty, and other measures designed to ensure a baseline of transparency and balance between the two nuclear superpowers—no longer exists. Both countries also have rough parity in offensive cyber-capabilities, featuring weapons far more attainable, usable, and destabilizing than anything used in the first Cold War. And, sadly but not surprisingly, the deep political divisions within the United States are playing out in the contest with Russia as well, with many elected leaders continuing to prioritize political expediency over national security. That's a reality well understood by Putin, and one that he surely factored into his decision to invade Ukraine again.

I hadn't yet been born when the Cuban Missile Crisis happened. I don't remember the duck-and-cover drills at school for preparedness in the event of a nuclear attack. I never worried about the prospect of nuclear annihilation from a military conflict that spiraled out of control. For three decades now, that simply has not been an active concern of global policymakers.

Today, we can no longer make that claim. We have tragically returned to a world where direct conflict between two of the world's military superpowers is a matter of pressing concern, where Europe has once again become a frontline battleground for global military tensions, and where the consequences of unchecked escalation are unthinkable, yet frighteningly real.

I'm not going to sugarcoat it: this complicated things. It's much harder to marshal the resources to fight a pandemic, combat climate change, and govern disruptive technologies when global supply chains are disrupted by economic, financial, and technological sanctions, and when the Russian government is engaged in unrestrained cyberwarfare and disinformation to undermine global governance. A more decoupled world is not only a less wealthy and efficient world—it's also a world of greater impunity, where rogue actors have more space to act in their own interests without fear of punishment.

And yet—even without a global sheriff, even with a dysfunctional and divided American political response, even with a US-China relationship lacking any of the trust required to reduce tensions and avert direct military conflict—there are good reasons to believe this latest geopolitical flare-up won't derail our collective ability to respond to crises.

After all, the United States and its allies are working much more closely together. Following decades of growing concern that the transatlantic relationship was deteriorating, that NATO was becoming obsolete, that Europeans were free riding on Washington, that the Americans were unilateral, transactional, and leaving Europe behind, the critical mission of the alliance came back into sharp focus. In the face of the Russian threat to European security, it's become crystal clear why NATO matters, why American military might matters, and why collective security matters. Putin's determination to restore the Russian empire reinvigorated a group of democracies whose resolve had atrophied due to a lack of challenging-enough tests. The level of coordination and unity of purpose mustered by the Western alliance was significantly higher than the one elicited by America's withdrawal from Afghanistan less than a year prior. Sometimes, it takes a crisis.

And then there's China. President Xi Jinping met with Putin during the opening ceremony of the 2022 Beijing Winter Olympics, where they released a joint statement nominally bringing the two countries the closest they had ever been. But if the Russian president is looking to break the current global order and embrace a new Cold War, the Chinese leadership wants none of it. China's globalized economy relies on continued interdependence with the West; Putin's quarrel with Europe is certainly not Xi's. In conversation with French president Emmanuel Macron, President Xi made clear that China continues to recognize Ukraine's territorial integrity and called for a diplomatic settlement to the conflict. Certainly, he has no interest in endorsing an exclusively Russian "sphere of influence" in China's own backyard. Could China become a force for stability by restraining Putin's imperial efforts? Sometimes, it takes a crisis.

These are dangerous times. It's painful to watch Europe once again become a military battlefield. A piece of the Berlin Wall was the must-have geopolitical souvenir of the twentieth century; will rubble from Kyiv's Maidan become the twenty-first-century equivalent? Perhaps.

But the new Cold War could also be the conflict that helps forge new leadership, a new global architecture, new institutions, and new ideologies. For two generations now, the world has largely neglected the inherent perils of globalization: from the animal-to-human and human-to-human transmission that led to a new infectious disease to the carbon emissions that drove climate change, the innovation explosion that engendered new disruptive technologies, and the countries—Russia the most powerful among them—and people that were left behind by it. We've never had feasible long-term strategies to address these challenges. Instead, we have always waited until the issues became urgent enough that we're forced to act . . . or else. The time is now.

—Ian Bremmer, February 2022

ACKNOWLEDGMENTS

The more advanced we become as a society, the more the risks we face become existential. That's why I study politics.

And damned if it's not true . . . but I'm feeling more optimistic these days. Maybe it's because we've made it through (nearly) the pandemic. Or maybe because the older you get, the more you appreciate the world around you. Either way, it's nice to write a book that isn't about how the world is falling apart. Or, more to the point, a book that's about what we are going to do about it.

"Who's we?" my mum would've asked. "You got a rat in your pocket?"

Not exactly. But I am deeply grateful to my friends and colleagues, always ready to rip into ideas on our toughest issues. And themselves not a small part of the solution. A few in particular I'd like to mention here: Carl Bildt, Borge Brende, Mark Carney, Vint Cerf, Jared Cohen, Chris Coons, Ivo Daalder, David Dollar, Kristalina Georgieva, Adam Grant, Antonio Guterres, Richard Haass, Christoph Heusgen, Robert Kagan, Zach Karabell, Joe Kennedy, Parag Khanna, Daniel Kurtz-Phelan, Christine Lagarde, Kai-Fu Lee, David Lipton, David Miliband, James Murdoch, Evan Osnos, Meghan O'Sullivan, Niko Pfund, Kevin Rudd, Eric Schmidt, Mustafa Suleyman, Larry Summers, Nick Thompson, Steve Walt, Gernot Wanger, and Fareed Zakaria.

Then there's our incredible team at Eurasia Group. We're now almost two hundred folks, and together we try to figure out how the world works. It's not as easy as it sounds. But it's easier than when it was just me back in 1998. My warm appreciation to Kevin Allison, Gerry Butts, Rohitesh Dhawan, Robert Kahn, Leon Levy, Mikaela McQuade, Maziar Minovi, Scott Rosenstein, Marietje Schaake, and Paul Triolo.

Willis Sparks is tremendous. We've worked hand in glove on six books together now, for nearly two decades. Don't know how we'd have built Eurasia Group to where we are today without our connection. Our small but intense research team includes Sebastian Strauss, brilliant and seamlessly connected despite pandemic conditions, and Megan O'Neill and Paige Williams, two extremely smart interns who helped with book research.

Alex Sanford is critical to all things I do involving media and generally public-facing stuff and helped orchestrate getting this from paper into your hands. A big shout-out to Greg Roth, our director of communications, and Sam Matino and Edana Ng for driving our book campaign. Kim Tran and Strax Matejic keep my life running smoothly and my various hats from falling off. Sarah Henning, my chief of staff, orchestrates it all like the unflappable maestro she is.

And my (new!) publisher, Jon Karp, and my editorial sharpshooter Eamon Dolan. Both showed infectious enthusiasm and personal commitment to publishing a great book together . . . and at somebody else's book party, no less. I suspect this will not be our last rodeo. Rafe Sagalyn is my agent for at least a decade, maybe longer. He exudes competence without beating you over the head with it; it's a quality I admire and enjoy.

To my chickie, Ann, just as delightful three years into a global pandemic. To my friends and family, who remain solid when everything else gets shut down. And to Moose the dog, small but courageous.

NOTES

Chapter 1: Two Collisions—Us vs. Them, at Home and Abroad

16 *"A report from the Pew Research Center published in"*: Pew Research Center, "Partisan Antipathy: More Intense, More Personal," October 10, 2019, pewresearch.org/politics/2019/10/10/partisan -antipathy-more-intense-more-personal/.

17 *"In a Gallup poll published in"*: Lydia Saad, "Americans' Political Ideology Held Steady in 2020," Gallup, January 11, 2021, https:// news.gallup.com/poll/328367/americans-political-ideology-held -steady-2020.aspx.

18 *"Within the thirty-eight-member Organization for Economic Co-operation and Development"*: "Income Distribution and Poverty," OECD.StatExtracts, https://web.archive.org/web/20150402093506 /http://stats.oecd.org/index.aspx?queryid=46189.

19 *"According to a 2021 study"*: *2021 Edelman Trust Barometer*, Global Report, Edelman, edelman.com/sites/g/files/aatuss191/files /2021-01/2021-edelman-trust-barometer.pdf.

20 *"a 2010 Supreme Court decision allowed corporations"*: Tim Lau, "Citizens United Explained," Brennan Center for Justice, December 12, 2019, brennancenter.org/our-work/research-reports /citizens-united-explained.

22 *"the newly created Federal Housing Authority"*: Terry Gross, "A 'Forgotten History' of How the U.S. Government Segregated America," May 3, 2017, npr.org/2017/05/03/526655831/a -forgotten-history-of-how-the-u-s-government-segregated-america.

23 *"the median wealth for a white family"*: Lisa J. Dettling, Joanne W. Hsu, Lindsay Jacobs, et al., "Recent Trends in Wealth-Holding by Race and Ethnicity: Evidence from the Survey of Consumer Finances," Board of Governors of the Federal Reserve System, September 27, 2017, federalreserve.gov/econres/notes/feds-notes /recent-trends-in-wealth-holding-by-race-and-ethnicity-evidence -from-the-survey-of-consumer-finances-20170927.htm.

23 *"Asian American immigrant women"*: "Not All Women Gained the Vote in 1920," PBS.org, July 6, 2020, pbs.org/wgbh/american experience/features/vote-not-all-women-gained-right-to-vote-in -1920/.

23 *"the US is expected to become"*: William H. Frey, "The US Will Become 'Minority White' in 2045, Census Projects," The Brookings Institution, March 14, 2018, brookings.edu/blog/the-avenue /2018/03/14/the-us-will-become-minority-white-in-2045-census -projects/.

23 *"Local laws targeted at making it more difficult"*: "Voting Laws Roundup: February 2021," Brennan Center for Justice, February 8, 2021, brennancenter.org/our-work/research-reports/voting-laws -roundup-february-2021.

25 *"States like California, Florida, Illinois, and Massachusetts"*: Zack Friedman, "These 20 States Are Raising the Minimum Wage Starting Today," January 1, 2021, forbes.com/sites/zackfriedman /2021/01/01/minimum-wage-increases-in-these-21-states /?sh=3d5c0ab81551.

29 *"he went much further in detailing his vision"*: Evan Osnos, "Making China Great Again," *The New Yorker*, January 1, 2018, newyorker.com/magazine/2018/01/08/making-china-great-again?reload=true.

32 *"over 80 percent of the world's countries traded"*: Alyssa Leng and Roland Rajah, "Chart of the Week: Global Trade Through a US-China Lens," The Lowy Institute, December 18, 2019, lowyinstitute.org/the-interpreter/chart-week-global-trade-through-us-china-lens.

33 *"the World Intellectual Property Organization received"*: "China Becomes Top Filer of International Patents in 2019 amid Robust Growth for WIPO's IP Services, Treaties and Finances," World Intellectual Property Organization, April 7, 2020, wipo.int/pressroom/en/articles/2020/article_0005.html.

33 *"it has contributed more UN peacekeeping troops"*: Patrick Wintour, "China Starts to Assert Its World View at UN as Influence Grows," *The Guardian*, September 24, 2018, theguardian.com/world/2018/sep/24/china-starts-to-assert-its-world-view-at-un-as-influence-grows.

34 *"Most Americans want President Biden and Congress"*: Zach Hrynowski, "Several Issues Tie as Most Important in 2020 Election," Gallup, January 13, 2020, https://news.gallup.com/poll/276932/several-issues-tie-important-2020-election.aspx.

35 *"once referred to the TPP as the"*: Glenn Kessler, "Fact Check: Clinton Did Call TPP the 'Gold Standard,' " Fact Checker: The Truth Behind the Rhetoric, *Washington Post*, September 26, 2016, washingtonpost.com/politics/2016/live-updates/general-election/real-time-fact-checking-and-analysis-of-the-first-presidential-debate/fact-check-clinton-dod-call-tpp-the-gold-standard/.

36 *"The US has military bases in forty countries"*: Jacques Attali, "China Is Not the Only Candidate for a 21st Century Superpower," Nikkei Asia, June 11, 2020, https://asia.nikkei.com/Opinion/China-is-not-the-only-candidate-for-a-21st-century-superpower.

37 *"This idea that champion and challenger"*: Graham Allison, "The Thucydides Trap: Are the US and China Headed for War?," *The Atlantic*, September 24, 2015, theatlantic.com/international/archive/2015/09/united-states-china-war-thucydides-trap/406756/.

37 *"the Peloponnesian War between Athens and Sparta"*: See Graham Allison's excellent book, *Destined for War: Can America and China Escape Thucydides's Trap?* (New York: Houghton Mifflin Harcourt, 2017).

38 *"there were some seventy thousand US companies"*: Evan Osnos, "The Future of America's Contest with China," *The New Yorker*, January 6, 2020, newyorker.com/magazine/2020/01/13/the-future-of-americas-contest-with-china.

41 *"4 percent of Italians"*: Katherine Butler, "Coronavirus: Europeans Say EU Was 'Irrelevant' During Pandemic," *The Guardian*, June 24, 2020, theguardian.com/world/2020/jun/23/europeans-believe-in-more-cohesion-despite-eus-covid-19-failings?CMP=share_btn_tw.

41 *"state media was playing up the story"*: Lulu Yilun Chen, "Alibaba's Jack Ma Sends Boxes of Coronavirus Test Kits and Masks to U.S.," *Time*, March 16, 2020, https://time.com/5803791/jack-ma-alibaba-coronavirus/.

41 *"In a survey from Pew Research conducted in March"*: Kat Devlin, Laura Silver, and Christine Huang, "U.S. Views of China Increasingly Negative Amid Coronavirus Outbreak," Pew Research Center, April 21, 2020, pewresearch.org/global/2020/04/21/u-s-views-of-china-increasingly-negative-amid-coronavirus-outbreak/?utm_source=Eurasia+Group+Signal&utm_campaign=68ea440b29-EMAIL_CAMPAIGN_2020_06_15_11_06&utm_medium=email&utm_term=0_e605619869-68ea440b29-134306173.

42 *"Kurt Campbell, Biden's lead Asia adviser"*: Peter Martin, "Biden's Asia Czar Says Era of Engagement with China Is Over," *Bloomberg*, May 26, 2021, bloomberg.com/news/articles/2021-05-26/biden-s-asia-czar-says-era-of-engagement-with-xi-s-china-is-over.

42 *"reported that President Xi had called"*: "China's Xi Jinping Tells People's Liberation Army to Get Ready for Combat," Radio Free Asia, March 10, 2021, rfa.org/english/news/china/combat-03102021110542.html.

43 *"A top US admiral warned"*: Helen Davidson, "China Could Invade Taiwan in Next Six Years, Top US Admiral Warns," *The Guardian*, March 9, 2021, theguardian.com/world/2021/mar/10/china-could-invade-taiwan-in-next-six-years-top-us-admiral-warns.

47 *"cost US taxpayers trillions of dollars"*: Reality Check team, "Afghanistan: What Has the Conflict Cost the US and Its Allies?" BBC News, September 3, 2021, bbc.com/news/world-47391821.

47 *"a multilateral lender that includes seventy-eight member countries"*: "Members and Prospective Members of the Bank," Asia Infrastructure Investment Bank, aiib.org/en/about-aiib/governance/members-of-bank/index.html.

47 *"the AIIB approved a $750 million loan to help"*: Cissy Zhou, "India-China Tensions Will Not Influence AIIB as Newly Re-elected President Vows to Keep Lender an 'Apolitical Institution,'" *South China Morning Post*, July 29, 2020, scmp.com/economy/global-economy/article/3095106/china-india-tensions-will-not-influence-aiib-newly-re.

47 *"it remains a major contributor to the IMF"*: Evan A. Feigenbaum, "Reluctant Stakeholder: Why China's Highly Strategic Brand of Revisionism Is More Challenging than Washington Thinks," Macro-Polo, April 27, 2018, https://macropolo.org/analysis/reluctant-stakeholder-why-chinas-highly-strategic-brand-of-revisionism-is-more-challenging-than-washington-thinks/.

49 *"arguably the largest in history in terms of trade volume"*: Peter A. Petri and Michael Plummer, "RCEP: A New Trade Agreement That Will Shape Global Economics and Politics," The Brookings Institution, November 16, 2020, brookings.edu/blog/order-from-chaos/2020/11/16/rcep-a-new-trade-agreement-that-will-shape-global-economics-and-politics/.

50 *"Sri Lanka* did *default on Chinese loans"*: Evan Osnos, "The

Future of America's Contest with China," *The New Yorker*, January 6, 2020, newyorker.com/magazine/2020/01/13/the-future-of-americas-contest-with-china.

51 *"The US has accepted more than three million refugees"*: "U.S. Resettles Fewer Refugees, Even as Global Number of Displaced People Grows," Pew Research Center, October 12, 2017, pewresearch.org/global/2017/10/12/u-s-resettles-fewer-refugees-even-as-global-number-of-displaced-people-grows/.

51 *"It has arrested and forcibly returned"*: *World Report 2020: China*, Human Rights Watch, hrw.org/world-report/2020/country-chapters/china-and-tibet#.

51 *"Less than one-tenth of 1 percent"*: Viola Zhou and Arman Dzidzovic, "China's Draft Bill on Permanent Residency Unleashes Hostile Comments against Foreigners," *Inkstone*, March 9, 2020, inkstonenews.com/society/chinas-draft-bill-permanent-residency-unleashes-hostile-comments-against-foreigners/article/3074244.

51 *"'If a person cannot walk into the middle of the town square'"*: Natan Sharansky with Ron Dermer, *The Case for Democracy: The Power of Freedom to Overcome Tyranny and Terror* (New York: Public Affairs, 2004), 40–41.

52 *"Xi Jinping's Communist Party banned all discussion"*: "How Much Is a Hardline Party Directive Shaping China's Current Political Climate?," Document 9: A ChinaFile Translation, *China File*, November 8, 2013, chinafile.com/document-9-chinafile-translation.

52 *"Teachers and professors seen to wander off the official path"*: Alice Su, "Spied on. Fired. Publicly shamed. China's Crackdown on Professors Reminds Many of Mao Era," *Los Angeles Times*, June 27, 2020, latimes.com/world-nation/story/2020-06-27/in-chinas-universities-targeted-attacks-on-intellectuals-raise-memories-of-the-cultural-revolution.

52 *"the Chinese state has regularly forced pregnancy checks"*: "China Cuts Uighur Births with IUDs, Abortion, Sterilization," Associated Press, June 29, 2020, https://apnews.com

/article/ap-top-news-international-news-weekend-reads-china
-health-269b3de1af34e17c1941a514f78d764c?utm_campaign
=SocialFlow&utm_source=Twitter&utm_medium=AP.

53 *"Human rights groups have uncovered evidence"*: Austin Ramzy
and Chris Buckley, " 'Absolutely No Mercy': Leaked Files Expose
How China Organized Mass Detentions of Muslims," *New York
Times*, November 16, 2019, nytimes.com/interactive/2019/11/16
/world/asia/china-xinjiang-documents.html.

53 *"The state has also given itself the right"*: Andrew Grotto and
Martin Schallbruch, "The Great Anti-China Tech Alliance,"
Foreign Policy, September 16, 2019, https://foreignpolicy
.com/2019/09/16/the-west-will-regret-letting-china-win-the
-tech-race/?utm_source=Fareed%27s+Global+Briefing&utm
_campaign=4de6dd711f-EMAIL_CAMPAIGN_2019_09_17
_09_04&utm_medium=email&utm_term=0_6f2e93382a-4de
6dd711f-84041237.

54 *"Apple removed an app"*: Jack Nicas, "Apple Removes App That
Helps Hong Kong Protesters Track the Police," *New York Times*,
October 9, 2019, nytimes.com/2019/10/09/technology/apple
-hong-kong-app.html.

54 *"Chinese police had spent three years collecting blood samples"*:
Emile Dirks and Dr. James Leibold, "Genomic Surveillance," Australian Strategic Policy Institute, June 17, 2020, aspi.org.au/report
/genomic-surveillance.

54 *"It's one more step toward a surveillance society"*: Sui-Lee Wee,
"China Is Collecting DNA from Tens of Millions of Men and Boys,
Using U.S. Equipment," *New York Times*, June 17, 2020, nytimes
.com/2020/06/17/world/asia/China-DNA-surveillance.html
?action=click&module=Top%20Stories&pgtype=Homepage.

56 *"it's the first known use of artificial intelligence to automate racism"*: "The Chinese Surveillance State, Part 1," *New York Times*,
May 6, 2019, nytimes.com/2019/05/06/podcasts/the-daily/china
-surveillance-uighurs.html?module=inline.

56 *"As when CloudWalk, an AI company, reportedly sold facial rec-*

ognition software": Lynsey Chutel, "China Is Exporting Facial Recognition Software to Africa, Expanding Its Vast Database," *Quartz Africa*, May 25, 2018, https://qz.com/africa/1287675/china-is-exporting-facial-recognition-to-africa-ensuring-ai-dominance-through-diversity/.

57 *"China has provided training for three dozen more countries"*: Paul Mozur, Jonah M. Kessel, and Melissa Chan, "Made in China, Exported to the World: The Surveillance State," *New York Times*, April 24, 2019, nytimes.com/2019/04/24/technology/ecuador-surveillance-cameras-police-government.html%20%20%20cfr.org/blog/exporting-repression-chinas-artificial-intelligence-push-africa.

57 *"American big data firms like Palantir have come under international scrutiny"*: Michael Steinberger, "Does Palantir See Too Much?," October 21, 2020, *New York Times Magazine*, nytimes.com/interactive/2020/10/21/magazine/palantir-alex-karp.html.

58 *"'We find ourselves once again with a peace that is no peace'"*: Niall Ferguson, "Is the United States in a New Cold War with China?," Silverado Policy Accelerator: Debate Series, November 17, 2020, YouTube, 18:15, youtube.com/watch?v=DtqO7KFhMJE.

58 *"'A new Cold War has begun'"*: Robert D. Kaplan, "A New Cold War Has Begun," *Foreign Policy*, January 7, 2019, https://foreignpolicy.com/2019/01/07/a-new-cold-war-has-begun/.

58 *"'new Cold War between the United States and China has already begun'"*: Richard Percival, " 'Cold War Has Begun!' China Warning Issued as Tensions Erupt—'It Will Shape This Century,' " *Express*, September 29, 2020, express.co.uk/news/world/1341266/china-news-US-europe-EU-war-germany-Peter-Beyer.

Chapter 2: Pandemic Politics

63 *"In less than three months"*: "Timeline: How the Global Coronavirus Pandemic Unfolded," Reuters, September 28, 2020, reuters.com/article/us-health-coronavirus-timeline/timeline-how-the-global-coronavirus-pandemic-unfolded-idUSKBN26K0AQ.

64 *"There may and likely will come a time"*: "Remarks by the President on Research for Potential Ebola Vaccines," White House Press Release, The White House, Office of the Press Secretary, December 2, 2014, https://obamawhitehouse.archives.gov/the-press-office/2014/12/02/remarks-president-research-potential-ebola-vaccines.

65 *"'The world as a whole doesn't have the preparedness for epidemics'"*: Betsy McKay, "Ebola Crisis Offers Lessons, Warnings on Epidemics, Bill Gates Says," *Wall Street Journal*, November 4, 2014, wsj.com/articles/ebola-crisis-offers-lessons-warnings-on-epidemics-bill-gates-says-1415051462.

66 *"never saw that number climb higher than 45.8 percent"*: Five ThirtyEight, "How (Un)Popular Is Donald Trump?," January 20, 2021, https://projects.fivethirtyeight.com/trump-approval-ratings/?ex_cid=rrpromo.

67 *"It was the only major economy"*: Jonathan Cheng, "China Is the Only Major Economy to Report Economic Growth for 2020," *Wall Street Journal*, January 18, 2021, wsj.com/articles/china-is-the-only-major-economy-to-report-economic-growth-for-2020-11610936187.

67 *"the European Commission accused China"*: Jennifer Rankin, "EU Says China Behind 'Huge Wave' of COVID-19 Disinformation," *The Guardian*, June 10, 2020, theguardian.com/world/2020/jun/10/eu-says-china-behind-huge-wave-covid-19-disinformation-campaign.

67 *"A report from Pew Research published in October 2020"*: Laura Silver, Kat Devlin, and Christine Huang, "Unfavorable Views of China Reach Historic Highs in Many Countries," Pew Research Center, October 6, 2020, pewresearch.org/global/2020/10/06/unfavorable-views-of-china-reach-historic-highs-in-many-countries/.

68 *"Brazil and Britain"*: "Mortality Analyses," Johns Hopkins Coronavirus Resource Center, https://coronavirus.jhu.edu/data/mortality.

71 *"The World Bank predicted in October 2020"*: "Extreme Poverty Set for First Rise Since 1998, World Bank Warns," BBC News, October 7, 2020, bbc.com/news/business-54448589.

71 *"data from the Ebola epidemic in West Africa"*: Bill Gates and Melinda French Gates, "COVID-19: A Global Perspective," Bill and Melinda Gates Foundation, September 2020, gatesfoundation.org /goalkeepers/report/2020-report/#GlobalPerspective.

71 *"COVID pushed more women"*: Ginette Azcona, Antra Bhatt, and Serge Kapto, "The COVID-19 Boomerang Effect: New Forecasts Predict Sharp Increases in Female Poverty," UN Women, September 2, 2020, https://data.unwomen.org/features/covid-19 -boomerang-poverty.

71 *"A report from the independent nonprofit foundation the Global Fund"*: *Results Report 2020*, The Global Fund, theglobalfund .org/media/10103/corporate_2020resultsreport_report_en .pdf?u=637356227598900000.

72 *"Scientists have discovered more than forty new lethal pathogens"*: Stewart M. Patrick, "The Time to Start Preparing for the Next Pandemic Is Now," *World Politics Review*, October 12, 2020, worldpoliticsreview.com/articles/29123/u-s-must-update -pandemic-playbook-after-failed-trump-coronavirus-response.

72 *"Genetic analysis has shown"*: Sue Sturgis, "Swine Flu Genes Traced to North Carolina Factory Farm," *Facing South*, May 5, 2009, facingsouth.org/2009/05/swine-flu-genes-traced-to-north -carolina-hog-farm.html.

77 *"Had they not, the country might not have become"*: "The Iranian Regime Risks Exacerbating the Outbreak of COVID-19," *The Economist*, February 24, 2020, economist.com/middle-east -and-africa/2020/02/24/the-iranian-regime-risks-exacerbating-the -outbreak-of-covid-19.

78 *"'Predict was an approach to heading off pandemics'"*: Donald G. McNeil Jr., "Scientists Were Hunting for the Next Ebola. Now the U.S. Has Cut Off Their Funding," *New York Times*, October 25, 2019, nytimes.com/2019/10/25/health/predict-usaid -viruses.html.

80 *"He didn't peddle fake herbal remedies"*: Aryn Baker, " 'Could It Work as a Cure? Maybe.' A Herbal Remedy for Coronavirus Is

a Hit in Africa, But Experts Have Their Doubts," *Time*, May 22, 2020, https://time.com/5840148/coronavirus-cure-covid-organic-madagascar/.

80 *"Unlike Belarus's president, Alexander Lukashenko"*: Sam Meredith, "Belarus' President Dismisses Coronavirus Risk, Encourages Citizens to Drink Vodka and Visit Saunas," CNBC, March 31, 2020, cnbc.com/2020/03/31/coronavirus-belarus-urges-citizens-to-drink-vodka-visit-saunas.html.

80 *"he didn't deliberately attack the integrity and credibility"*: Charles Piller, "Undermining CDC," *Science*, October 14, 2020, sciencemag.org/news/2020/10/inside-story-how-trumps-covid-19-coordinator-undermined-cdc.

80 *"Moon's Democratic Party was rewarded with a landslide victory"*: Do Kyung Ryuk, JeongHyeon Oh, and Yewon Sung, "Elections During a Pandemic: South Korea Shows How to Safely Hold a National Election During the COVID-19 Crisis," Wilson Center, May 19, 2020, wilsoncenter.org/blog-post/elections-during-pandemic-south-korea-shows-how-safely-hold-national-election-during.

81 *"the World Health Organization was buffeted by criticism"*: Roz Krasny and Tony Czuczka, "US Officials Air Concerns about WHO's COVID Origin Report," *Bloomberg*, March 28, 2021, bloomberg.com/news/articles/2021-03-29/u-s-officials-air-concerns-about-who-s-covid-origin-report.

82 *"COVAX faces similar hurdles"*: "172 Countries and Multiple Candidate Vaccines Engaged in COVID-19 Global Access Facility," World Health Organization, August 24, 2020, who.int/news/item/24-08-2020-172-countries-and-multiple-candidate-vaccines-engaged-in-covid-19-vaccine-global-access-facility.

82 *"'constrained by multilateral organizations'"*: Emily Rauhala and Yasmeen Abutaleb, "U.S. Says It Won't Join WHO-linked Effort to Develop, Distribute Coronavirus Vaccine," *Washington Post*, September 1, 2020, washingtonpost.com/world/coronavirus-vaccine-trump/2020/09/01/b44b42be-e965-11ea-bf44-0d31c85838a5_story.html.

82 *"President Biden recommitted the US to COVAX"*: "Fact Sheet: President Biden to Take Action on Global Health through Support of COVAX and Calling for Health Security Financing," White House press release, February 18, 2021, whitehouse.gov/briefing -room/statements-releases/2021/02/18/fact-sheet-president-biden -to-take-action-on-global-health-through-support-of-covax-and -calling-for-health-security-financing/.

84 *"European governments agreed in 2020 on a recovery package"*: "COVID-19: The EU's Response to the Economic Fallout," European Council, Council of the European Union, consilium.europa.eu /en/policies/coronavirus/covid-19-economy/.

85 *"These financial packages also include stimulus"*: "5 Ways the EU and Member States Work Together against COVID-19," European Council, Council of the European Union, consilium.europa.eu/en /covid-eu-solidarity/.

85 *"'We were late to authorize'"*: "Covid: What's the Problem with the EU Vaccine Rollout?," BBC News, March 4, 2021, bbc.com/news /explainers-56286235.

86 *"the leaders of twenty-three countries joined the WHO"*: Maria Cheng, "World Leaders Call for Pandemic Treaty, Short on Details," Associated Press, March 30, 2021, https://apnews.com/art icle/pandemics-mario-draghi-rwanda-coronavirus-pandemic-covid -19-pandemic-9b5db1741b963094736ff1e2606b4326.

Chapter 3: Climate Emergency

88 *"travel 7,500 miles west from Damascus to Central America"*: Nina Lakhani, " 'People Are Dying': How the Climate Crisis Has Sparked an Exodus to the US," *The Guardian*, July 29, 2019, theguardian.com/global-development/2019/jul/29/guatemala -climate-crisis-migration-drought-famine.

88 *"hundreds of thousands of people fled the region"*: John Gramlich and Alissa Scheller, "What's Happening at the U.S.-Mexico Border in 7 Charts," Pew Research Center, November 9, 2021, pewresearch

.org/fact-tank/2021/11/09/whats-happening-at-the-u-s-mexico
-border-in-7-charts/.

89 *"climate disasters will push* hundreds of millions *onto the road"*: Jack
A. Goldstone and Larry Diamond, "How Will Demographic Trans-
formations Affect Democracy in the Coming Decades?," Hoover
Institution, Spring Series, Issue 719, May 14, 2019, hoover.org/re
search/how-will-demographic-transformations-affect-democracy
-coming-decades?utm_source=Fareed%27s+Global+Briefing&utm
_campaign=3e6af6e493-EMAIL_CAMPAIGN_2019_05_13_09
_09&utm_medium=email&utm_term=0_6f2e93382a-3e6af6e493
-84041237.

89 *"Populations will surge in Africa"*: Anthony Cilluffo and Neil G.
Ruiz, "World's Population Is Projected to Nearly Stop Growing
by the End of the Century," Pew Research Center, June 17, 2019,
pewresearch.org/fact-tank/2019/06/17/worlds-population-is
-projected-to-nearly-stop-growing-by-the-end-of-the-century/.

90 *"the number of undernourished people"*: "Climate Change Is an
Increasing Threat to Africa," United Nations, October 27, 2020,
https://unfccc.int/news/climate-change-is-an-increasing-threat-to
-africa.

90 *"climate change can create overlapping disasters"*: Thomas Fuller
and Christopher Flavelle, "A Climate Reckoning in Fire-Stricken
California," *New York Times*, September 10, 2020, nytimes
.com/2020/09/10/us/climate-change-california-wildfires.html
?action=click&module=Top%20Stories&pgtype=Homepage.

90 *"Studies show that by 2050"*: Al Shaw, Abrahm Lustgarten, Pro-
Publica, and Jeremy W. Goldsmith, "New Climate Maps Show a
Transformed United States," ProPublica, September 15, 2020,
https://projects.propublica.org/climate-migration/.

91 *"This is the impact of the Anthropocene,"*: Joseph Stromberg,
"What Is the Anthropocene and Are We in It?" *Smithsonian*, January 2013, smithsonianmag.com/science-nature/what-is-the-anthrop
ocene-and-are-we-in-it-164801414/.

91 *"One-sixth of all the carbon emissions"*: David Fickling, "The 2010s

Wrecked the Planet. Don't Despair Yet," *Bloomberg*, January 1, 2020, bloomberg.com/opinion/articles/2020-01-02/power-sector -shows-world-the-way-on-carbon-emissions?sref=75vWZjCW.

91 *"The Amazon lost more forest cover in 2019"*: Neil Giardino, "Amazon Rainforest Lost Area the Size of Israel in 2020," ABC News, February 5, 2021, https://abcnews.go.com/International /amazon-rainforest-lost-area-size-israel-2020/story?id=75683477.

91 *"more than one-third of all destruction"*: Henry Fountain, " 'Going in the Wrong Direction': More Tropical Forest Loss in 2019," *New York Times*, June 2, 2020, nytimes.com/2020/06/02/climate /deforestation-climate-change.html.

92 *"During the industrial age"*: Daisy Dunne, "Scientists Discover New 'Human Fingerprint' on Global Drought Patterns," World Economic Forum, July 14, 2020, weforum.org/agenda/2020/07 /human-fingerprinting-drought-rainfall-africa-asia-america.

92 *"Melting ice around the poles"*: Justin Worland, "The Leaders of These Sinking Countries Are Fighting to Stop Climate Change. Here's What the Rest of the World Can Learn," *Time*, June 13, 2019, https://time.com/longform/sinking-islands-climate-change /?utm_medium=socialflowtw&xid=time_socialflow_twitter&utm _campaign=time&utm_source=twitter.com.

92 *"about 1 percent of the earth's surface"*: Abrahm Lustgarten, "The Great Climate Migration Has Begun," *New York Times Magazine*, July 23, 2020, nytimes.com/interactive/2020/07/23/magazine /climate-migration.html.

92 *"We are the first generation"*: *Living Planet Report 2018: Aiming Higher*, World Wildlife Fund, wwf.org.uk/sites/default/files/2018 -10/wwfintl_livingplanet_full.pdf.

93 *"because 65 percent of global oil reserves are now held"*: "Share of Oil Reserves, Oil Production and Oil Upstream Investment by Company Type, 2018," International Energy Agency, January 17, 2020, iea.org/data-and-statistics/charts/share-of-oil-reserves-oil-produc tion-and-oil-upstream-investment-by-company-type-2018.

93 *"still rely heavily on coal"*: Joshua W. Busby, Sarang Shidore, Jo-

hannes Urpelainen, and Morgan D. Bazilian, "The Case for US Co-operation with India on a Just Transition Away from Coal," The Brookings Institution, April 20, 2021, brookings.edu/research/the-case-for-us-cooperation-with-india-on-a-just-transition-away-from-coal/, and Evelyn Cheng, "China Has 'No Other Choice' but to Rely on Coal Power for Now, Official Says," CNBC, April 29, 2021, cnbc.com/2021/04/29/climate-china-has-no-other-choice-but-to-rely-on-coal-power-for-now.html.

93 *"Saudi Arabia's Vision 2030 plan"*: "Saudi Vision 2030: An Ambitious Vision for an Ambitious Nation," vision2030.gov.sa/v2030/overview/.

94 *"The ten companies responsible for the biggest surges"*: Adam Tooze, "Welcome to the Final Battle for the Climate," *Foreign Policy*, October 17, 2020, https://foreignpolicy.com/2020/10/17/great-power-competition-climate-china-europe-japan/.

95 *"A 2019 study conducted by"*: Elisabeth Behrmann, "Twilight of Combustion Engine Comes for Germany," *Automotive News Europe*, April 11, 2019, https://europe.autonews.com/automakers/twilight-combustion-engine-comes-germany.

95 *"But countries as poor as Ecuador"*: Alexandra Valencia, "Ecuador's Moreno Scraps Fuel Subsidy Cuts in Big Win for Indigenous Groups," Reuters, October 14, 2019, reuters.com/article/us-ecuador-protests/ecuadors-moreno-scraps-fuel-subsidy-cuts-in-big-win-for-indigenous-groups-idUSKBN1WT265, and Davide Natalini, "Gilets Jaunes May Be the Start of a Worldwide Revolt against Climate Action," *The Conversation*, April 1, 2019, https://theconversation.com/gilets-jaunes-may-be-the-start-of-a-worldwide-revolt-against-climate-action-112636.

96 *"the United States and Europe combined for 8.9 gigatons"*: Adam Tooze, "Welcome to the Final Battle for the Climate," *Foreign Policy*, October 17, 2020, https://foreignpolicy.com/2020/10/17/great-power-competition-climate-china-europe-japan/.

98 *"half the people on earth will be living"*: Alberto Boretti and Lorenzo Rosa, "Reassessing the Projections of the World Water De-

velopment Report," *npj Clean Water*, Nature.com, July 31, 2019, nature.com/articles/s41545-019-0039-9.

98 *"but also of more frequent severe storms"*: Jen Christensen, "Fact Check: Pence Says There Are No More Hurricanes Now than 100 Years Ago," Facts First, CNN, October 8, 2020, cnn.com/2020/10/08/politics/fact-check-pence-hurricanes/index.html?utm_source=feedburner&utm_medium=feed&utm_campaign=Feed%3A+rss%2Fcnn_allpolitics+%28RSS%3A+CNN+-+Politics%29.

98 *"higher sea levels caused by warming"*: Desmond Ng, "Why Jakarta Is the Fastest Sinking City in the World," Channel News Asia, February 28, 2020, channelnewsasia.com/cnainsider/why-jakarta-is-world-fastest-sinking-city-floods-climate-change-781491.

98 *"More than ninety American cities"*: Robert Muggah, "The World's Coastal Cities Are Going Under. Here's How Some Are Fighting Back," World Economic Forum, January 16, 2019, weforum.org/agenda/2019/01/the-world-s-coastal-cities-are-going-under-here-is-how-some-are-fighting-back/.

99 *"Hundreds of millions of people on both sides"*: Alejandra Borunda, "The World's Supply of Fresh Water Is in Trouble as Mountain Ice Vanishes," *National Geographic*, December 9, 2019, nationalgeographic.com/science/article/water-towers-high-mountains-are-in-trouble-perpetual.

100 *"India would have violated the Indus River Treaty"*: "Indus Water Treaty: Everything You Need to Know," ClearIAS, November 26, 2016, clearias.com/indus-water-treaty/.

100 *"Water is already a powerful weapon for India"*: Jeffrey Gettleman, "India Threatens a New Weapon against Pakistan: Water," *New York Times*, February 21, 2019, nytimes.com/2019/02/21/world/asia/india-pakistan-water-kashmir.html.

101 *"India will join this importing club as it passes China"*: Hannah Ritchie, "India Will Soon Overtake China to Become the Most Populous Country in the World," Our World in Data, April 16,

2019, https://ourworldindata.org/india-will-soon-overtake-china-to
-become-the-most-populous-country-in-the-world.

102 *"some worst-case estimates warn that as many as thirty million
people"*: Abrahm Lustgarten, "The Great Climate Migration Has
Begun," *New York Times Magazine*, July 23, 2020, nytimes.com
/interactive/2020/07/23/magazine/climate-migration.html.

102 *"The twenty-six-country open border zone in Europe"*: "Schengen
Area," VisaGuide.world, https://visaguide.world/europe/schengen
-visa/schengen-area-countries-list/.

102 *"Developing countries host 85 percent of the world's migrants"*:
"The World's Refugees in Numbers," Amnesty International,
amnesty.org/en/what-we-do/refugees-asylum-seekers-and
-migrants/global-refugee-crisis-statistics-and-facts/.

102 *"The first country that climate change will completely destroy"*:
Mike Ives, "A Remote Pacific Nation, Threatened by Rising Seas,"
New York Times, July 2, 2016, nytimes.com/2016/07/03/world
/asia/climate-change-kiribati.html.

103 *"More than forty-five million Bangladeshis live in coastal areas"*:
"Climate Displacement in Bangladesh," Environmental Justice
Foundation, https://ejfoundation.org/reports/climate-displacement
-in-bangladesh.

103 *"A 2019 report from the US National Academy of Sciences"*: Jonathan L. Bamber, Michael Oppenheimer, Robert E. Kopp, et al.,
"Ice Sheet Contributions to Sea-Level Rise from Structured Expert
Judgment," *Proceedings of the National Academy of Sciences*, June
4, 2019, pnas.org/content/116/23/11195.

104 *"Scientists have warned that rising sea levels could create"*: "The
Cost of Doing Nothing: The Humanitarian Price of Climate Change
and How It Can Be Avoided," International Federation of Red
Cross, September 19, 2019, https://reliefweb.int/report/world
/cost-doing-nothing-humanitarian-price-climate-change-and-how
-it-can-be-avoided.

105 *"an already overcrowded city whose sewers frequently burst"*:

Poppy McPherson, "The Dysfunctional Megacity: Why Dhaka Is Bursting at the Sewers," *The Guardian*, March 21, 2018, theguardian.com/cities/2018/mar/21/people-pouring-dhaka -bursting-sewers-overpopulation-bangladesh.

105 *"the Bolivian town of Cochabamba"*: "Leasing the Rain," William Finnegan, *The New Yorker*, March 31, 2002, newyorker.com /magazine/2002/04/08/leasing-the-rain.

106 *"erratic weather continues"*: "Impact Story: Addressing a Water Crisis in Bolivia," Stockholm Environment Institute, May 23, 2018, sei.org/featured/growing-water-crisis-bolivia/.

106 *"According to a 2019 report from the World Resources Institute"*: Rutger Willem Hofste, Paul Reig, and Leah Schleifer, "17 Countries, Home to One-Quarter of the World's Population, Face Extremely High Water Stress," World Resources Institute, August 6, 2019, wri.org/insights/17-countries-home-one-quarter-worlds -population-face-extremely-high-water-stress.

108 *"Parts of the Siberian tundra and Canada alone are estimated to store"*: Laura Millan Lombrana, "Where Climate Scientists See Danger, Russia Sees an Opportunity," *Bloomberg*, March 15, 2021, bloomberg.com/news/articles/2021-03-15/where-climate-scientists -see-danger-russia-sees-an-opportunity?sref=75vWZjCW.

108 *"UN experts have warned that poorer countries"*: "'Climate Apartheid' between Rich and Poor Looms, UN Expert Warns," BBC News, June 25, 2019, bbc.com/news/world-48755154.

108 *"A half century of poverty reduction"*: Damian Carrington, " 'Climate Apartheid': UN Expert Says Human Rights May Not Survive," *The Guardian*, June 25, 2019, theguardian.com/environment/2019 /jun/25/climate-apartheid-united-nations-expert-says-human -rights-may-not-survive-crisis?CMP=Share_iOSApp_Other.

109 *"designed to address the problem of carbon in the atmosphere through climate manipulation"*: Daniel Grossman, "Geoengineering: A Worst-Case Plan B? Or a Fuse Not to Be Lit?," Yale Climate Connections, June 8, 2021, https://yaleclimateconnections.org/2021 /06/geoengineering-a-worst-case-plan-b-or-a-fuse-not-to-be-lit/.

111 *"Multinational development banks have collectively pledged loans"*: "Net-Zero Emissions Must Be Met by 2050 or COVID-19 Impact on Global Economies Will Pale beside Climate Crisis, Secretary-General Tells Finance Summit," United Nations, November 12, 2020, un.org/press/en/2020/sgsm20411.doc.htm.

113 *"Some of the world's largest companies have made carbon pledges"*: Leo Kelion, "Apple's 2030 Carbon-Neutral Pledge Covers Itself and Suppliers," July 21, 2020, bbc.com/news/technology-53485560.

113 *"a lobbying organization that represents more"*: Valerie Volcovici, "Business Roundtable CEO Group Announces Its Support for Carbon Pricing to Help Fight Climate Change," *Business Insider*, September 16, 2020, businessinsider.com/us-ceo-group -says-it-supports-carbon-pricing-to-fight-climate-change-2020 -9?r=US&IR=T#:~:text=Business%20Roundtable%2C%20a%20 lobbying%20group,levels%20by%20the%20year%202050.

114 *"The leaders of imperiled island nations"*: Justin Worland, "The Leaders of These Sinking Countries Are Fighting to Stop Climate Change. Here's What the Rest of the World Can Learn," *Time*, June 13, 2019, https://time.com/longform/sinking-islands-climate -change/?utm_medium=socialflowtw&xid=time_socialflow_ twitter&utm_campaign=time&utm_source=twitter.com.

115 *"a CEO who named his son"*: Avery Hartmans and Rosie Perper, "Elon Musk Said His and Grimes' New Baby Is Named X Æ A-12. Grimes Broke Down the Meaning Behind Each Letter of the Bizarre Moniker," *Business Insider*, May 5, 2020, businessinsider .com/x-ae-a-12-elon-musk-grimes-baby-name-meaning-2020-5.

117 *"leading the way on carbon pricing"*: "The World Urgently Needs to Expand Its Use of Carbon Prices," *The Economist*, May 23, 2020, economist.com/briefing/2020/05/23/the-world-urgently- needs-to-expand-its-use-of-carbon-prices.

118 *"Retail giant Walmart pledged in 2020"*: Lucy Handley, "Walmart Has a Grand Plan to Help Suppliers Club Together to Buy Green Energy," CNBC, October 23, 2020, cnbc.com/2020/10/23/walmart -wants-suppliers-to-buy-renewable-energy-collectively.html.

118 *"Multinational consumer goods company Unilever is using satellite imagery"*: Lucy Handley, "Unilever Is Using Geolocation Data and Satellite Imagery to Check for Deforestation in Its Supply Chain," CNBC, September 24, 2020, cnbc.com/2020/09/24 /unilever-in-data-pilot-to-check-for-deforestation-in-its-supply -chain.html.

119 *"Software giant Salesforce announced in early 2020"*: "One Trillion Trees to Combat Climate Change: Why It's Not So Outlandish," Salesforce, January 22, 2020, salesforce.com/news/stories /one-trillion-trees-to-combat-climate-change-why-its-not-so -outlandish/.

119 *"That helps explain why climate change is made worse"*: Henry Fountain, "'Going in the Wrong Direction': More Tropical Forest Loss in 2019, *New York Times*, June 2, 2020, nytimes.com/2020 /06/02/climate/deforestation-climate-change.html.

124 *"is trying to jump-start the effort"*: "Final Announcement of the Recommendation for the New Governance Body Composition," Taskforce on Scaling Voluntary Carbon Markets, iif.com/tsvcm.

Chapter 4: Disruptive Technologies

128 *"Specially made drones helped deliver lifesaving medicine"*: Harry Kretchmer, "How Drones Are Helping to Battle COVID-19 in Africa—and Beyond," World Economic Forum, May 8, 2020, weforum.org/agenda/2020/05/medical-delivery-drones-corona virus-africa-us/.

128 *"helped hospitals predict how many beds"*: Owen Hughes, "This AI Tool Helps Hospitals Predict COVID-19 Bed and Ventilator Demand," ZDNet, April 21, 2020, zdnet.com/article/this-ai-tool -helps-hospitals-predict-covid-19-bed-and-ventilator-demand/.

128 *"A spike in Google searches using phrases"*: Seth Stephens-Davidowitz, "Google Searches Can Help Us Find Emerging COVID-19 Outbreaks," *New York Times*, April 5, 2020, nytimes .com/2020/04/05/opinion/coronavirus-google-searches.html.

128 *"AI played a crucial role in vaccine development"*: Jo Best, "AI and the Coronavirus Fight: How Artificial Intelligence Is Taking on COVID-19," ZDNet, April 9, 2020, zdnet.com/article/ai-and-the-coronavirus-fight-how-artificial-intelligence-is-taking-on-covid-19/.

128 *"Contact tracing and smartphone apps that tracked"*: Simon Sharwood, "Pan-European Group Plans Cross-Border Contact-Tracing App—and Promises GDPR Compliance," *The Register*, April 6, 2020, theregister.com/2020/04/06/pan_european_privacy_preserving_proximity_tracing_plan/.

130 *"Aadhaar brought an unprecedented number of people"*: "Top 10 Insights," State of Aadhaar, stateofaadhaar.in/top-10-insights.php.

131 *"Those who live in them"*: "Urban Development Overview," World Bank, worldbank.org/en/topic/urbandevelopment/overview#1.

131 *"Traffic accidents kill more than one million people"*: "Road Traffic Deaths Data by Country," Global Health Observatory Data Repository, World Health Organization, https://apps.who.int/gho/data/node.main.A997?lang=en.

133 *"uses automatic license plate scanners"*: James Bridle, "How Britain Exported Next-Generation Surveillance," *Matter*, December 18, 2013, https://medium.com/matter/how-britain-exported-next-generation-surveillance-d15b5801b79e.

133 *"film star Will Smith told interviewer Stephen Colbert"*: "Will Smith: 'Racism Is Not Getting Worse, It's Getting Filmed,'" *Hollywood Reporter*, August 3, 2016, hollywoodreporter.com/tv/tv-news/will-smith-colbert-race-relations-obama-politics-sings-summertime-916816/.

134 *"researchers published a paper in the journal* Science*"*: Starre Vartan, "Racial Bias Found in a Major Health Care Risk Algorithm," *Scientific American*, October 24, 2019, scientificamerican.com/article/racial-bias-found-in-a-major-health-care-risk-algorithm/.

135 *"presented evidence that facial recognition algorithms"*: "Algorithmic Bias Persists," The Gender Shades Project, MIT Media Lab, Massachusetts Institute of Technology, media.mit.edu/projects/gender-shades/overview/.

137 *"A 2018 study from McKinsey & Company"*: Michael Chui, James Manyika, Mehdi Miremadi, et al., "Notes from the AI Frontier: Applications and Value of Deep Learning," McKinsey Global Institute, April 17, 2018, mckinsey.com/featured-insights/artificial -intelligence/notes-from-the-ai-frontier-applications-and-value-of -deep-learning.

137 *"Reports from Oxford Economics and McKinsey"*: "How Robots Change the World," Oxford Economics, https://resources.oxford economics.com/how-robots-change-the-world?source=recent -releases.

138 *"the World Economic Forum described it"*: Nicholas Davis, "What Is the Fourth Industrial Revolution?," World Economic Forum, January 19, 2016, weforum.org/agenda/2016/01/what-is-the -fourth-industrial-revolution/.

138 *"President Obama's Council of Economic Advisers forecast that"*: Carl Benedikt Frey, "COVID-19 Will Only Increase Automation Anxiety," *Financial Times*, April 21, 2020, ft.com/content /817228a2-82e1-11ea-b6e9-a94cffd1d9bf.

139 *"The US and some European governments are gradually accepting the need"*: "Coronavirus: Spain Set for Basic Income to Ease Crisis Pain," BBC News, May 18, 2020, bbc.com/news/world-europe -52707551.

140 *"The average person born today in Japan"*: "Life Expectancy of the World Population," Worldometer, worldometers.info/demograph ics/life-expectancy/.

142 *"but a 2020 study from Pew Research found that only about one-third of Americans"*: John Gramlich, "10 Facts about Americans and Facebook," Pew Research Center, June 1, 2021, pewresearch .org/fact-tank/2021/06/01/facts-about-americans-and-facebook/.

142 *"Many Americans read that the fires may have deliberately been set"*: Ashley Gold, "Exclusive: False Fire Rumors Keep Spreading on Facebook Despite Ban," *Axios*, September 16, 2020, axios.com /facebook-false-fire-rumors-keep-spreading-despite-ban-a014ee1c -8bd7-4fe1-a644-928f2a580e19.html.

143 *"just 39.6 percent of Africans had internet access"*: Hafez Gha-
nem, "Shooting for the Moon: An Agenda to Bridge Africa's Digital
Divide," The Brookings Institution, February 7, 2020, brookings
.edu/blog/africa-in-focus/2020/02/07/shooting-for-the-moon-an
-agenda-to-bridge-africas-digital-divide/.

144 *"'If you want to liberate a society'"*: Nicholas Thompson and Ian
Bremmer, "The AI Cold War That Threatens Us All," *Wired*, October
23, 2018, wired.com/story/ai-cold-war-china-could-doom-us-all/.

145 *"Russia also helped Assad disseminate digital propaganda"*: Karl
Nicolas Lindenlaub, "The Syrian Online War of Narratives," Atlantic Council, July 8, 2020, atlanticcouncil.org/blogs/menasource
/the-syrian-online-war-of-narratives/.

146 *"China's social credit system"*: Amanda Lee, "What Is China's Social Credit System and Why Is It Controversial?," *South
China Morning Post*, August 9, 2020, scmp.com/economy/china
-economy/article/3096090/what-chinas-social-credit-system-and
-why-it-controversial.

146 *"The data used to power China's social credit system"*: Ibid.

147 *"'akin to the Centers for Disease Control and Prevention using apps
from Amazon and Facebook'"*: Paul Mozur, Raymond Zhong, and
Aaron Krolik, "In Coronavirus Fight, China Gives Citizens a Color
Code, with Red Flags," *New York Times*, March 1, 2020, nytimes
.com/2020/03/01/business/china-coronavirus-surveillance.html.

147 *"Chinese companies have already helped"*: Joe Parkinson, Nicholas Bariyo, and Josh Chin, "Huawei Technicians Helped African
Governments Spy on Political Opponents," *Wall Street Journal*,
August 15, 2019, wsj.com/articles/huawei-technicians-helped
-african-governments-spy-on-political-opponents-11565793017.

147 *"the biggest companies in American history"*: John Laidler, "High
Tech Is Watching You," *Harvard Gazette*, March 4, 2019, https://
news.harvard.edu/gazette/story/2019/03/harvard-professor-says
-surveillance-capitalism-is-undermining-democracy/.

147–48 *"All that information is being gathered"*: "Big Brother Is
Watching You. (And You. And You. And You, Too.)," GZERO

Media, June 10, 2019, gzeromedia.com/big-brother-is-watching -you-and-you-and-you-and-you-too.

148 *"the average American is caught on security cameras"*: Dan Avery, "Most Americans Are Recorded 238 Times a Week by Security Cameras and a Majority of Filming Happens When Driving, Study Reveals," *Daily Mail*, September 25, 2020, dailymail.co.uk /sciencetech/article-8774151/Most-Americans-recorded-238 -TIMES-week-security-cameras-study-reveals.html.

148 *"The* New York Times *reported in January 2020"*: Kashmir Hill, "The Secretive Company That Might End Privacy as We Know It," *New York Times*, January 18, 2020, nytimes.com/2020/01/18 /technology/clearview-privacy-facial-recognition.html.

148 *"the US government broadened its use of warrantless surveillance"*: Nicholas Wright, "Coronavirus and the Future of Surveillance," *Foreign Affairs*, April 6, 2020, foreignaffairs.com/ articles/2020-04-06/coronavirus-and-future-surveillance?utm _medium=newsletters&utm_source=on_the_ballot&utm _campaign=on_the_ballot_2020_prospects&utm_content=202 00408&utm_term=prospects-OTB-021020.

149 *"And though participation in Aadhaar was once voluntary"*: Ananya Bhattacharya and Nupur Anand, "Aadhaar Is Voluntary— but Millions of Indians Are Already Trapped," *Quartz India*, September 26, 2018, https://qz.com/india/1351263/supreme-court -verdict-how-indias-aadhaar-id-became-mandatory/.

149 *"The questions looming in India"*: David Ariosto, "The World's Largest Democracy Scans Voters' Eyes," GZERO Media, May 6, 2019, gzeromedia.com/the-worlds-largest-democracy.

150 *"1G was the technology that allowed us"*: "Ain't Nuthin But a 5G Thang," GZERO Media, March 11, 2019, gzeromedia.com/aint -nuthin-but-a-5g-thang.

150 *"It's the foundation on which developers will build the Internet of Things"*: Jessica Rosenworcel, "Choosing the Wrong Lane in the Race to 5G," *Wired*, June 10, 2019, wired.com/story/choosing-the -wrong-lane-in-the-race-to-5g/.

150 *"It will even enable governments and companies to aggregate information"*: Nicholas Thompson and Ian Bremmer, "The AI Cold War That Threatens Us All," *Wired,* October 23, 2018, wired.com /story/ai-cold-war-china-could-doom-us-all/.

152 *"the global market for drone aircraft is expected to grow"*: "Global Unmanned Aerial Vehicle (UAV) Market Report 2021–2026," Globe Newswire, June 28, 2021, globenewswire.com/en/news-release /2021/06/28/2253654/28124/en/Global-Unmanned-Aerial -Vehicle-UAV-Market-Report-2021-2026-Rising-Demand-for -Contactless-Deliveries-of-Medical-Supplies-and-Other-Essentials -Using-Drones-Owing-to-COVID-19.html.

155 *"cyberweapons of various kinds have been deployed"*: "Cyber Threats with David Sanger," GZERO Media, August 6, 2018, gzeromedia.com/videos/cyber-threats-with-david-sanger.

155 *"Nor should we take much comfort"*: Robert D. Kaplan, "Why We Need Someone Like Ike," *Wall Street Journal,* July 17, 2019, wsj .com/articles/why-we-need-someone-like-ike-11563404275.

156 *"as when a Russian malware attack on Ukraine"*: "Six Russian GRU Officers Charged in Connection with Worldwide Deployment of Destructive Malware and Other Disruptive Actions in Cyberspace," The United States Department of Justice, October 19, 2020, justice.gov/opa/pr/six-russian-gru-officers-charged-con nection-worldwide-deployment-destructive-malware-and.

156 *"but they did significant and lasting damage"*: "Cyber Threats with David Sanger," GZERO Media, August 6, 2018, gzeromedia .com/videos/cyber-threats-with-david-sanger.

156 *"To combat what World Health Organization officials called"*: Matt Richtel, "W.H.O. Fights a Pandemic Besides Coronavirus: An 'Info demic,' " *New York Times,* February 6, 2020, nytimes.com/2020 /02/06/health/coronavirus-misinformation-social-media.html.

157 *"a twenty-one-year-old hacker from New Jersey"*: Nicky Woolf, "DDoS Attack That Disrupted Internet Was Largest of Its Kind in History, Experts Say," *The Guardian,* October 26, 2016, theguardian .com/technology/2016/oct/26/ddos-attack-dyn-mirai-botnet.

158 *"A 2019 study from the Brookings Institution"*: Mark Muro, Jacob Whiton, and Robert Maxim, "What Jobs Are Affected by AI? Better-Paid, Better-Educated Workers Face the Most Exposure," The Brookings Institution, November 20, 2019, brookings.edu /research/what-jobs-are-affected-by-ai-better-paid-better-educated -workers-face-the-most-exposure/.

158 *"AI is changing what it means to be human"*: Janna Anderson and Lee Rainie, "Artificial Intelligence and the Future of Humans," Pew Research Center, December 10, 2018, pewresearch.org/internet /2018/12/10/artificial-intelligence-and-the-future-of-humans/.

159 *"Russian president Vladimir Putin once predicted"*: Radina Gigova, "Who Putin Thinks Will Rule the World," CNN, September 2, 2017, cnn.com/2017/09/01/world/putin-artificial-intelligence -will-rule-world/index.html.

160 *"China's leaders then tasked the country's tech companies"*: Nicholas Thompson and Ian Bremmer, "The AI Cold War That Threatens Us All," *Wired*, October 23, 2018, wired.com/story/ai-cold -war-china-could-doom-us-all/.

161 *"China will have two big advantages"*: Ibid.

163 *"Chinese technologies will be cheaper"*: Fareed Zakaria, "The Blacklisting of Huawei Might Be China's Sputnik Moment," FareedZakaria.com, May 23, 2019, https://fareedzakaria.com/col umns/2019/5/23/the-blacklisting-of-huawei-might-be-chinas -sputnik-moment.

166 *"YouTube launched a project to refine the way"*: Clive Thompson, "YouTube's Plot to Silence Conspiracy Theories," *Wired*, September 18, 2020, wired.com/story/youtube-algorithm-silence-con spiracy-theories/.

167 *"Facebook hasn't yet followed YouTube's lead"*: Tate Ryan-Mosley, "Why Facebook's Political-Ad Ban Is Taking on the Wrong Problem," *MIT Technology Review*, September 6, 2020, technology review.com/2020/09/06/1008192/why-facebooks-political-ad -ban-is-taking-on-the-wrong-problem/.

167 *"machines can be taught that addictions aren't healthy"*: Jim

Guszcza, "AI Needs Human-Centered Design," *Wired*, wired.com /brandlab/2018/05/ai-needs-human-centered-design/.

170 *"the Biden administration partnered with Japan, India, and Australia"*: "Major Countries Propose Priorities for Biden Administration, World Leaders: Leaders of Australia, India, Japan and the United States Shape a New Era of Cooperation," Boston Global Forum, January 7, 2021, https://bostonglobalforum.org/news -and-events/news/major-countries-propose-priorities-for-biden -administration-world-leaders-leaders-of-australia-india-japan-and -the-united-states-shape-a-new-era-of-cooperation/.

Conclusion

176 *"There was no intelligent life on our planet"*: Jeff Desjardins, "Animation: Human Population Growth Over All of History," Visual Capitalist, January 31, 2018, visualcapitalist.com/animation -population-growth-history/.

180 *"we've also extended our capacity for cooperation"*: For a persuasive elaboration of this theory, see Robert Wright, *Nonzero: The Logic of Human Destiny* (New York: Pantheon Books, 1999).

188 *"172 countries signed on to the COVAX project"*: "172 Countries and Multiple Candidate Vaccines Engaged in COVID-19 Vaccine Global Access Facility," World Health Organization, August 24, 2020, who.int/news/item/24-08-2020-172-countries-and-multiple -candidate-vaccines-engaged-in-covid-19-vaccine-global-access -facility.

192 *"The EU has used COVID-19 to combat climate change"*: *Greenness of Stimulus Index*, February 2021, Vivid Economics, 44–45, vivideconomics.com/wp-content/uploads/2021/02/Greennes-of -Stimulus-Index-5th-Edition-FINAL-VERSION-09.02.21.pdf.

INDEX

Aadhaar, 130–31, 149
Afghanistan, 46–47, 51, 141
Africa, 50, 65, 71, 78, 87–90, 92,
  99, 101, 104, 107, 117, 143
African Americans, 22–24, 34
African Development Bank,
  47–48
agriculture, 72, 99, 101, 106–7,
  119, 120
algorithms, 7, 22, 132, 134–35,
  142, 161, 166–68, 178
Alibaba, 160–61, 194–97, 201
Alphabet, 127
Alston, Philip, 108
Amazon (company), 113, 127,
  193–96, 198
Amazon rainforest, 91, 119, 120
Antarctic, 103
Ant Group, 195
Anthropocene period, 91
antifa, 142
Apple, 54, 113, 127, 162,
  193–96
Arab Spring, 87–89, 100

Arctic, 103, 107, 108
Armstrong, Neil, 177
artificial intelligence (AI), 7, 55,
  57–58, 132, 134, 135, 147,
  157–58, 165, 167, 170, 178,
  190, 196, 198
  algorithms in, 7, 22, 132,
    134–35, 142, 161, 166–68,
    178
  artificial general intelligence
    (AGI), 157
  China and, 28, 44, 147,
    160–61, 172
  countries' strategic advantage
    in, 159–62
  COVID and, 128
  facial recognition, 55–57, 135,
    146, 148, 161, 171
  greatest risk of, 159
  lack of US national strategy
    for, 161
  multinational institution
    needed for, 169
  racial bias and, 56–57, 134–35

artificial intelligence (AI)
(*Continued*)
in surveillance, 54–58, 133,
147, 158, 161
war and, 160
and what it means to human,
158, 178
Asia, 78, 89, 92, 99, 104, 194
COVID and, 76–77, 125
military power in, 43
Asian Americans, 23
Asian Development Bank, 47
Asian Infrastructure Investment
Bank (AIIB), 29, 47–48
al-Assad, Bashar, 145
Associated Press, 52
Athens, 37
atmosphere, 91
Australia, 27, 35, 47, 67, 94,
125, 170
Australian Strategic Policy
Institute, 54
authoritarianism, 29, 31, 32, 44,
52, 69, 78, 79, 164, 199
digital, 29–30, 136, 143–51,
164, 168, 171, 172, 190
automation, 33, 135–39, 170
automobile industry, 94–95, 115,
117, 192
driverless cars, 131–32, 150,
161, 170

Baidu, 161
bailouts, 71, 88
Balkans, 50
Bangladesh, 103–5
bank accounts, 149
banks, 8, 111, 114–15, 187, 202
Belarus, 80

Belt and Road Initiative (BRI),
29, 40, 45, 47, 48, 50, 56,
71–72
Berners-Lee, Tim, 176
Beyer, Peter, 58
Big Tech companies, *see*
technology companies
biometric identification systems,
130–31, 149
bird flu, 73, 78
birds, 72, 91
black Americans, 22–24, 34
Black Lives Matter, 142
Biden, Joe, 17, 19, 27, 34, 42, 43,
71, 82, 88–89, 97, 105, 112,
117, 169, 170
Bill & Melinda Gates Foundation,
65, 70, 71
Bolivia, 105–6, 120
Bolsonaro, Jair, 91, 120
Borneo, 98
Brazil, 9, 44, 68, 79, 91–92, 101,
111, 114, 120, 142
Brexit, 84, 85
Brin, Sergey, 197
Britain, 8, 68, 202
Brookings Institution, 158
bubonic plague, 176
Buolamwini, Joy, 135
Burkina Faso, 104
Burundi, 143
Bush, George W., 64, 66, 78
Business Roundtable, 113
ByteDance, 194, 196–97, 201

cable news channels, 142
California, 117, 202
cameras, security, 148, 161
Campbell, Kurt, 42

Canada, 8, 58, 79, 108, 125, 170, 202
Cape Town, 107
capitalism, 19–20, 43
  surveillance, 147
Capitol, storming of, 16, 17, 193
carbon dioxide (CO2) emissions, 91–94, 96–97, 103, 109–11, 113, 116–19, 124, 192
  net zero goal for, 93–97, 111–13, 125, 126, 189
Carney, Mark, 124
cars, 94–95, 115, 117
  driverless, 131–32, 150, 161, 170
Carter, Jimmy, 30
Case for Democracy, The (Sharansky), 51
Central America, 88, 89, 98, 101, 104
Central Intelligence Agency (CIA), 57
centrists, 17
Chad, 104
Chevron, 118
Chile, 18
China, 3, 5, 9, 13, 27, 86, 170, 190, 199, 200
  aging population in, 34, 72
  Americans' view of, 41–42
  artificial intelligence and, 28, 44, 147, 160–61, 172
  Belt and Road Initiative (BRI) of, 29, 40, 45, 47, 48, 50, 56, 71–72
  "birth control" in, 52
  climate change and, 93, 94, 96, 107, 111–14, 117, 120
  Communist Party in, 33, 42, 50–52, 77, 112, 160, 168, 180, 194
  COVID and, 29–30, 39–41, 46, 47, 63, 65–69, 72–74, 77, 81, 84, 128, 146–47
  cyber-sovereignty in, 53–54
  cyberweapons and, 154, 155
  data and, 170, 172
  economic growth of, 28–33, 38–40, 49, 52, 67
  food supplies in, 101
  global strategy of, 31
  Hong Kong and, 29, 41, 54, 59, 67, 124
  infrastructure aid to other countries provided by, 29, 35, 45, 47–48, 50, 169
  intellectual property and, 33, 38, 168–69
  internet and, 53–54, 145, 160, 162–64, 172
  loans to other countries from, 48, 50
  Made in China 2025 plan of, 28
  North Korea and, 36, 43, 51
  outsourcing of jobs to, 33, 137
  People's Liberation Army in, 36, 50
  rise of, 32–38, 45–58, 60, 142, 160
  risk of financial crisis in, 34
  social credit system in, 55–56, 146
  South China Sea and, 29, 43, 59, 67, 124, 150
  state intrusion and repression in, 52–55, 146–47
  surveillance technologies in, 54–58, 147

China (*Continued*)
Taiwan and, 29, 42–43, 59, 67, 150, 185
technology and, 43–45, 54, 163, 169–72
technology companies and, 54, 161–62, 195, 200–201
Tiananmen Square in, 51–52
trade and, 33–34, 39, 46, 48–49, 59
Uighurs in, 52–53, 56
United Nations and, 33
weapons of, 42, 43, 151
Xi in, 28–30, 33, 39, 40, 42–43, 50, 52, 53, 67, 160–61
China-US relations, 3–6, 11, 14, 15, 28–61, 86, 126, 190–91, 198, 200
China's rise and, 32–38
and China's rise as dangerous, 49–58
and China's rise as offering opportunities, 45–49
Cold War possibility in, 43–45, 58–60, 163, 165, 190, 193, 194, 200, 201
collaboration in, 81
confrontation possibility in, 43, 58–60, 160, 185, 190–91, 197
COVID and, 5, 6, 8, 39–42
decoupling in, 39, 42
emerging trap in, 37–42
5G and, 150–51
flashpoints in, 42–45
interdependence in, 37–39, 59
rivalry partnership in, 31, 36, 42, 163

supply chains in, 38
trade and, 33–34, 39
cities, 131–32
smart, 133, 150, 160, 161
City of London, 132–33
civil wars, 71, 88–90, 107, 123, 145
Clearview AI, 148
climate change, 4, 6–7, 10–12, 14, 27, 31, 46, 83–84, 86, 87–126, 143, 166, 172–73, 177, 185–87, 190, 195, 197, 202
agriculture and, 99, 101, 106–7, 119, 120
automobile industry and, 94–95, 115, 117
carbon dioxide (CO2) emissions and, 91–94, 96–97, 103, 109–11, 113, 116–19, 124, 192
carbon net zero goal and, 93–97, 111–13, 125, 189, 126, 189
China and, 93, 94, 96, 107, 111–14, 117, 120
civil wars and, 88–90
competition and, 99–101, 107
COVID and, 84, 125, 126, 187
as crisis we need, 111–24
drought and, 87–90, 92, 101, 104, 119
Europe and, 94, 99, 104, 117, 184, 191, 192
extinctions and, 91, 92
financing of plans for, 120–22
floods and, 89, 90, 92, 98–99, 103, 104, 106

forests and, 91–92, 119–21
fossil fuels and, 84, 91, 93–96,
  107–8, 112, 117–18, 123
geo-engineering and, 109–10
glaciers and ice sheets and,
  100, 103, 104, 107, 108
Green Marshall Plan needed
  for, 123–24, 189
Green New Deal and, 123–24
India and, 93, 94, 96, 99–101,
  104, 105, 111, 114, 120
inequality and "climate
  apartheid" caused by, 108–9
joint R&D and, 115–16
Kyoto Protocol and, 124
legislation on, 118
Paris accord on, 27, 93, 97,
  112–14, 118, 202
politics and, 92–96
refugees and, 88–90, 101–5,
  122–23
risks of, 97–100
rule setting and, 114–15
Russia and, 93, 94, 96, 107,
  108, 112
sea levels and, 92, 98, 99,
  102–4, 121, 122
smaller countries' role in
  addressing, 114
technologies and, 97
Trump and, 27, 93, 97, 112,
  125, 202
United Nations and, 92, 93,
  108, 169, 189–90
unrest and conflict and,
  105–8
water and, 97–101, 105–7,
  121

wildfires and, 90, 92, 119,
  142
world leaders and, 113–14
Clinton, Bill, 30, 42, 43
Clinton, Hillary, 17, 35, 156
cloud computing, 170, 196, 198
CloudWalk, 56–57
cloud whitening, 109
Cochabamba, 105–6
Colbert, Stephen, 133
Cold War
  US-China, 43–45, 58–60, 163,
    165, 190, 193, 194, 200, 201
  US-Soviet, 2, 5, 10, 27, 37, 43,
    46, 58, 154, 160, 162, 163,
    165, 166
Colombia, 102
communication, *see* information
  and communication
Communism, 8, 11, 43, 85
  in China, 33, 42, 50–52, 77,
    112, 160, 168, 180, 194
  in Soviet Union, 180
computing, 28, 134, 197
  algorithms in, 7, 22, 132,
    134–35, 142, 161, 166–68,
    178
  cloud, 170, 196, 198
  COVID and, 196
  hacking and, 152, 157, 198
  quantum, 28, 159–60, 173
  see also artificial intelligence;
    data
Congo, 119
Congress, US, 18, 25, 34, 105,
  161
conservatives, 17
  see also Republicans

conspiracy theories, 166
cooperation, practical, 178–84,
    203–4
  positive vision for, 187–88
Council of Economic Advisers,
    138
COVAX, 82, 125, 187, 188
COVID-19 pandemic, 2–4, 6–11,
    13, 16, 40–41, 46, 63–86,
    90, 108, 116, 126, 143, 164,
    166, 178, 186–87, 195, 199
  artificial intelligence and, 128
  Asian countries' response to,
    76–77, 125
  burden sharing and, 81–82
  China and, 29–30, 39–41, 46,
    47, 63, 65–69, 72–74, 77,
    81, 84, 128, 146–47
  China-US relations and, 5, 6,
    8, 39–42
  climate change and, 84, 125,
    126, 187
  computing infrastructure and,
    196
  disinformation and, 67,
    156–57, 167
  economic damage and recovery
    from, 26, 30, 40, 67, 69, 70,
    83, 96, 105, 115, 117, 135,
    136, 186
  Europe and, 41, 84–85, 191,
    192
  G-Zero response to, 66–68
  inequality worsened by, 68–72
  information sharing and,
    77–81, 173
  lessons from, 6, 63–64, 72–86
  masks in, 66
  media and, 66
  political dysfunction and, 66,
    67, 73, 77
  preparation and investment
    and, 73–77
  schools and, 70, 71, 196, 202
  supply chains and, 40, 101,
    115
  technology and, 127–29, 135
  testing in, 41, 63, 78–80, 84
  Trump and, 27, 39–41, 65, 66,
    79–80, 82, 187
  and underfunding of public
    health agencies, 75
  vaccines in, 8, 13–14, 16, 42,
    67, 69, 82–85, 115, 118,
    125, 126, 128, 153, 167,
    178, 186–88
  warnings of, 6, 64–65
  workers and, 70, 84, 136–39,
    153, 192, 196, 202
crack cocaine, 23
crime, 23, 148, 151–53, 198
crises, 11–12
  Goldilocks, 186–87
Cuban Missile Crisis, 11, 166
culture wars, 21, 66
cyberweapons, 36–37, 43, 44,
    152–57, 165, 173

D10 countries, 170
Damascus, 87, 88
data, 44, 134, 146, 147–50, 157,
    160, 161, 171–72
  China and, 170, 172
  European Union and, 192–93
  privacy and, see privacy
  size of datasphere, 195
  World Data Organization for,
    168–72, 187, 189–90

debt forgiveness, 71
Defense Department, 83
dehumanization, 129, 135–39
democracy(ies), 8, 25, 27, 29, 32,
    34, 37, 44, 51, 57, 59, 60, 67,
    139, 141, 168, 169, 179–80,
    182, 185, 190, 193, 195
  American values and, 179
  social media and, 142
  surveillance and, 148
  technology and, 170–73
Democrats, 16–18, 21, 24–27,
    38, 42, 45, 73, 127
Deng Xiaoping, 28
Dhaka, 105
Dickens, Charles, 28
disinformation and
    misinformation, 22, 24, 67,
    145, 156–57, 166–68
disruptive technologies, see
    technology
distributed denial-of-service
    (DDoS) attacks, 157
DNA, 141
drones, 151–52
drought, 87–90, 92, 101, 104,
    119
drugs, pharmaceutical, 7, 80–81,
    83, 118, 128
drug use, 23, 141, 178, 195
Dyn, 157

East India Company, 194
Ebola, 65, 71
Ecuador, 95
education, 24, 81
  college degrees, 18, 23
  COVID and online learning,
    70, 71, 84, 186–87, 196, 202

Egypt, 87, 100–101, 120, 144
elections, 25, 34, 139, 180, 195
  of 2016, 17, 156
  of 2020, 16, 17, 19, 20,
    163–64, 167, 193
  of 2024, 27, 190
El Salvador, 88, 89, 104
encryption, 159–60
energy, 12, 131, 202
  from fossil fuels, 84, 91, 93–96,
    107–8, 112, 117–18, 123
  renewable, 84, 93, 96, 107,
    113, 115, 118, 123, 189, 202
entrepreneurs, 19, 26, 195
epidemics, see pandemics
Eritrea, 104
ESG (environmental, social, and
    governance) investments,
    114–15
Ethiopia, 100–101, 120
Eurasia Group, 82
European Bank for
    Reconstruction and
    Development, 48
European Commission, 67, 191
European Council on Foreign
    Relations, 41
Europe and European Union
    (EU), 13, 21–22, 27, 41,
    42, 44, 45, 48, 50, 51, 71,
    84–86, 88, 101, 111, 141,
    180, 183–84
  Brexit and, 84, 85
  climate change and, 94, 99,
    104, 117, 184, 191, 192
  COVID and, 41, 84–85, 191,
    192
  data use and privacy and,
    192–93, 195

Europe and European Union
(EU) (*Continued*)
immigration and refugees in,
71, 88, 108
Schengen Area in, 102
taxation and, 191, 192
technology and, 170–72, 184,
191, 197
European Green Deal, 111
European Parliament, 111
Every Nation for Itself
(Bremmer), 8
extinctions, 91, 92
ExxonMobil, 118

Face++, 135
Facebook, 127, 142, 144, 156,
162, 167, 193–96
facial recognition technologies,
55–57, 135, 146, 148, 161,
171
farming, 72, 99, 101, 106–7, 119,
120
Federal Housing Authority, 22
Ferguson, Niall, 58
Fiji, 102–4, 114
filter bubbles, 142, 163, 164, 167
financial crisis of 2008–2010,
9, 10, 46, 84, 88, 136, 141,
191, 199
Fitzgerald, F. Scott, 59
5G technology, 44, 132, 150–51,
161, 196
floods, 89, 90, 92, 98–99, 103,
104, 106
Floyd, George, 133
food
agriculture, 72, 99, 101, 106–7

companies, 167–68
stockpiles, 101
Foreign Policy, 58
forests, 91–92, 119–21
fossil fuels, 84, 91, 93–96, 107–8,
112, 117–18, 123
4chan, 21
fourth industrial revolution,
138
Fox, 21
France, 8, 47, 67, 85, 95, 170,
202
Freedom House, 57

G7 (Group of Seven), 8–9
G20 (Group of 20), 9
Gagarin, Yuri, 176–77, 180
Gallup, 17
Gates, Bill, 65
Gates Foundation, 65, 70, 71
GDP, global, 131, 170
Generation Z, 202–3
genetics, 141, 150
geo-engineering, 109–10
geopolitical recessions, 9, 10
Germany, 8, 47, 79, 85, 95, 170,
181
Ghonim, Wael, 144
GI Bill, 23
Gilded Age, 18
global financial crisis, 9, 10, 46,
84, 88, 136, 141, 191, 199
Global Forest Watch, 119
Global Fund, 71
global GDP, 131, 170
globalism, 14, 28, 29, 193
technology companies and,
196–201

globalization, 26, 31, 45, 74, 90–91, 140, 143, 164, 180, 202, 203
global middle class, 68, 109, 142, 176
global population, 176
global warming, *see* climate change
Goldilocks crisis, 186–87
Google, 113, 156, 162, 193–97
Gorbachev, Mikhail, 1–2, 12, 14, 15, 166, 203
Grand Ethiopian Renaissance Dam, 100–101
Great Resignation, 139
Greece, 79, 191
greenhouse effect, 91
Green Marshall Plan, 123–24, 189
Green New Deal, 123–24
Guatemala, 88, 89, 104
G-Zero, 8–10, 86, 110
    COVID and, 66–68
    net zero and, 96–97, 126

hacking, 152, 157, 198
Haiti, 46
health care, 12, 25
    access to, 140–41
    medicines, 7, 80–81, 83, 118, 128
    and racial bias in artificial intelligence, 134
Honduras, 88, 89, 104
Hong Kong, 29, 41, 54, 59, 67, 124
housing, 22
Huawei, 151, 161, 168

human history, 176, 180
humanitarian aid, 40
human rights, 34, 41, 42, 53, 60, 108, 122, 123, 133, 158, 169, 184
Hussein, Saddam, 49

IBM, 135
identification systems, biometric, 130–31, 149
iFlyTek, 161
immigration, 19, 23, 34
    in Europe, 71
    jobs and, 138
    Trump and, 51, 71, 88
Immigration and Customs Enforcement, 57
income
    guaranteed, 139
    inequality in, *see* inequality
    median family, 23
independents, 17
India, 9, 27, 44, 47, 67, 79, 105, 125, 142, 170, 195, 202
    Aadhaar system in, 130–31, 149
    climate change and, 93, 94, 96, 99–101, 104, 105, 111, 114, 120
    technology and, 129–31, 171–72
individualism, 19
Indonesia, 9, 40, 98, 119
Indus River, 99–100
inequality, 14, 18–19, 59, 81, 84, 123, 138, 141, 158, 165–66, 177, 180–81, 195
    climate apartheid, 108–9
    COVID and, 68–72

information and communication,
141–45, 161, 164, 176
filter bubbles and, 142, 163,
164, 167
misinformation and
disinformation, 22, 24, 67,
145, 156–57, 166–68
see also media
infrastructure, 171
China's aid to other countries
for, 29, 35, 45, 47–48, 50,
169
encryption and, 159–60
5G and, 150, 151
innovation, 7, 16, 76, 83, 115,
125, 158, 186
in China, 33
see also technology
intellectual property, 190
China and, 33, 38, 168–69
of pharmaceutical companies,
80–81
intelligent life, 12–13, 176
International Monetary Fund
(IMF), 47, 81, 183
internet, 44, 70, 142–45, 162–64,
170, 195
American ecosystem of, 44, 45
China and, 53–54, 145, 160,
162–64, 172
conspiracy theories on, 166
invention of, 176
privacy and, see privacy
social media, see social media
"splinternet" and, 45, 163, 164
see also information and
communication
Internet of Things (IoT), 44, 145,
149, 150, 157, 163, 196

Iran, 27, 51, 77, 154–56
Iraq, 46, 49, 141, 153
Irish Republican Army, 133
Islamic Development Bank, 47
Islamic State, 153–54
Israel, 47
Italy, 8, 40, 41, 99, 170, 181, 191

Jakarta, 98
Japan, 8, 22, 27, 35, 40, 44, 59,
79, 95, 125, 140, 170–72,
181
jobs, see work, workers
Jordan, 51, 88, 101, 102

Kaplan, Robert, 58
Kashmir, 100
Kennedy, John F., 143
Kenya, 143
Kiribati, 102–4, 122
Kuwait, 49
Kyoto Protocol, 124

labor unions, 18
Latin America, 50, 141
League of Nations, 181
Lebanon, 88, 102
liberals, 17
see also Democrats
Libya, 87
life expectancy, 140
Li Keqiang, 146
London, 103, 132–33
Lukashenko, Alexander, 80

Ma, Jack, 41, 200–201
machine learning, see artificial
intelligence
Macron, Emmanuel, 85

Madagascar, 80
Malaysia, 50
Mali, 104
malware, 156
Mao Zedong, 5, 33
Markey, Edward, 123
Mars, 16, 177, 197
Marshall Plan, 11, 48, 189
  Green Marshall Plan, 123–24,
    189
mass transit systems, 132
Mauritania, 104
McKinsey & Company, 131, 137
media, 21–22, 24, 59, 127
  cable news, 142
  COVID and, 66
  newspapers, 144
  social, *see* social media
medicines, 7, 80–81, 83, 118, 128
Merkel, Angela, 85
Metaverse, 164
Mexico, 9, 18, 68, 79, 88, 117,
    125, 137
Miami, Fla., 99
Microsoft, 113, 135, 194, 196,
    198
middle class, 14
  black, 23
  global, 68, 109, 142, 176
Middle East, 27, 71, 89, 104,
    107, 112
migrants and refugees, 51, 70,
    71, 84, 88–90, 101–5, 108,
    116, 122–23, 191
Mirai botnet, 157
misinformation and
  disinformation, 22, 24, 67,
    145, 156–57, 166–68
MIT Media Lab, 135

moderates, 17
Modi, Narendra, 149
money in politics, 20, 21
Moon Jae-in, 80
moon landing, 177
Morales, Evo, 106
mRNA technologies, 83
MSNBC, 21
Mubarak, Hosni, 144
Musk, Elon, 115, 197, 200

NASA, 177
National Academy of Sciences,
    103
National Institute of Standards
    and Technology, 135
National Institutes of Health, 83
nationalism, 60, 179, 180
  technology companies and,
    196–201
National Public Radio, 25
Nepal, 100, 104
Netflix, 127
Netherlands, 99
New Deal, 22
news, *see* information and
    communication; media
newspapers, 144
New York, N.Y., 25, 99, 103, 202
New York Times, 56, 78, 147,
    148
New Zealand, 79, 122
NGOs, 81, 82, 202
Nicaragua, 104
Niger, 104
Nigeria, 96, 104, 140
Nile, 100–101, 103
9/11 attacks, 10, 47, 66, 133,
    148, 149

Nixon, Richard, 5
North Atlantic Treaty
    Organization (NATO), 10,
    35, 46, 49, 207
North Korea, 36, 43, 51, 154,
    156
NotPetya, 156
nuclear weapons, 2, 11, 12, 27,
    36, 43, 154–55, 160, 166,
    169, 173, 176

OANN, 21
Obama, Barack, 27, 35, 64–65,
    138
Obamacare, 25
Ocasio-Cortez, Alexandria, 123
oceans, 110
oil, gas, and coal companies,
    84, 91, 93–96, 107–8, 112,
    117–18, 123, 194
1t.org, 119
opioid epidemic, 23, 195
Organization for Economic
    Cooperation and
    Development (OECD), 18
Oxford Economics, 137

Page, Larry, 197
Pakistan, 48, 99–100, 104, 120
Palantir, 57
Panama, 46, 104
pandemics, 65
    bubonic plague, 176
    COVID-19, see COVID-19
    pandemic
    warnings of, 6, 64–65
pandemics, future, 14, 27, 31,
    63–64, 72–82, 143, 185, 186
    burden sharing and, 81–82
    family and individual planning
        for, 76
    information sharing and, 77–81
    Predict project and, 78
    preparation and investment
        for, 73–77
Paris climate accord, 27, 93, 97,
    112–14, 118, 202
Parler, 193
Pascal, Blaise, 79
Pasteur, Louis, 175
Peloponnesian War, 37
People's Bank of China, 146
People's Daily, 42
Pew Research Center, 16, 67, 142
pharmaceuticals, 7, 80–81, 83,
    118, 128
Philippines, 35, 43
phones, cellular, 176
    smartphones, 133, 145, 147,
        149, 150, 161
planets, intelligent life on, 12–13
police brutality, 24, 34, 133
politics
    climate change and, 92–96
    money in, 20, 21
    polarization in, 17
    see also United States, political
        dysfunction in
Pompeo, Mike, 60
populism, 10, 14, 26, 28, 84
postindustrial shock, 138
poverty, 70–71, 81, 90, 104, 123,
    142, 180
    climate change and, 108–9
Predict project, 78
privacy, 54–55, 130, 145–46,
    151, 157, 158, 161, 168,
    170, 190

encryption and, 159–60
European Union and, 192–93,
195
security and, 148
surveillance and, 54–58, 133,
147, 148, 158, 161, 168, 170
private sector, 19–20, 76, 115,
117–18, 124, 162, 165, 173,
196
Public Broadcast System, 24–25
Putin, Vladimir, 159, 205–8

QAnon, 21
Quadrilateral Security Dialogue
(Quad), 170
quantum computing, 28, 159–60,
173

racial bias in artificial
intelligence, 56–57, 134–35
racism, 22–24, 51, 123, 133,
141, 168
radio, 143, 144
Rajoelina, Andry, 80
ransomware, 152–53
Reagan, Ronald, 3, 6, 14, 15,
143, 186
Gorbachev and, 1–2, 12, 14,
15, 166, 203
redlining, 22
Refugee Convention, 51
refugees and migrants, 51, 70,
71, 84, 88–90, 101–5, 108,
116, 122–23, 191
Regional Comprehensive
Economic Partnership
(RCEP), 29, 48–49
Republicans, 16–18, 20, 21,
23–27, 38, 42, 45, 73, 127

robotics, 28, 137, 152, 157
Roosevelt, Franklin, 22, 143
Russia, 9, 36, 46, 67, 81, 94,
145, 151, 154, 156, 159,
171, 199, 202
climate change and, 93, 94,
96, 107, 108, 112
US presidential election of
2016 and, 156
Russia, czarist, 180
Rwanda, 47

Safety.com, 148
Sahara desert, 104
Salesforce, 119
Sana'a, 107
Saudi Arabia, 49, 93–94
Schengen Area, 102
Schmidt, Eric, 31
science, 125
Science, 134
Science and Technology Daily,
57
sea levels, 92, 98, 99, 102–4,
121, 122
security cameras, 148, 161
Senegal, 104
September 11 terrorist attacks,
10, 47, 66, 133, 148, 149
Shanghai, 103
Sharansky, Natan, 51
Shell, 118
Siberia, 108
Silicon Valley, 161, 162, 197
see also technology
companies
Singapore, 76, 79
Al-Sisi, Abdel Fattah, 144
smart cities, 133, 150, 160, 161

smartphones, 133, 145, 147, 149, 150, 161
Smith, Will, 133
social credit system, 55–56, 146
social media, 21, 22, 24–25, 41, 66, 133, 144, 145, 164, 167, 170, 195, 202
  conspiracy theories on, 166
  democracy and, 142
  Facebook, 127, 142, 144, 156, 162, 167, 193–96
  Russia and, 156
social safety nets, 20, 34, 72, 84, 86, 139, 158, 165, 180
Social Security Act, 22–23
Somalia, 46
South China Sea, 29, 43, 59, 67, 124, 150
South Korea, 9, 27, 35, 44, 47, 79, 80, 95, 117, 133, 170, 171
Soviet Union, 1–2, 43, 48, 50, 59, 169
  in Cold War, 2, 5, 10, 27, 37, 43, 46, 58, 154, 160, 162, 163, 165, 166
  collapse of, 154
  communism in, 180
  space program of, 32, 176–77
space programs, 16, 32, 176–77, 197
SpaceX, 197
Spain, 68, 99, 191
Sparta, 37
Sputnik, 32
Sri Lanka, 50, 104
Steele, Tanya, 92
Strait of Hormuz, 50
Sudan, 100, 104, 120

supply chains, 29, 38, 74, 75, 112, 113, 118–19, 161, 168, 180
  COVID and, 40, 101, 115
Supreme Court, US, 20
surveillance, 54–58, 133, 147, 148, 158, 161, 168, 170
sustainable development, 81
swine flu, 72
Syria, 71, 87–90, 98, 101, 104, 123, 145, 153

Taiwan, 76
  China and, 29, 42–43, 59, 67, 150, 185
taxes, 20, 124, 130
  carbon, 116–17
  European Union and, 191, 192
technology, 4, 7–8, 11–12, 14, 27, 31, 46, 58, 59, 86, 126, 127–73, 185–87, 195
  and acceleration of human development, 176–78
  artificial intelligence, see artificial intelligence
  authoritarianism and, 29–30, 136, 143–51, 164, 168, 171, 172, 190
  catastrophic risks from, 154–57
  China and, 43–45, 54, 163, 169–72
  cities improved by, 131–32
  climate change and, 97
  computing, see computing
  COVID and, 127–29, 135
  data and, see data
  dehumanization from, 129, 135–39

democracy and, 170–73
digital divide and, 139–43
discussions among world
  leaders needed for, 172–73
disruptive, as crisis we need,
  164–68
European Union and, 170–72,
  184, 191, 197
5G, 44, 132, 150–51, 161,
  196
fourth industrial revolution,
  138
genetics and, 141, 150
geo-engineering, 109–10
health care access and, 140–41
India and, 129–31, 171–72
intellectual property and, *see*
  intellectual property
internet, *see* internet
mRNA, 83
outlaw risk and, 151–54
parallel ecosystems of, 45
postindustrial shock and, 138
privacy and, *see* privacy
risks of, 129, 134–57
smart cities, 133, 150, 160,
  161
smartphone, *see* smartphones
surveillance, 54–58, 133, 147,
  148, 158, 161, 168, 170
work and, 7, 19, 33, 128, 129,
  135–39, 157–58, 181
technology companies, 115, 118,
  127, 132, 145–47, 160, 161,
  167, 168, 171, 173, 193–94,
  196–99, 201, 193–201
China and, 54, 161–62, 195,
  200–201
globalist goals in, 196–201

government and, 161–62
nationalist goals in, 196–201
techno-utopian goals in,
  196–98, 200–201
Teitiota, Ioane, 122, 123
television, 143, 144
Tencent, 161, 194, 196–97, 201
terrorism, 46, 133, 151–54, 168,
  173
  Islamic State, 153–54
  9/11 attacks, 10, 47, 66, 133,
    148, 149
Tesla, 95, 115, 197
Texas, 16
Thailand, 106
Thucydides, 37
Thunberg, Greta, 203
TikTok, 201
tobacco, 167–68, 178
Total Information Awareness,
  148
town square test, 51–52
trade, 10, 34, 44, 60, 164, 176,
  182
  China and, 33–34, 39, 46,
    48–49, 59
  in food, 101
  Regional Comprehensive
    Economic Partnership, 29,
    48–49
  Trans-Pacific Partnership, 35,
    48
  World Trade Organization, 30,
    169–71, 183, 190
traffic accidents, 131
trains, 132
transit, mass, 132
Trans-Pacific Partnership (TPP),
  35, 48

trees, 91–92, 119–21
Trump, Donald, 10, 27, 29, 30,
    35, 42, 66, 105, 161, 168, 190
  Capitol riot and, 16, 17, 193
  China and, 30, 35, 38–39
  climate change and, 27, 93,
    97, 112, 125, 202
  COVID and, 27, 39–41, 65,
    66, 79–80, 82, 187
  deplatforming of, 193–94
  in election of 2016, 17, 156
  in election of 2020, 16, 17, 19,
    163–64, 193
  immigration and, 51, 71, 88
  Predict project and, 78
  Trans-Pacific Partnership and,
    35, 48
Tunisia, 87, 144
Turkey, 9, 18, 51, 88, 102
Tuvalu, 104
Twitter, 144, 156, 193, 195

Uighur Muslims, 52–53, 56
Ukraine, 156, 205–8
Unilever, 118–19
United Arab Emirates, 94
United Kingdom, 47, 79, 170
United Nations (UN), 10, 81, 183
  China and, 33
  climate change and, 92, 93,
    108, 169, 189–90
  creation of, 182
  refugees and, 104–5, 122, 123
  sustainable development goals
    of, 81
United States, 8, 13
  China's relations with, see
    China-US relations

Congress, 18, 25, 34, 105, 161
  defense treaties of, 36, 43
  diversity of opinions in, 179
  foreign policies of, 26, 36, 43,
    48–50, 169–70
  global financial crisis and, 46
  humanitarian aid from, 40
  loans to allies from, 48
  military interventions of,
    46–47, 49–50, 154
  military power of, 36, 39, 154,
    162
  refugees accepted by, 51
  technology ecosystem of, 44, 45
United States, political
    dysfunction in, 3, 4, 11,
    15–28, 32, 59, 184–85, 190
  capitalism and, 19–20
  COVID and, 66, 67, 73, 77
  geographical component to, 17
  in government, 17–18
  leadership crippled by, 26–27
  media and, 21–22
  and money in politics, 20, 21
  racism and, 22–24
  solutions to, 24–26
  wealth gap and, 18–19
US Agency for International
    Development (USAID), 78
US National Academy of
    Sciences, 103

vaccines, 83, 116
  COVID, 8, 13–14, 16, 42, 67,
    69, 82–85, 115, 118, 125,
    126, 128, 153, 167, 178,
    186–88
  mRNA, 83

Vanuatu, 104
Venezuela, 94, 96, 102
Vietnam, 43, 76, 79
viruses
  animal-to-human transmission
    of, 72, 73, 78
  Predict project and, 78
  see also pandemics;
    pandemics, future
von der Leyen, Ursula, 85
voting laws, 23

Walmart, 118
war(s), 181, 184
  artificial intelligence and, 160
  balance of power and, 37, 43,
    156
  civil, 71, 88–90, 107, 123, 145
  European Union and, 184
  mutually assured destruction
    in, 160
  World War I, 181, 182
  World War II, 11, 165, 176,
    181–82, 184
  World War III, 173
  see also weapons
War Games, 165
water, 97–101, 105–7, 121
  drought, 87–90, 92, 101, 104,
    119
  floods, 89, 90, 92, 98–99, 103,
    104, 106
  sea levels, 92, 98, 99, 102–4,
    121, 122
wealth inequality, see inequality
wealth, median family, 23
weapons, 129, 177–78
  autonomous, 151–52, 165

of China, 42, 43, 151
  cyber, 36–37, 43, 44, 129,
    152–57, 165, 173
  geo-engineering, 110
  nuclear, 2, 11, 12, 27, 36, 43,
    154–55, 160, 166, 169, 173,
    176
  US-China confrontation and,
    43
wildfires, 90, 92, 119, 142
women and girls, 71, 81
work, workers, 19–20, 25, 26,
    34, 86, 136, 165
  automation and, 33, 135–39,
    170
  benefits for, 20, 24
  college degrees and, 18, 23
  COVID and, 70, 84, 136–39,
    153, 192, 196, 202
  gig economy, 24
  Great Resignation and, 139
  green energy jobs, 96, 123
  immigrants and, 138
  outsourcing of jobs, 18, 33, 137
  postindustrial shock and, 138
  remote, 70, 84, 153, 186–87
  Social Security and, 22–23
  technology and, 7, 19, 33, 128,
    129, 135–39, 157–58, 181
  wages for, 18, 20, 25
World Bank, 47, 71, 100, 131
World Carbon Organization, 116,
    124
World Economic Forum, 28, 119,
    138
World Health Organization
    (WHO), 10, 27, 40, 68, 77,
    81–82, 86, 156

World Intellectual Property
  Organization, 33
World Resources Institute,
  106
World Trade Organization, 30,
  169–71, 183, 190
World War I, 181, 182
World War II, 11, 165, 176,
  181–82, 184
World War III, 173
World Wildlife Fund, 92
Wright brothers, 176, 177

Xi Jinping, 28–30, 33, 39, 40,
  42–43, 50, 52, 53, 67,
  160–61, 207–8

Yemen, 107
YouGov, 17
YouTube, 166–67, 194–95
Yugoslavia, 46, 49, 50

Zakaria, Fareed, 142
Zimbabwe, 56–57
Zuckerberg, Mark, 197, 200